Causal Systems Theory

A New Theory of Psychology

Bret Scott Miles

CST Publishing
2026

First edition

Published by CST Publishing

ISBN 979-8-9950979-0-7 (paperback)
ISBN 979-8-9950979-1-4 (hardcover)

Library of Congress Control Number: 2026905605

Cover and interior design by the author

Printed in the United States of America

Dedication

To those who feel drawn toward a deeper understanding of the subtle systems within us and the vast systems that surround us.

To my wife, whose unwavering love, patience, and encouragement sustained me through the long and quiet hours of this work—an ever-steadfast presence, constant in spirit, tireless in heart, and always believing.

To my sister, the iron against which my thoughts were sharpened. For her persistence, her devotion to understanding, and for sharing with me the same restless curiosity—perhaps, as we often say, written into our very genes.

To my brother, whose devotion to detail and quiet pursuit of excellence has long stood as a guiding example in my life, always searching for a better way to accomplish what needs to be done.

How to Read This Book

This book is cumulative. Each chapter builds on structural commitments established earlier. The terms introduced are not metaphors. They are components of a mechanical model. If a term appears unfamiliar, it is not decorative. It carries load within the architecture.

The argument proceeds from constraint to stabilization to behavior and only afterward to experience. Many readers are accustomed to beginning with inner life and working outward. This book reverses that order. It begins with what any finite system must be like before psychology is possible at all.

This volume is meant to introduce the basic architecture of Causal Systems Theory, not to exhaust every implication of it. Many of the claims made here could expand into chapters of their own, and many chapters could become books of their own. They are not expanded here because too much detail at once would obscure the structure being established. The aim is to make the foundational architecture visible first. Once that architecture is clear, further expansion becomes easier to follow.

Consequently, some arguments are presented at the level of principle rather than full expansion. Some implications are named without elaboration into the domains they touch. This is not because the structure ends there, but because readers must understand the main architecture in view. It is better to see the frame clearly before adding further layers of detail.

A Note on Language

This book does not use much of the vocabulary most readers associate with psychology. Words such as choice, decision, intention, and control are largely absent. They are not omitted for effect. They are omitted because the framework presented here does not require them.

For many readers, this produces friction. Agency-based language functions as a default explanatory shortcut in everyday life. When it is removed, the remaining description can initially feel unfamiliar, as though something essential is missing. What is missing is not lived experience. What is missing is a customary way of packaging it. The structure described in these pages operates without reference to an inner author.

Because of this shift, some passages may feel denser than conventional psychological writing. The density is not complexity alone. It is the absence of familiar compression. The reader is asked to follow constraint, stabilization, and consequence without returning to inner-control language.

The chapters are designed to be read in order. Skipping ahead may create confusion, as later claims depend on earlier structural foundations. If a section feels dense, pause is appropriate. Allow the architecture to assemble before evaluating its implications.

Nothing in this book asks the reader to adopt a belief. It asks only that the mechanical constraints described be examined carefully and followed wherever they lead.

Table of Contents

Prologue

What a Life Does

Every life leaves an effect

Before we speak about systems, frames, stabilization, it is worth grounding ourselves in the single fact that does not depend on belief, worldview, or philosophy. This book does not determine that a life is meaningful or meaningless, that it matters or does not matter. The only factual statement that can be made without stepping outside the boundaries of what is observable is this:

Your life will have an impact.
Your existence will have an effect on what follows.
You cannot prevent it.

A system cannot exist without altering the systems around it. A body cannot occupy space without changing the flow of energy, attention, and behavior in other bodies. A mind cannot stabilize in a moment without imprinting that stabilization onto the next one. And organisms like us — complex, sensitive, constantly reorganizing — send ripples through the world whether we intend to or not.

This is true for every form of life: the tree bending under wind, the fox tracking scent in snow, the child learning the rules of a household, the adult navigating the tightening demands of work and life. None of them choose their place in the causal chain; each is a conduit carrying causation forward. No moment of experience, however quiet or private, is without consequence. Even in stillness, the system is shaping its next stabilization. Even in silence, the world is being rearranged.

You will touch other lives.
You will alter someone's stability, even if only by a fraction.
You will contribute to the long chain of causes that produced you and will continue beyond your existence.

This book does not ask you to see this as good or bad, right or wrong. It asks only for accuracy—for clear contact with what is. Nothing is required here. Only noticing. Clarity does not demand action. It requires only contact.

Causal Systems Theory (CST) is not a philosophy of purpose. It is a description of how systems unfold and the residue they leave behind. And because every system leaves an effect simply by existing, this book is no exception. Before anything else can be said, we begin with one orientation: you are already in motion, already carrying conditions forward, already reshaping the world through the ways your system stabilizes. Whether you name it purpose, fate, chance, will, or something else entirely, the machinery remains the same. Your existence will have an effect. It will shape what comes next.

Every life is an intersection of forces it did not generate.
Every life exerts force it cannot help but generate.
Your presence—like every presence—has consequences.

This is where the story begins.
Not with what a life *means*.
But with **what a life *does***.

Part I

The Physics of Being a System

What any system must be like before psychology is even possible

Chapter 1

What This Book Is About

Reframing Mind and Behavior Through Constraint and Stabilization

Most books about psychology offer new descriptions of the same underlying picture — new theories, terms, stories, and explanations. But underneath, the same basic assumption usually remains the same: a person who chooses, a mind that decides, an inner agent that stands somehow apart from the machinery and steers it.

This book does something different. It starts from a simpler and more uncomfortable place. Human beings are not an exception to how the rest of reality works. We are systems among systems. We do not sit outside the machinery of the world. We are made of it. Whatever else we may be, we are finite, physical systems that have to operate under the same kinds of constraints as every other finite system that persists in time. Those constraints are not psychological, cultural, or moral. They are mechanical.

These mechanical constraints define how any system can exist at all: how it moves from state to state, carries forward, stabilizes, accumulates history, breaks, and changes. They apply to cells and storms, to engines and ecosystems, and they apply just as much to nervous systems and human lives.

In the physical sciences, new kinds of behavior do not appear because we describe old parts more cleverly. They appear when the same parts are bound together under new constraints. Water is not a better description of hydrogen and oxygen. It is what happens when they are organized in a particular way. The same components, held under a different structure, become a different kind of thing. The same is true here.

This book does not add new forces, new faculties, or new inner actors. It does not propose a new story about what people "really are." It takes the same physical, biological, and informational processes we already know and binds them under a different causal grammar: load, stability, constraint, and carry.

Once those constraints are made explicit, familiar features of mental life begin to look different. Effort stops looking like a virtue and starts looking like a cost. Emotion stops looking like a guide and starts looking like a signal. Identity stops looking like a core and starts looking like a long-term shape. Trauma stops looking like damage and starts looking like overfitting. Awareness stops looking like a driver and starts looking like a surface signature. Change stops looking like something you initiate and starts looking like something that happens when structure can no longer be carried.

These features of mental life start looking like consequences. Not consequences of your beliefs. Not consequences of your choices. Consequences of the kind of physical system you are. This is not a better description of the same psychology. It is a different kind of causal framework. It does not begin with meaning, intention, or purpose. It begins with the question of what kinds of physical systems can exist at all, what constraints they must obey, and what must follow from that.

If you change the instrument used to measure, you change what becomes visible. You do not create a new world. You reveal a different structure in the one that is already there. What follows in this book is grounded in the consequences of how physical systems work — not in speculation about inner authors, free choice, or mental command. It is a psychology built from the mechanics of the system we are, and from the lawful constraints under which any such system must operate. Because of this, it can account for many psychological extremes that agency-based psychology cannot explain, and it provides a coherent foundation for understanding how human systems operate, and for shaping more effective therapeutic conditions for helping others.

The opening part of this book develops the mechanical foundations of the system we are. It examines constraint, measurement, stabilization, and structure in careful detail. This material can be demanding because it replaces familiar psychological language with a physical and architectural one. But this groundwork is necessary. Once these mechanics are clear, patterns of experience, behavior, suffering, and change become simpler and easier to understand, reducing the load carried by your system.

Chapter 2

The Telescope and the Instrument We Live Inside

How Measurement Limits the World a System Can Have

On a cold autumn night in 1995, a young astronomer named Elena stood alone on a roof in New Mexico, staring into what she believed was nothing. The sky above her was clear and black, a black so deep it seemed to swallow the stars and leave only their sharpest points. But Elena was not looking at the stars. She was looking at everything between them—at the regions where human eyes register only emptiness.

Her telescope was powerful for an amateur instrument, yet the dark patches she loved revealed almost nothing. Still, something about them kept pulling her back. Night after night, she returned to the same empty regions, unable to shake the sense that "nothing" might not be the whole story. Later that evening, she examined her images. As expected, they showed only grainy darkness. She saved the files and moved on.

Years passed. Eventually, Elena joined a team working with a newly launched space telescope. When observation time became available, she proposed a simple and unpopular idea: instead of pointing the telescope at bright objects, aim it at a region that appeared empty. The area she chose was tiny—no bigger than a grain of sand held at arm's length. Her colleagues hesitated. Telescope time was precious. Why spend it looking at nothing? But the proposal was approved.

When the first deep-field images arrived, Elena stared at the screen as if the floor had dropped out beneath her. The patch of sky that had seemed empty was overflowing with galaxies—not stars, but galaxies—thousands of them, scattered at every depth. Spirals, ellipses, ancient red systems, newborn blue ones erupting with light. The void she had studied for years had never been empty. It had been invisible.

The sky had not changed. The instrument had. The telescope did not create galaxies. It altered what could be detected. Patterns appeared. Structures became visible—not because the universe reorganized, but because the means of observing it had changed. What can be encountered depends on the instrument doing the encountering. What remains unseen is often hidden not by absence, but by the limits of the measuring system in use.

The Instrument We Live Inside

Elena revealed something fundamental about any system that can only encounter the world through measurement. We do not encounter the world directly. We encounter the world through a measuring architecture.

The human system is not a camera copying reality. It is a layered measuring and stabilizing structure composed of many narrow channels: pressure sensing, motion extraction, posture sampling, tension tracking, internal state monitoring, and social pattern detection. Each channel is bounded and shaped by development and history. At every moment these processes operate in parallel, and their activity is reduced into a single internal state. That state is what the moment is like.

A measuring system can register only what it is built to register. Anything outside its range is not encountered, even if fully present. The architecture does not reveal the world in its full extent. It reveals only what it can carry. By the time anything appears in awareness, the measuring work is already complete.

Before a shift in tone is felt, it has been measured. Before a room feels tense or calm, many small cues have been combined. Before something feels threatening or safe, body and environment have already converged into a single state. Awareness does not select among possibilities. It receives the result. It is where the system's internal state becomes available, not where it is produced.

What you experience is not the world itself. It is the output of your measuring architecture—an instrument shaped by early conditions, repeated stabilizations, learned sensitivities, and long-established pathways. It has blind spots. It has preferred routes of resolution. Two people can stand in the same room and stabilize different internal worlds, not because the room differs, but because their instruments measure it differently.

What Measurement Makes Real

Experience is measurement-dependent. A system cannot encounter what it cannot register. To the system, what is unmeasured is indistinguishable from what is absent. A sunflower cannot smell the manure in the field it grows in. The molecules are present, but nothing in its architecture can register them. For that system, they do not exist. A metal detector can be passed over a wooden table forever and never find the grain of the wood. A thermometer can sit in sunlight and never register the color of the sky. Each system lives within the range of what it can transduce. What lies outside that range is not hidden. It is simply not part of that system's world. This is not a special case. It follows from having any measurement boundary at all.

Measurement as Partitioning

Measurement does more than convert. It partitions. Once physical variation is transduced into the system's medium, the continuous world is automatically divided into the categories the architecture can sustain— warm or cool, bright or dim, motion or stillness. These distinctions feel like properties of the environment, yet they arise from the structure of the measuring apparatus.

A flatbed scanner does not capture a page as it exists. It samples light at fixed intervals, assigns each sample to a limited intensity range, and outputs a grid of discrete units. The image is not the page. It is the scanner's rendering shaped by its measurement thresholds and stabilization limits. The mind operates the same way. A continuous world is rendered into discrete internal distinctions because the architecture cannot operate otherwise. It must reduce incoming variation into a finite set of carryable states. The divisions are not in the world. They arise from what can be transduced and stabilized.

Why Measurement Must Simplify

Measurement always discards far more than it preserves, because the space of possible structure exceeds what any finite architecture can transduce. Most of the world never becomes part of experience—not because it is ignored, but because it cannot be translated into the system's medium at all.

Receptors have fixed sensitivities and thresholds. Anything outside them never enters the system. This simplification is not optional. A finite architecture cannot sustain infinite input. Measurement compresses the world into a narrow band the system can carry without disintegration. The world is vast. The architecture is not. Measurement sits between them, and boundaries always simplify. Experience therefore cannot reveal the world "as it is." It reveals only what the architecture allows to pass.

Convergence

Measurement alone does not produce a moment. It produces too much. At every instant, the architecture is struck by a vast parallel field: light, pressure, posture, temperature, internal state, residue, social cues. All arrive simultaneously. None arrive in sequence. A finite system cannot inhabit this simultaneity. It cannot carry multiple incompatible states forward. Coherence requires one configuration. Therefore, the parallel field must converge into a single carryable state. This occurs by constraint, not selection. Only one arrangement can remain—the configuration the system can sustain without disorganization under current conditions. This convergence occurs before anything is experienced. By the time a moment has any felt character, the work is already done. Measurement determines what can enter. Convergence determines what can remain.

When Measurement Becomes Compressed

A measuring system does not continue resolving everything with equal intensity. Repeated configurations require fewer distinctions to stabilize. Measurement does not vanish; it becomes compressed. What was once actively sampled becomes implicitly registered. The system has not lost detail. It has lost the need to re-measure it. Any instrument, once calibrated to a stable signal, stops resolving unnecessary variation. Because of this, familiarity is not knowing more. It is measuring less.

What a system encounters in everyday life is therefore not the full structure of what is present, but a reduced rendering that is sufficient for recognition. Objects, environments, and people appear settled, obvious, already known—not because they lack detail, but because the system no longer needs to extract that detail to produce a usable internal state. When repetition is interrupted, compression loosens. Measurement briefly expands. Features that were always present become visible again—not as new information, but as newly measured structure.

The Face You Thought You Knew

A man has been married for twenty years. He has seen his wife's face tens of thousands of times. Her presence is familiar, efficient, already settled. Then she leaves for two months to care for her dying mother. When she returns, he stands in the airport and watches her approach. For a moment, he does not speak. Nothing about her face has changed. Yet it is not the same face. He notices the curve of her cheek, the asymmetry of her smile, the shape of her hands, the way her voice occupies space. He is not recovering lost information. He is measuring differently. During her absence, the grooves that usually compress her into "already-known" loosened. The architecture is briefly sampling again. For a few days he continues to encounter her this way. Then familiar stabilizations return. The extra detail fades—not because it is gone, but because it is no longer required. He does not lose her beauty. He loses the need to measure it.

The First Constraint: Measurement and Convergence

A system never encounters the world directly. It encounters only what its instrument can measure, and it can inhabit only what those measurements can converge into as a carryable state.

Nothing inside the system occurs in response to "the world." It occurs in response to whatever was measured and stabilized. Anything the instrument cannot measure does not exist for the system. Anything that cannot converge cannot be inhabited. This is not unique to human systems. Any finite architecture with a boundary must first convert external variation into its own form, and must then force that variation into a single configuration it can carry forward. These two operations define the entire domain of what the system can encounter. Everything that follows depends on this: why people can live in the same environment yet inhabit different internal worlds, why awareness is always downstream of the machinery that produces the state, and why altering the measuring structure alters the world that can be lived in.

Constraints Established So Far

Constraint 1 — Measurement and Convergence: A system never encounters the world directly. It only ever encounters what its own measurement architecture can transduce and converge into a stable, carryable state.

Chapter 3

Nothing Happens All at Once

Why a System Can Only Ever Produce Its Next State

The System Cannot Act on the Present

Every system that exists in sequence faces a constraint it cannot escape: it cannot act on what is happening now. By the time anything exists for the system, it already belongs to what has already occurred. This is not a philosophical claim. It is mechanical ordering. A system can be in only one state at a time. For it to be in another state, something must change. And for something to change, something else must already have happened.

A simple assembly line makes this visible. One station completes its operation and passes the part to the next. The next station can work only on what it has already received. There is no point where the line works on a part while it is still being made. Every operation is performed on a completed handoff.

The same ordering remains when the scale compresses to microseconds. A camera sensor integrates light, the signal is read out, processed, and written. By the time an image exists anywhere in the system, the light that produced it is already gone. Faster hardware does not remove the sequence. It only tightens it. The system still works only on what has already been converted into an internal state.

Mechanically, there is no place where a system reaches into a forming state and reshapes it. It produces the next state from the one before. There is always a before and an after. There is always a handoff. We speak as if things happen "in the moment," but there is no such operating zone. There is only a boundary where one completed state gives rise to another. By the time a state exists with any felt character, the process that produced it has already finished. The present is not something a system acts on. It is something a system becomes. Imagine a row of falling dominoes. Each domino falls because the one before it fell. No domino needs an extra force to decide. The sequence is sufficient.

The Chain Never Breaks

A system is no different. Its current state is what it is because of the state before it. Its next state will be what it will be because of the state it is in now, together with whatever influences reach it. There is no place in the chain where the system steps outside the sequence. There is only the sequence. This remains true no matter how complicated the system becomes. Your body is in one configuration, then another. Muscles contract because signals arrive. Signals arise because prior conditions drove them. Even the fastest reflexes obey the same ordering. By the time movement occurs, the state that produced it has already been replaced. The process advances like a propagating wave: each stage responds only to what the previous stage has completed.

Experience feels immediate. The machinery is sequential. From inside experience, it can feel as if action occurs in real time. But that felt immediacy is itself something that appears only after a state has already been produced. By the time anything feels like a decision, the conditions that made that outcome unavoidable have already done their work.

A cursor on a screen feels like it moves continuously under your hand. But the computer is not working on "the motion." It reads an input, updates an internal state, and redraws the display. By the time the new position appears, the input that produced it has already been processed and replaced by the next. Smoothness is a display outcome. The machinery is a sequence of completed steps. There is no exemption for nervous systems. There is no break in the chain where something uncaused enters. The brain is not outside causation. It is an extremely complicated part of it. A neuron cannot fire without being driven into that state by prior signals. Those signals were produced by earlier states, and those by earlier still. The brain does not interrupt causation. It is built entirely out of it.

Awareness Is Downstream

There is also another subsystem positioned later in the sequence. In Chapter 2, we saw that awareness receives only the output of the system's internal machinery. Not only does the system advance by handoffs; the part that registers what has occurred sits downstream from the processes that produce it. By the time fear is felt, the bodily state of fear has already been assembled. By the time calm is felt, the system has already stabilized. By the time something feels like a choice, the state that produced that outcome already exists.

Consider a sudden threat. First, sensory channels register a sharp change in the environment. That input propagates and reorganizes the body: heart rate rises, breathing tightens, muscles contract, hands begin to shake. Only after this new configuration is in place does the experience of fear appear. Experience does not initiate the state. It marks that the state has already been entered. When the threat passes, the sequence does not reverse by declaration. The bodily configuration unwinds according to its own dynamics: heart rate slows, breathing lengthens, muscle tension releases, and only then does the experience of calm appear. Again, experience does not drive the transition. It registers that the transition has already occurred. Awareness is late by structure. It cannot be otherwise.

What This Means and What It Doesn't Mean

It is easy to hear this and conclude that everything is fixed in the sense of being simple or rigid. In one sense, it is fixed: whatever happens will happen because the system, in that state, could not have produced a different next state. There is no break in the chain and no place where something uncaused enters.

But this does not imply simplicity, rigidity, or easy prediction. A system can be extraordinarily sensitive to its current configuration. Small differences can produce radically different trajectories. History reshapes what is even possible. Structure determines which paths are open and which are closed. None of this escapes causation. It only means causation is rich. The future is not written in advance as a script. But whatever future arrives will arrive because of what already exists, and could not have arrived any other way.

The Second System Constraint: Sequential Causation

This can now be stated as a constraint. *A system can only ever produce its next state from its current state. It cannot act on a forming state, it cannot reach into what has not yet been produced, and it cannot skip steps. Every change is a handoff. Every state is the result of the one before it.*

Everything that follows depends on this: why effort feels the way it does, why change takes time, why habits have momentum, why trauma persists, why insight so often does nothing, why systems get stuck in grooves, and why no amount of wanting can bypass structure. Once this is seen, the question shifts. The question is no longer, "Why did I choose that in that moment?" It becomes, "What kind of system was I, that this was the only next state available?" That question does not blame, judge, or moralize. It describes. And description is where mechanics begins. If a system can only move forward one state at a time, the next question is unavoidable: what kinds of states can it occupy at all? Not everything is possible for every architecture. Some states simply cannot exist for a given system. The next chapter is about that.

Constraints Established So Far

Constraint 1 — Measurement and Convergence: A system never encounters the world directly. It only ever encounters what its own measurement architecture can transduce and converge into a stable, carryable state.

Constraint 2 — Sequential Causation: A system can only ever produce its next state from its current state. It cannot act on the present, reach into the future, or skip steps. Every state is the result of a prior state.

Chapter 4

Not Every State Is Possible

How Structure Defines What a System Can Be

If a system can only ever produce its next state from its current state, then the next question is unavoidable: what kinds of states can it occupy at all? The answer is not "any." A system does not move through open space. It moves within a domain defined by its own structure. Some states are reachable. Most are not. This limitation is not imposed by the world. It is imposed by the system itself. A ladder cannot become a chair. A radio cannot become a telescope. A camera cannot become a Geiger counter. Not because the world forbids it, but because their internal organization does. The parts they contain, the way those parts are arranged, and the interfaces they expose define what states can ever occur. A system's possible states are defined by its structure.

Structure Is a Set of Constraints

Every system consists of parts arranged in specific ways, with specific modes of interaction. That organization is not merely how the system works. It is what the system is. From that organization follows a strict boundary: a finite set of structurally realizable states, and an infinite set that are not. A gearbox can be in first gear, second gear, third gear, or neutral. It cannot be in "half a gear" except by failing. A digital register can hold any value within its bit width. It cannot hold a value outside that range. A bridge can sustain certain load distributions and not others. When forced into an impossible configuration, it does not enter a new state. It fails. Structure does not sit on top of behavior. It generates the space within which behavior can occur. What we call behavior is motion within that space.

The State Space of Structure

It is useful to think of a system's possible configurations as forming a structured space. Each point corresponds to a state the system can, in principle, occupy. Movement occurs one state at a time, always within what structure allows. This is what is meant by a *state space.*

Some regions of this space are densely connected. Some are isolated. Some are easily reachable from many directions. Others require long chains of intermediate transitions. Many are unreachable because no path exists through the system's existing organization.

This is not abstraction. Any networked system has this character. A nervous system, for example, is not a uniform field of possibilities. It is a patterned connectivity in which some configurations lie one step apart, others require extended propagation, and many cannot occur because no pathway connects them. The connectivity does not merely influence movement. It defines where movement can occur at all.

At any moment, the system does not invent its possibilities as it moves. The space of possible states is implied by its current structure. Movement always occurs within an already-constrained geometry. But that geometry is not static. History reshapes it. Learning, wear, damage, reinforcement, and reorganization alter which configurations are reachable. Change does not occur outside the state space. It deforms the space itself.

Impossible States Do Not Appear

When a state cannot be occupied, it does not present itself as a difficult option or a forbidden choice. It does not appear. A calculator does not refuse to play music. A thermometer does not decline to measure color. These are not failures. They are outside the space of realizable states. The same holds for more complex systems. A body cannot fold into arbitrary shapes. A nervous system cannot enter arbitrary activation patterns. These impossibilities are not felt as resistance. They are absent. There is no experience of what cannot occur.

Movement Is Always Within the Allowed Geometry

When a system changes, it does not move from any state to any other. It moves from one allowed configuration to another, along paths permitted by its structure. Even dramatic reorganization remains within what is structurally realizable at that moment. When a bridge collapses, it does not become a helicopter. When a hard drive fails, it does not become a radio.

When a body is injured, it does not enter arbitrary new modes of being. It transitions into a different region of its own constrained state space.

Structure Is History That Has Become Constraint

In many systems, structure is not fixed. It is shaped by prior states. Wear, growth, deformation, learning, and damage all reshape the geometry of possible configurations. A bent axle has a different range of movement than a straight one. A trained neural network has a different set of reachable internal states than an untrained one. A scarred body has a different movement space than an uninjured one. These changes become new constraints. History does not add freedom. It reshapes what is possible.

There Is No Jump Outside the Space

Because a system can only produce its next state from its current state, and because both states must lie within its structurally defined space, there is no mechanism by which it can leap outside its own possibilities.

Imagine a person who has fallen into a twenty-foot-deep steel shaft with smooth walls. From that configuration, only a limited set of next states are physically realizable: standing, sitting, lying down, climbing briefly, or falling back. There is no sequence of bodily movements that leads from that state to outside the shaft. Jumping out or flying out is not difficult. It is structurally unavailable. If the person later appears outside the shaft, it is not because the body moved there through its own state space. It is because the conditions changed—a ladder lowered, a rope introduced, the walls altered. From the original configuration, escape was not reachable. There is no move that escapes structure. There is no transition unconstrained by what the system is. This is not pessimism. It is mechanics.

Constraint Does Not Mean Rigidity

Constraint does not imply narrowness or stagnation. A system's state space can be enormous—far larger than could ever be fully explored. Small structural changes can open vast new regions. Learning and reorganization can dramatically reshape what is reachable. But none of this escapes constraint. It only alters the geometry of the allowed space. Chess is fully deterministic and rule-bound. No piece moves illegally. No board position appears except through a valid sequence. Yet the number of possible positions exceeds the number of atoms in the observable universe. From almost any position, small changes open entirely new regions of possibility. The system never leaves its constraints, and yet the space it defines is effectively inexhaustible. Novelty does not come from stepping outside structure. It comes from moving into regions that were previously unreachable.

The Third System Constraint: State Space

This can now be stated cleanly as a constraint.

Every system has a state space defined by its structure. It can occupy only states within that space. Transitions occur only between configurations that are structurally realizable. A system cannot become what its structure does not permit.

Everything that follows depends on this: why some changes are easy and others impossible, why patterns repeat, why certain breakdowns recur while others never occur, why history matters, and why architecture is destiny in a literal sense. Once this is clear, another question becomes unavoidable. If a system has many possible states, why does it occupy some more than others? Why do some persist while others vanish immediately? The next chapter addresses that.

Constraints Established So Far

Constraint 1 — Measurement and Convergence: A system never encounters the world directly. It only ever encounters what its own measurement architecture can transduce and converge into a stable, carryable state.

Constraint 2 — Sequential Causation: A system can only ever produce its next state from its current state. It cannot act on the present, reach into the future, or skip steps. Every state is the result of a prior state.

Constraint 3 — State Space: Every system has a space of possible states defined by its structure. The system can only ever occupy states within that space, and can only transition between states that are structurally realizable. A system cannot become what its structure does not permit.

Chapter 5

Why Stability Comes First

How Only Some States Can Persist

In the previous chapter, we saw that every system has a space of possible states defined by its structure. Some states are reachable, but most are not. Yet reachability is not the same as viability. A system can enter many configurations it cannot remain in. Some are only briefly reachable before the system is forced out of them. Some impose demands that cannot be sustained. Others destroy the very conditions that made them possible. A state can be structurally possible and still not be carryable.

A bridge can briefly sustain a load that exceeds its long-term tolerance. For a moment nothing appears wrong, but joints begin to slip, materials deform, and the structure must either shed the load or fail. That configuration was reachable but not maintainable. An engine can spin at a speed its bearings cannot sustain. Friction, heat, and vibration accumulate faster than they can be dissipated, forcing reorganization or breakdown. A body can enter a level of exertion its cardiovascular and respiratory systems cannot support. Oxygen debt, heat, and metabolic byproducts accumulate until the state cannot persist. In each case, structural possibility and structural viability diverge. Only some reachable states can actually be carried.

What It Means to Carry a State

A state is not merely a momentary configuration. It must be carryable across time. To carry a state is to sustain a configuration that fits within the system's current structure—one that can be integrated without disintegration, forced reorganization, or loss of coherence. A bridge must not only enter a loaded configuration; it must remain there. A processor must not only represent a value; it must hold it without overheating or corruption. A body must not only assume a posture; it must sustain it without breakdown. A state that cannot be carried is not a state the system can live in. It is a configuration that immediately forces transition.

Stability Is Not a Goal, It Is a Condition

Stability is often described as something systems pursue. Mechanically, this is incorrect. Stability is not a goal, preference, or strategy. It is the condition under which a system can continue to exist at all. A system that cannot remain in any state cannot sustain organized behavior and cannot persist. Stability does not result from intention. It determines which states can exist in time.

The Suspension Bridge Under Load

A suspension bridge illustrates what it means to carry a state. Under ordinary conditions, forces are distributed across cables, towers, and anchors, and disturbances are absorbed without visible strain. The structure remains in a configuration it can carry. When heavier load or stronger wind arrives, the bridge does not instantly settle into a new stable configuration. It oscillates. Forces redistribute. Energy moves through the structure as excess motion is shed.

If redistribution succeeds, oscillations dampen and the bridge settles into a configuration that can sustain the load. If forces persist or exceed tolerance, deeper reorganization begins—deformation, narrowing tolerances, or structural failure. The visible motion is not instability itself. It is the trace of a system searching for a configuration it can carry. At every moment, only some reachable configurations are stable enough to persist.

The Domain of Carryable States

Within the larger space of possible states lies a smaller region: the set of dynamically maintainable configurations. Some impose little strain and require little internal work. Others are technically reachable but costly, requiring continuous redistribution of stress. Some cannot be carried at all and immediately force transition. A system therefore does not move through all possible states. It moves within the subset that can persist. Stability does not guide the system. It defines what can remain.

Failure Is Not a Separate Process

When a system cannot carry a state, it does not "try and fail." The configuration simply cannot persist. Instability forces transition to another configuration. An overloaded bridge does not attempt to remain a bridge and then decide to fall. A processor does not choose to shut down. A body does not decide to collapse. Each enters a configuration that cannot be carried and transitions according to its structure. Failure is not a special event. It is the outcome of non-carryable states.

Stability Is Local, Not Absolute

No state is stable under all conditions. Stability exists only within a range of surrounding circumstances. Change the load, environment, internal parameters, or history, and a previously stable configuration may become unstable. A ladder is stable under its own weight and a climber's load. Add lateral force or shift the ground, and the same configuration becomes unstable. A moving bicycle is dynamically stable, yet the same configuration at rest would fall. Stability is therefore not a property of a state alone. It is a relationship between a state and the conditions acting upon it.

Why Systems Settle

Unstable states cannot persist. High-strain states cannot endure when lower-strain alternatives exist. Configurations that impose less structural work persist longer. This is not because the system seeks comfort or efficiency. It is because only these configurations can remain. A system does not prefer stability. Stability is what remains when non-carryable configurations fall away, in the same way water flows along channels of least resistance without intention.

Stability Is the Gatekeeper of Experience

Because a system can only exist in states it can carry, everything it ever experiences has already passed through this constraint. A configuration that cannot be sustained is never inhabited. It is passed through or forces transition. Novelty becomes real only if it becomes stable. Experience is therefore not a record of what is possible. It is a record of what is carryable.

The Fourth System Constraint: Stability (Carryability)

This can now be stated cleanly.

A system can persist only in states it can carry. States that cannot be maintained force transition, breakdown, or reorganization. Stability is not a goal. It is the structural condition for continued existence.

Everything that follows depends on this: why systems settle into patterns, why some changes do not last, why breakdowns occur, why recovery requires new stability, and why some configurations feel effortless while others feel strained. Once this is clear, another question becomes unavoidable. If some states impose less load and others impose more, how does that difference shape what systems actually do over time? The next chapter addresses that.

Constraints Established So Far

Constraint 1 — Measurement and Convergence: A system never encounters the world directly. It only ever encounters what its own measurement architecture can transduce and converge into a stable, carryable state.

Constraint 2 — Sequential Causation: A system can only ever produce its next state from its current state. It cannot act on the present, reach into the future, or skip steps. Every state is the result of a prior state.

Constraint 3 — State Space: Every system has a space of possible states defined by its structure. The system can only ever occupy states within that space, and can only transition between states that are structurally realizable. A system cannot become what its structure does not permit.

Constraint 4 — Stability (Carryability): A system can persist only in states it can carry. States that cannot be maintained force transition, breakdown, or reorganization. Stability is not a goal. It is the structural condition for continued existence.

Chapter 6

The Shape of Cost

How Cost Emerges from What Is Hard to Carry

In the previous chapter, we saw that a system can exist only in states it can carry. States that cannot be maintained force transition or reorganization. But stability alone is not enough. Among the states a system can carry, some are easy to maintain while others require continuous internal work. Both may persist, but not at the same cost. A further distinction therefore appears: not just between carryable and uncarryable states, but between lower-cost and higher-cost states.

What Cost Is

Cost is not a price the system decides to pay. It is the amount of internal work required to maintain coherence under constraint. A bridge under light load is stable at lower cost than the same bridge under heavy load, even if both remain stable. Under heavier load, internal stresses must be continuously redistributed and absorbed. The configuration persists, but only through ongoing work. A processor at low utilization operates at low cost. Near its thermal limits, it may still function, but only because cooling, throttling, and correction mechanisms work continuously to prevent failure. A body standing at rest is stable at low cost. The same body holding an awkward posture may remain upright only through continuous compensation. Cost is not whether a state can be carried. It is how much internal work is required to carry it.

Load

When a system must continuously work to remain in a configuration, it is under load. Load is the internal burden created by maintaining a state that does not naturally sustain itself. Two systems can be equally stable yet under very different load: one coasting, the other straining. A person standing in a

20

relaxed posture remains stable with little internal work. Holding a heavy box at arm's length or maintaining a twisted posture requires continuous muscular activation, joint bracing, and rapid correction. Stability persists, but under load.

A Cost-Shaped Landscape

State space is not only divided into possible and impossible, or stable and unstable. It is shaped by gradients of cost. It is useful to think of this space as a landscape. Some regions resemble valleys; others resemble slopes, ridges, or narrow passes. Some configurations are easy to sustain. Others require strain and redistribution, and can be held only briefly.

A physical example makes this visible. On a calm day, the atmosphere is relatively even in temperature and pressure. Disturbances fade, and the system maintains coherence with little internal redistribution. This corresponds to a low-cost region of the landscape where nearby conditions are easy to sustain.

A thunderstorm is different. Strong gradients, rising moisture, and unstable air require continuous internal redistribution. Small disturbances grow rather than fade, and coherence must be actively maintained. The configuration persists, but at high cost. When the atmosphere can no longer sustain that internal work, it reorganizes into a calmer state.

Cost is not a number the system computes. It is the physical difficulty of carrying a configuration: strain across structure, tension among subsystems, and the rate at which instability accumulates. Low-cost states are configurations the system can sustain with little internal stress, like resting in a basin. High-cost states load the structure and require continuous work, like remaining on an incline or balancing near an edge.

The shape of this landscape is not fixed. History reshapes it. Repetition lowers cost along some paths. Strain erodes others. Learning, injury, and adaptation alter which configurations are easy, difficult, or unreachable. Movement occurs along slopes and channels defined by this geometry. A system can be forced uphill temporarily, but unless the terrain itself changes, it cannot remain there.

Throughout this book, behavior and change will be described using this landscape language: basins, ridges, corridors, and slopes. These are not metaphors for experience. They describe the geometry of what a finite system can sustain. A state space has shape, and that shape determines both the cost of transition and the cost of persistence.

Basins and Ridges

Low-cost regions are often called attractors. In CST terms, an attractor is simply a basin-shaped region of state space. Nothing pulls the system toward it. The geometry makes nearby configurations settle there because remaining is inexpensive and leaving requires work. Standing at the bottom of a basin requires little effort. Small disturbances fade. Standing partway up requires continuous work; without that work, the system returns downward. On a slope, the system does not remain. On a ridge, it must balance precisely. At a cliff, no state can be carried at all. On a flat, persistence is easy but displacement is also easy. These regions represent distinct structural conditions, not preferences.

What a Cost-Shaped Landscape Means

A system moves within a terrain shaped by what is inexpensive, costly, unstable, or impossible to sustain. Later chapters will show how history and repetition carve channels through this terrain, deepening some basins and narrowing others.

Why Systems Drift

Costly states require continuous internal work and are therefore fragile. If that work is reduced or overwhelmed, the configuration cannot be maintained. Low-cost states require little work and are robust. Systems therefore drift toward regions of lower cost, not because they seek ease, but because only those configurations can persist without continuous strain. Drift is not randomness. It is movement governed by geometry and constraint — the system traversing its landscape because its current configuration cannot be sustained where it is.

Lowest Cost Is Not "Better"

Low-cost states are not inherently superior. They are simply easier to maintain. Some preserve function; others degrade it. An addictive loop can become low cost after the system reorganizes around it. Remaining in the loop requires little reconfiguration. Leaving requires sustained, costly change. The loop is low cost not because it is good, but because the architecture has been shaped to make it easy to repeat. Cost describes how a state is maintained, not whether it should be.

An addicted smoker provides a clear illustration. After repeated nicotine exposure, neural pathways reorganize around the cue–craving–inhalation sequence. Environmental triggers, internal tension states, and motor routines become tightly coupled. Remaining in the smoking loop requires little reconfiguration. The cues arise, the action follows, the chemistry stabilizes, and the state persists at relatively low cost for that reorganized system. Attempting to exit the loop, however, requires sustained internal work: craving signals intensify, regulation mechanisms strain, and alternative pathways must be stabilized repeatedly. The loop is low cost not because it preserves health, but because the architecture has been shaped to make it easy to repeat.

When Cost Accumulates

A system can remain in a high-cost state for long periods, but internal work consumes margin. Components wear, tolerance narrows, and brittleness increases. A configuration once barely sustainable becomes unstable under smaller additional load. A body can maintain chronic overwork and sleep loss for years through continuous compensation. Over time, recovery weakens, regulation narrows, and minor disturbances produce large effects. Eventually, the same workload becomes uncarryable and the system reorganizes. The system does not fail by decision. It exhausts structural margin and has to reorganize.

The Fifth System Constraint: Cost (Load)

This can now be stated clearly.

Among the states a system can carry, some require more internal compensatory work than others. That work is load. The load required to maintain a state is its cost. Systems do not remain in low-cost states by preference. They remain there because only those states can persist without continuous strain.

At this point, several constraints are in place. A system can exist only in states it can carry. Among those states, cost varies. Regions of the state space therefore differ in geometry: basins, slopes, ridges, flats, and cliffs. High-cost states consume margin; when margin disappears, reorganization follows. Change does not arise from intensifying compensation within the same configuration. It arises from entering a different configuration. If a system is forced into a state it cannot afford to carry, what happens next? The next chapter addresses that.

Constraints Established So Far

Constraint 1 — Measurement and Convergence: A system never encounters the world directly. It only ever encounters what its own measurement architecture can transduce and converge into a stable, carryable state.

Constraint 2 — Sequential Causation: A system can only ever produce its next state from its current state. It cannot act on the present, reach into the future, or skip steps. Every state is the result of a prior state.

Constraint 3 — State Space: Every system has a space of possible states defined by its structure. The system can only ever occupy states within that space, and can only transition between states that are structurally realizable. A system cannot become what its structure does not permit.

Constraint 4 — Stability (Carryability): A system can persist only in states it can carry. States that cannot be maintained force transition, breakdown, or reorganization. Stability is not a goal. It is the structural condition for continued existence.

Constraint 5 — Cost (Load): Among the states a system can carry, some require more internal compensatory work than others. That work is load. The amount of load required to maintain a state is its cost. Systems do not remain in low-cost states by preference. They remain there because only those states can persist without continuous strain.

Chapter 7

Grooves, Channels, and Residue

How History Carves the Landscape

In the previous chapters, we described a system moving within a cost-shaped landscape. Some regions are easy to occupy, others are costly, and some cannot be carried at all. Basins, slopes, ridges, plateaus, and cliffs describe the geometry of what a system can and cannot sustain at any moment. But this landscape is not a fixed stage. It is gradually reshaped by the system's own motion. Each time a configuration is stabilized under load, the adjustments that made that stabilization possible slightly alter the structure itself. Each redistribution leaves a small deformation. Over time, these changes accumulate. The terrain is carved by the traffic that passes through it. What the system inhabits now is therefore not only a position in a landscape, but a landscape already shaped by everything the system has previously been forced to carry.

Residue and Condition

A system does not reset after each moment. When a configuration is stabilized, the internal modifications that made it carryable do not vanish. They remain as structural change—shifted thresholds, altered coordination, changed sensitivities, redistributed tolerances. CST calls the persistent footprint of these changes *residue*.

Residue is not stored information and not a record. It is the architecture itself, slightly reshaped by stabilization. Over time, accumulated residue does not merely mark where the system has been. It changes the geometry of what the system can carry next—deepening basins, raising ridges, narrowing corridors, and carving channels.

This history-written geometry is what CST calls condition. Condition is not a trait and not an identity. It names the current shape of the system's structure as it now exists, produced by its own prior stabilizations. What the system can easily carry now, what it can barely carry, and what it cannot carry at all are consequences of this accumulated residue.

How Repetition Carves Channels

When a system repeatedly passes through the same regions of its state space, transitions through those regions become easier because the surrounding structure is already organized to support them. In systems where motion feeds back into structure, repetition also reshapes the structure itself, lowering resistance along those routes.

A forest path does not begin as a path. Early crossings push aside vegetation and compress uneven ground. With enough repetition, the soil compacts, the edges clear, and water begins to run there. Each passage makes the next one easier. Other routes, used less often, gradually become harder. No one plans the trail. It emerges because repeated motion reshapes the terrain. The same principle applies to any system whose stabilizations alter its own constraints. Over time, certain sequences of stabilization become channels through the landscape. CST calls these channels grooves.

A groove is not a preference and not a commitment. It is a deformation of possibility: a region of the landscape made easier to traverse and easier to remain in because it has been traversed and occupied many times before. In an engine, repeated motion seats surfaces and reduces friction along some paths. In a nervous system, repeated activation lowers the effective cost of the same activation pattern, making the same transitions occur more readily. In a riverbed, repeated flow deepens one channel and leaves others to silt and rise. Different substrates, same geometry: motion that feeds back into structure sculpts its own corridors.

Grooves and the Distribution of Cost

Grooves are not merely habits. They are regions of reduced cost. When a system enters a well-carved channel, less internal work is required to remain coherent there. Coordination is already aligned. Thresholds already match. Redistribution is minimal. Outside these channels, the opposite holds. Regions that are rarely visited become more expensive to enter and harder to stabilize. A configuration that was once moderately difficult can, after long disuse, become extremely costly or practically unreachable.

A simple physical case shows the mechanism. Repeated friction on the skin produces a callus. Each episode forces minor redistribution and repair. A small structural change remains. Over many repetitions, that specific form of load is carried at lower cost in that specific region. The system has not stored an instruction. It has acquired a new shape. The same applies across scales. Repeated traversal of a coordination pattern does not preserve a script to be retrieved later. It alters thresholds, timings, and coupling in the substrate itself. What was once unstable and expensive becomes stable and inexpensive because the architecture has been rebuilt to carry it.

Path Dependence

Because the landscape is reshaped by history, future motion is constrained not only by what is possible in principle, but by what has already occurred. Two systems with similar basic designs but different histories no longer inhabit the same cost landscape. Their basins differ. Their ridges differ. Their easy routes differ. This is why two people can enter the same situation and not pay the same cost to remain there. For one system, the configuration lies near a prepared channel and stabilizes with little internal work. For the other, the same configuration lies far from any supported route and requires continuous compensation. Nothing in the present moment explains the difference. The difference lies in how the landscapes have been carved. History does not dictate what must happen next, but it removes many alternatives before the next moment arrives by reshaping what is reachable at low cost.

Enjoys the music   Overwhelmed by the noise

Why Change Is Structurally Difficult

When a system is sitting in a deep, well-carved basin, leaving requires passing through regions of higher cost. It requires entering configurations less supported by the current structure and therefore demanding more redistribution. This is not resistance and not reluctance. It is geometry. A marble does not leave a deep channel without being pushed across ridges and unstable terrain. Likewise, a system does not leave a deep groove without passing through states that are harder to carry. Sometimes it can tolerate that passage. Sometimes it cannot. In every case, the difficulty lies in the shape of the landscape, not in any decision made within it.

Grooves Are Not Goals

It is tempting to describe grooves as if they were maintained by intent. That is not correct. The system does not seek grooves. Grooves are what remain after repeated stabilization under constraint. They are not chosen. They are produced. A river does not choose its channel. Where resistance is slightly lower, more flow occurs. That flow lowers resistance further. Over time, what began as a small irregularity becomes a stable corridor. The river does not find its way. The way is what is left after everything else has been made harder to traverse. The system behaves in the same way. Motion reshapes the landscape. The reshaped landscape biases future motion. No intention is required anywhere in this loop.

What This Means Going Forward

By this point, three facts are in place. A system can persist only in states it can carry. Among those states, cost varies. And repeated occupation reshapes the landscape itself, carving grooves that make some futures easy and others costly or unreachable. The system is therefore not only moving within a landscape. Its structure is continuously reshaping that landscape. This explains why patterns persist, why change is difficult, and why history matters even when the present moment looks identical. It also sets up the next constraint: as grooves deepen, the range of low-cost alternatives shrinks. The landscape narrows. The next chapter describes that narrowing—and how stability itself can become a trap.

Chapter 8

Corridors and Narrowing

How Possibility Shrinks Over Time

In the previous chapters, we saw that a system can only persist in states it can carry, and that among those states some are inexpensive to hold while others require continuous internal work. We also saw that the system moves within a cost-shaped landscape whose geometry determines which configurations it can remain in and which it must leave. But this landscape is not static. The system's own stabilizations reshape the space it moves within. Every stabilization, every repeated transition, every sustained configuration, leaves structural consequences. Some regions of the landscape become easier to occupy and easier to traverse. Others become steeper, more fragile, or effectively unreachable. Over time, the distribution of what the system can still do changes, even if the abstract structural space of what is possible in principle does not. Nothing in this process requires planning, preference, or selection. It is the mechanical result of history acting on structure.

From Space to Corridor

Early in a system's life, many transitions may be available. The landscape may be wide, with many shallow basins and gentle slopes, and many possible routes between regions. Even if not all of these regions are low cost or stable, many of them are at least reachable. The structure resembles a smooth sandstone face before prolonged weathering, with few deep channels and little enforced routing. With time and repeated traversal, that surface does not remain smooth. It develops a small number of deep channels that capture most of the flow, while other routes gradually become steeper and more expensive.

A large river basin makes this visible at scale. The Colorado River system, for example, did not always occupy only the single dominant channel seen today. Earlier in its history, water spread across multiple routes, leaving behind many carved paths in the surrounding rock. Over geological time, flow concentrated. One channel deepened, captured more of the drainage, and became dominant, while other routes were left stranded as dry canyons and abandoned cuts in the landscape. The old paths still exist as geometry, but they no longer carry flow.

In a system, this flow corresponds to conditions that converge into stabilized states. Flow does not remain evenly distributed. Some configurations are stabilized again and again. Some transitions are used repeatedly. Some regions are entered so often that the structure gradually reshapes to support them. At the same time, other regions are visited rarely or not at all. The paths leading to them are not reinforced. Their surrounding terrain is not smoothed. Their access routes become relatively more expensive, more fragile, or more easily disrupted.

Over time, the system's effective field of movement contracts. What remains is no longer a broad space, but a narrower region through which most successful transitions now pass. This is what CST calls a corridor. A corridor is not a chosen path. It is the remaining region of state space the current structure can still traverse and stabilize at lowest cost. Outside it lie configurations that may still exist in principle, but no longer exist as viable futures for this particular system, because reaching them would require passing through regions of higher cost or instability that the system cannot survive or integrate — like a damaged bridge that cannot bear the load required to reach the far side, even though the far side still exists.

Narrowing Is Not Preference

Narrowing is not a change in desire, strategy, or attitude. It is a geometric change in the landscape itself. Each time a system stabilizes in a particular region, residue leaves its effect there, and that region becomes slightly easier to return to. Each time a region fails to carry a stable configuration and must be abandoned, no supportive structure is laid down there. Over many repetitions, these small asymmetries accumulate. Basins deepen. Slopes steepen. Ridges sharpen. Some passages effectively close. No avoidance occurs. No resistance is required. The system is not "choosing" the narrower route. The lower-cost path is the one that remains carryable; wider routes no longer exist as traversable sequences of states. From the inside, this does not register as a loss of possibility. It registers as certainty, as the sense that there is only one way this can go.

History Becomes Geometry

Because the system's own activity reshapes its constraints, the future is not determined only by structure in the abstract. Two systems with similar initial designs but different histories do not inhabit the same landscape anymore. They do not merely differ in what they tend to do. They differ in what they can still do at all. One system may still have wide regions of low-cost movement available. Another may be confined to a narrow channel where only a small family of configurations can be reached without loss of coherence or reorganization. Both may still function. Both may still be stable. But their futures are no longer drawn from the same space. This is not a psychological fact. It is a structural one.

Why Narrowing Produces Fragility

When a system can move within a wide region of its landscape, disturbances can often be absorbed by smaller rerouting. If one path becomes costly, another nearby path may still be available. As corridors narrow, this flexibility disappears. When movement is confined to a small region of state space, the same disturbances become decisive. There are fewer alternate routes. Fewer transitions remain carryable. The system becomes brittle not because it has less strength, but because it has less geometry. The loss is not power. It is room.

Why Corridors Feel Like "How Things Are"

From the inside, corridor narrowing appears as repetition. The same kinds of situations recur. The same ranges of response appear. The same transitions succeed. Other outcomes never occur, not because they are forbidden or suppressed, but because the system no longer has a viable route to them. Nothing here requires belief, commitment, identity, or intention. The system is not "stuck." It is confined to the region of its landscape that remains traversable at lowest cost under its current structure. At this stage, the corridor is only a constraint on traversal. It shapes what transitions are still possible. It does not yet explain why experience feels continuous, personal, or like it belongs to a single ongoing self. That requires one more layer of structure. The next chapter is about that.

Chapter 9

When Stability Becomes a Trap
How Systems Become Brittle Without Breaking

In the previous chapters, we saw how repeated traversal carves grooves and reshapes a system's landscape. Some paths become easier to traverse and easier to remain in. Others become harder to reach, harder to sustain, or disappear as viable routes. This is not a failure mode. It is how any finite system becomes reliable at all. A system that cannot settle into repeatable, carryable configurations cannot sustain coherent function for long. At first, this reshaping looks like improvement. Transitions become smoother. Fewer forced reorganizations occur. Day-to-day load decreases as the system spends more time in regions it can carry at lower cost. Nothing here requires planning or inner direction. It is what follows when a system remains where it can persist and is forced out of what it cannot carry.

Narrowing Is Not a Malfunction

The same mechanics that reduce cost also reshape the system to fit a narrower range of conditions. The grooves that lower daily strain are the grooves that remove alternatives. When a system repeatedly occupies a small region of state space, two structural changes occur together. Inside that region, coordination becomes easier because the architecture becomes better matched to the specific demands it repeatedly carries. Outside it, unvisited routes lose support: transitions become costlier, less stable, and eventually non-viable.

In human systems, the same trade appears without any damage. A system whose days are routed through a small set of familiar environments and demands becomes increasingly well-matched to that corridor. Coordination inside it becomes smoother and less expensive. Broader, more variable configurations are visited less, develop less supporting structure, and become progressively harder to stabilize. What were once reachable ways of being fade from the system's viable future, not by decision, but by geometry. Structural reshaping always trades breadth for fit: the system becomes more economical where it already is and less capable elsewhere.

Deep Grooves Are Narrow Grooves

A shallow basin allows easy movement in and out. A deep basin holds a system tightly and makes leaving difficult, because departure requires crossing higher-cost regions. As grooves deepen, stability inside the region increases while flexibility outside it decreases. Day-to-day load may fall, but the range of low-cost alternatives shrinks. This is why narrowing can look like stability while quietly becoming a trap. The system does not become trapped because it refuses to change. It becomes trapped because the remaining routes out require passing through configurations it cannot carry for long without overload or forced reorganization.

Overfitting as a Mechanical Process

Overfitting, in CST terms, is the progressive reshaping of a system's landscape such that it becomes highly matched to a narrow range of conditions and increasingly unable to carry states outside that range. It is specialization produced by repeated traversal: deep grooves, steep ridges, and the loss of alternative low-cost routes. In engineering, a model is called overfitted when it performs extremely well under a narrow set of conditions and poorly elsewhere.

The same structure appears in any system whose persistence reshapes its own constraints. When a system repeatedly persists under a particular pattern of load, it reorganizes to carry that pattern with lower internal work. The groove deepens. The familiar becomes less expensive. The architecture becomes tightly matched to what it has repeatedly had to carry. That precision has a structural cost. States outside the groove become harder to reach, harder to sustain, and sometimes unreachable because the connecting transitions no longer exist at tolerable cost. The system has become reliable by becoming specific.

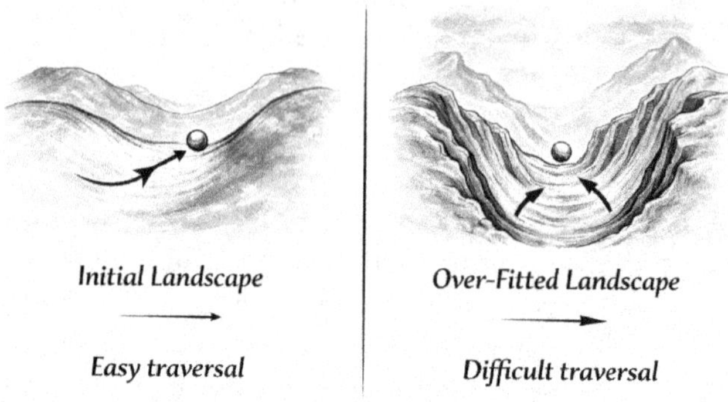

Brittleness

Brittleness is the condition produced at the limit of overfitting. A brittle system can remain coherent only inside a very narrow corridor and fails abruptly when pushed outside it. It is not an unstable system. Under the conditions it has been shaped for, it can be highly coherent, economical, and reliable. Brittleness appears when conditions shift or internal balances are disturbed. Because many low-cost transitions have been eliminated, adaptation is no longer gradual. The system is forced into high-cost states, breakdown, or reorganization—not for lack of effort, but for lack of carryable routes. Brittleness is not weakness. It is specialization taken to its mechanical limit: high stability inside a narrow corridor and high cost at the edges.

When Change Requires Instability

Once a system is deeply specialized, change can no longer occur through smooth, low-cost adjustment. To reach new regions of state space, the system must pass through higher-cost and less stable configurations, because there is no gentle path out of a deep groove. Load rises before it can drop. Existing stability is lost before a new carryable configuration can form. This is not refusal. It is geometry. The same mechanics that make a system reliable can therefore make it rigid. Narrowing is how systems become functional. Narrowing is also how systems become trapped. The next chapter turns to what happens when a system can no longer remain inside its own corridor at all—when the current groove is no longer carryable, and forced transition and reorganization follow.

Chapter 10

Breakdown, Reorganization, and Reset

What Happens When a System Cannot Stay Where It Is

Up to this point, we have been describing how systems persist by remaining inside states they can carry, and how history shapes those configurations into grooves, corridors, and narrowed landscapes. A system becomes reliable by remaining where it can stay stable at tolerable cost. It becomes constrained by the same process. But no state is carryable under all conditions. As load shifts and margins shrink, what was once barely sustainable can become impossible to maintain.

A simple bodily example makes this visible. When a hip joint begins to degrade, the body can often continue to function by redistributing load. Gait shifts slightly, and a limp develops. Other muscles and joints take on more work. At first, the state remains coherent, even though it requires more internal work to carry. Over time, the compensation becomes more pronounced and more consistent. For a time, the pattern holds together. But as strain accumulates and margins shrink, what once barely worked becomes uncarryable. Pain rises, stability fails, and the state can no longer be sustained. Nothing new has been "decided." The arrangement simply exceeds what the structure can now support, and a more radical reorganization becomes unavoidable. When this happens, the system does not face a choice. It faces a constraint. A state that cannot be carried does not continue. The system cannot remain where it is. Something must change. This is the mechanical meaning of what experience later calls breakdown.

Breakdown Is Not a Special Process

Breakdown is not a different kind of operation from ordinary functioning. It is not a failure mode added on top of normal mechanics. It is simply what happens when a state loses carryability. A bridge does not stop holding by effort or intent; a load configuration that cannot be sustained leads to a structural transition. That new state may involve deformation, partial loss of function, or total structural collapse, but the mechanism is the same as in every other transition: the prior state could not be carried, so it did not persist. A processor that overheats does not decide to shut down. It enters a thermal state that cannot be carried, and the system transitions accordingly. A body that faints does not choose to stop standing. It enters a metabolic or circulatory state that cannot be sustained, and posture disappears. In every case, breakdown is not a separate category of event, nor an event that is chosen. It is simply the point at which the current state ceases to be viable. The only thing that makes breakdown seem special is that it makes the loss of carryability visible.

When a Moment Will Not Fit

Every moment follows the same basic sequence. Incoming variation is measured. Measurement is reduced into a single state. That state is what the system must now carry forward. Usually, this stabilized state falls within what the current architecture can support. Stabilization proceeds with little structural change. But sometimes it does not. Sometimes the converged state exceeds the stability band of the active organization. The moment will not fit. This mismatch is not confusion and not uncertainty. It is structural strain. It is the internal tension that appears when an incoming state cannot be carried by the current structure without reorganization. The system has received a state it can register but not one it can sustain in its present form. When this happens, the system cannot simply continue. To remain coherent at all, the structure itself must change.

A simple mechanical example makes this visible. Consider a small vehicle designed to carry only a limited load. With a light load, it operates comfortably within its capacity. As additional load is added, the system can often continue to function by using up slack and redistributing weight. Tolerances are consumed. Margins shrink. For a time, the overall state remains coherent, though increasingly strained. The engine runs hotter. Response slows. Eventually, a further demand appears — a long incline, a heavier pull, a hotter day. Nothing about the vehicle has changed in principle. But the same state that was barely being carried is no longer sustainable. The engine overheats. Power drops. The system cannot continue in that form, not because anything is "wrong," but because the load now exceeds what the structure can carry in that state. The moment does not fit. The system has received a state it can register, but not one it can sustain without structural change.

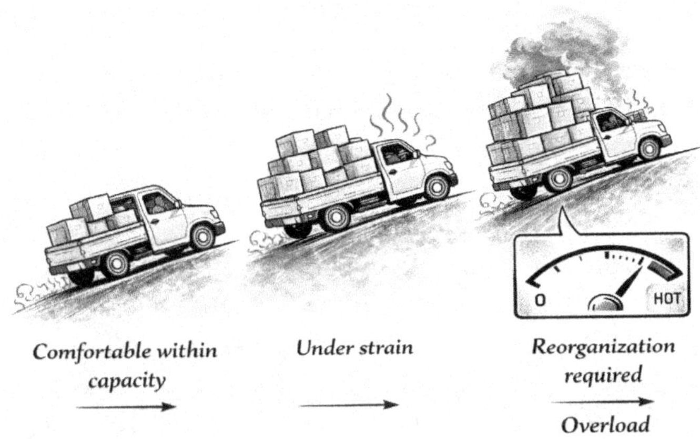

Reorganization as Forced Integration

Reorganization is not planning or problem solving. It is the mechanical redistribution of load and coordination across the system's parts in order to reach any state that can be carried. Sometimes this redistribution is small. A posture shifts. Attention narrows. A task is dropped. A subsystem takes over. Sometimes it is larger. Whole modes of operation are suspended. Energy is rerouted. Capacity is shed. And sometimes it is drastic. The structure fractures, stabilizes into a simpler form, or loses functions that can no longer be supported under the new conditions. The scale varies. The mechanism does not. A small exceedance produces a small adjustment. Repeated exceedance produces accumulating structural change. A large exceedance produces rapid and sometimes violent reorganization.

In a restaurant designed to hold a certain number of people, a slight exceedance may bring tables closer together and add a few chairs. As load increases, circulation narrows and coordination reorganizes. When capacity is greatly exceeded, tables and chairs may be removed entirely, leaving standing space only, as the structure abruptly reorganizes to remain carryable. In every case, change is forced by mismatch between the moment and the structure that must carry it. This is what CST means by strained integration. It is not understanding. It is not correction. It is the unavoidable consequence of a finite architecture encountering a state it cannot carry in its current form.

Another Simple Physical Example

When a system enters cold water, the temperature change is measured and converged immediately into a state. That new state either falls within what the current organization can carry at tolerable load, or it does not. If it does not, redistribution begins at once. Blood flow shifts. Muscle tone changes. Breathing reorganizes. Coordination patterns alter. None of this requires evaluating what the temperature "means." The architecture is responding to a constraint violation. The current state cannot be carried in its present form. If the cold exposure is brief, the system returns to its prior organization with little residue. If it is repeated or prolonged, thresholds change and tolerances shift. The architecture itself is altered. In both cases, the mechanism is the same. A state exceeded what could be carried. Reorganization occurred.

Why Reorganization Often Looks Like "Falling Apart"

From the inside, reorganization is often encountered as loss of control, loss of coherence, or loss of competence. Familiar capacities disappear. Coordination degrades. The system no longer does what it used to do. But mechanically, nothing has gone wrong. The system has simply stopped holding a state that has become impossible to carry and has reorganized accordingly. What experience calls "falling apart" is often the release of an arrangement that could only be maintained by exhausting the last remaining margin. The previous state does not vanish because something failed to try hard enough. It vanishes because the structure can no longer support it.

Reset as Reduction of Load

Sometimes the only way for a system to regain a carryable state is to become simpler. Sleep, fainting, shutdown, withdrawal, dissociation, and structural breakdown all belong to this category. They are not repairs. They are reductions of active load. A reset is not a solution. It is a retreat to a state with fewer active demands and lower coordination requirements. It is a way of making existence possible again when the current form is no longer sustainable. A system in reset is not improved. It is merely able to persist.

Awareness Only Sees the Surface

Reorganization itself does not appear in awareness. It is distributed, structural, and unfolds across many cycles of partial stabilization and failure. What are rendered are the surface consequences: strain, effort, disorientation, exhaustion, loss of capacity, or the sudden relief that appears when load drops. These are not the reorganization itself. They are the experiential signatures of the work being done to reach a carryable state again. Awareness does not guide this process. It registers its cost. The role of awareness in this architecture will be taken up in later chapters.

Breakdown Does Not Create New Capacity

Reorganization and reset do not, by themselves, produce a better system. They only produce a different one. If a system reorganizes into a state that still exceeds what it can carry, instability will continue. If it reorganizes into a state that falls within its current margins, stability returns. Nothing about this depends on meaning, insight, or intention. It depends only on whether the new arrangement fits within the system's carrying capacity.

A simple ecological example makes this visible. A beaver dam creates a stable water configuration by holding back flow. As long as the structure can carry the load imposed by the river, the basin persists. When rainfall increases, debris accumulates, or erosion weakens the structure, the same arrangement can become uncarryable. The dam fails. Water is rerouted. The landscape is reorganized. It happens because the previous configuration can no longer be carried. Sometimes reorganization destroys old grooves. Sometimes it opens access to regions of the landscape that were previously unreachable. But this is not because breakdown is beneficial. It is because the old corridor is no longer viable. Change happens here only because it could not happen earlier within the system's margins.

Why Breakdown Feels Sudden

From the outside, breakdown often looks abrupt. From the inside, it often feels like something snapped. Mechanically, this is because systems can remain in barely carryable states for long periods while margin is slowly consumed as internal work continues. Load is redistributed again and again. Partial corrections accumulate. Nothing dramatic happens until the margin is gone. When the margin is exhausted, the same state that was carried yesterday is no longer viable today. The transition appears sudden because the system has crossed a structural boundary.

The Same Rule at Every Scale

The same pattern appears everywhere. A body under chronic strain holds together until it does not. An organization under accumulating load continues to function until it cannot. A nervous system in prolonged overextension maintains coherence until a state is reached that can no longer be carried. A massive star does the same: it remains stable for millions of years as long as internal pressure can counterbalance gravity, and then, when that balance is no longer possible, it stabilizes abruptly into a different stabilization mode of structure. In every case, nothing "decides" to fail. A margin is slowly consumed. When it is gone, the same state that existed a moment before can no longer persist. There is no separate machinery for crisis. There is only the same rule: states that can be carried persist; states that cannot do not.

What This Chapter Establishes

This chapter establishes a simple mechanical fact. When a system can no longer remain what it currently is, it does not choose what comes next. It is forced into reorganization or reduction until a carryable state appears again. Breakdown is not the opposite of functioning. It is what functioning looks like at the point where the current form is no longer possible. Reset is not healing. It is survival. Reorganization is not improvement. It is transition. Everything that follows in this book about trauma, identity change, and therapy depends on this. No system changes because it wants to. It changes because its current form can no longer be carried. The next chapter turns to what determines which reorganizations persist and which do not: the machinery that turns stabilized states into lived experience.

Chapter 11

Widening and Integration

How Landscapes Become More Traversable

In the previous chapter, we saw what happens when a system is forced into states it cannot carry. Stability is lost. Load rises. The system is driven into reorganization because the current state has become unmaintainable. What follows such a transition is not a return to the same landscape. The structure itself has changed. Some pathways have been altered, some couplings redistributed, some margins consumed, and some constraints reshaped. Even when the system appears to have "recovered," it is now moving in a terrain that is no longer identical to the one it occupied before. From this point, two broad outcomes are possible. The landscape can become narrower and more brittle, or it can become wider and more traversable. The previous chapter described narrowing. This chapter describes the opposite case.

What Widening Means

Widening does not mean becoming better, wiser, or more capable in any psychological sense. It means something simpler and more mechanical. A landscape is wider when more states are carryable at low or moderate cost and more paths exist between regions without extreme load or instability. It is wider when the system can move between states without being forced into breakdown. In a narrow landscape, the system has only a few low-cost basins and only a few corridors between them. Most transitions require climbing steep slopes or crossing ridges. In a wider landscape, the same system has gentler slopes, broader passes, overlapping basins, and multiple routes between regions. Widening is not the creation of new states in principle. The state space was always defined by structure. Widening is a change in the cost geometry of that space: a change in which regions are easier to carry, which are harder, and how steep the transitions between them are.

Integration

When widening occurs, it occurs through integration. Integration is not a mental act and not a unification of meanings. It is a physical change in how parts of the system are connected, coordinated, and allowed to share load. A state that was previously costly to carry may become easier because the work required to sustain it is now distributed across more components or across better-aligned pathways. A transition that once required abrupt reorganization may become smooth because intermediate states have become stable enough to be traversed. Geometrically, integration thickens bridges between regions, broadens basins, lowers ridges, and turns narrow passes into wide corridors. Where there were once narrow passes, there may now be wide corridors. Where there were once isolated regions of stability, there may now be overlapping zones.

A simple engineering example makes this visible. Consider a computing system in which many components must communicate through a single narrow circuit-board bus system. As long as traffic is light, the system functions. As demands increase, that bus system becomes a bottleneck. Transitions that require coordination across components become slow, unstable, or are forced into abrupt scheduling and blocking. If the architecture is reorganized so that traffic can flow through multiple buses, caches, or parallel pathways, nothing about the individual computations change. Load that was previously forced through a single narrow route is now distributed across several. States that were once difficult to carry become easier. The system has not become unconstrained. It has become less tightly constrained by a single bottleneck.

Widening Is Distributed Load

The mechanical difference between narrowing and widening is simple. Narrowing concentrates load into fewer pathways and fewer states. Widening distributes load across more pathways and more states. When load is concentrated, the system becomes very stable locally and very brittle globally. When load is distributed, the system becomes less extreme in either direction. Fewer transitions require extreme compensation. Fewer regions of the landscape are separated by cliffs. A widened landscape is not flat. It still has slopes, basins, and ridges. Some states will always be harder to carry than others. Some transitions will always be more demanding than others.

But fewer necessary transitions require passage through regions of extreme load or instability.

Why Reorganization Sometimes Widens and Narrows

Widening occurs only when reorganization creates alternative load paths, overlapping regions of stability, or reduces the cost of intermediate states. But not every reorganization produces widening. Some reorganizations solve the immediate problem by further specializing the structure around a narrow set of conditions. The system becomes very good at surviving one kind of situation and much worse at surviving others. The groove becomes deeper. The corridor becomes narrower. Local stability increases. The range of reachable states decreases. Mechanically, this is the difference between concentrating strain (narrowing) and distributing it (widening).

Widening Is Not Effort

Widening does not happen because a system tries harder inside the same state. Increasing internal work within a narrow corridor does not change the shape of the corridor. It only increases the cost of staying in it. Widening requires that the landscape itself be reshaped. This is why many structural changes pass through periods of greater instability or drift before they result in greater freedom of movement. There is no smooth, low-cost path out of a deep groove. The system often has to cross higher-cost regions before it reaches a terrain that is genuinely broader.

How Widening Accumulates

Because structure is shaped by past load, widening is never instantaneous. Each time a state is carried that previously could not be carried, the landscape is altered slightly. Each time a transition occurs without breakdown that previously required it, a ridge is lowered or a pass is widened. Over time, these small changes accumulate into a terrain that has more routes, more overlap between regions, and fewer forced bottlenecks. This is not learning in the sense of acquiring information. It is plastic deformation of constraint — structural plasticity.

What This Completes in the Mechanical Story

At this point, the mechanical picture is complete. Measurement and convergence limit what can appear, state space and stability limit what can be lived in, cost shapes motion, history carves grooves and corridors, narrowing produces brittleness, breakdown forces reorganization, and widening reshapes what the system can carry. All of this is still purely mechanical. Nothing here depends on experience, meaning, or awareness. *This is the story of a finite physical system moving through its own constraints.* Only now are we in a position to ask the next question. If all of this happens before experience, how does any of it become experience at all?

This Completes the Mechanical Story

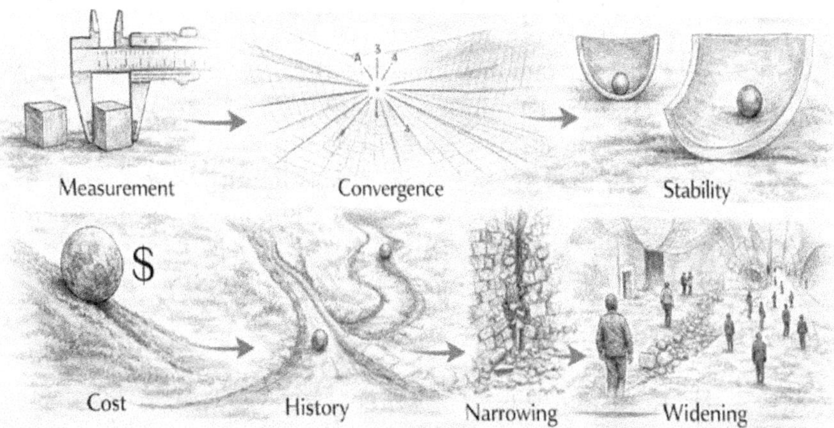

At this point, the mechanical picture is complete. Measurement and convergence limit what can appear as a state. State space, integration, and stability limit what can be sustained. Cost shapes motion, history carves grooves, narrowing produces brittleness, breakdown forces reorganization, and widening reshapes what the system can carry. All of it remains mechanical.

45

Part II

Constraint, Frames, and the Formation of a Moment

How Frames of Reference produce the moment the system inhabits

Chapter 12

Frames of Reference

How One Stabilized State Exists Across Layered Organization

Imagine a wide valley in the early morning. A thin, acrid smoke drifts through the lower ground. In the town below, people smell it. Their eyes sting. The air feels wrong. Yet no one can tell where it is coming from. The smoke seems everywhere and nowhere at once. No boundary can be drawn. No source can be fixed. What exists is a diffuse field of local signals that cannot yet organize into a coherent whole.

The difficulty is not lack of effort. It is structural. From within the valley, only short-range coordination is possible. Signals register locally, but they cannot integrate across distance or extended causal span. Momentary coherence forms at narrow range, yet the larger configuration those signals belong to cannot stabilize. The smoke exists physically, but it cannot yet stabilize as a globally coherent state within the system.

Far above the valley, the same physical reality organizes differently. From an expanded position of integration, the drifting smoke resolves into a bounded pattern. Its source becomes visible beyond a distant ridge. Direction, spread, and scale coordinate into a single configuration. Nothing about the smoke has changed. What has changed is the scale at which it can be carried and stabilized.

Like Elena and her telescope, the same sky resolves differently when resolving capacity expands. Nothing in the sky changes; what changes is the range of patterns that can be carried without fragmentation. When integration widens, signals that were previously diffused organize into a coherent state.

In CST, this shift in scale is called a change in Frame of Reference — a change in mode of organization. Nothing new is created, and the underlying condition does not change. What changes is the scale at which coherence can be sustained. A Frame of Reference is both the mode in which stabilization occurs and the stabilized configuration that results. It determines what patterns can hold together and at what scale they remain stable.

When the Frame shifts, configurations that previously could not stabilize may become carryable. This is not a change in viewpoint or understanding. It is a change in what configuration the system can sustain. Frames are not perspectives. They are structural conditions that determine the scale of coherence the system can stabilize.

Stabilization Does Not Occur in One Place

Stabilization does not occur in a single location or level. It unfolds across layered organization. A configuration remains stable only if it fits across the structures engaged in that moment. If stability fails in any active layer, the state cannot continue. Stability is layered. The same stabilized configuration appears differently depending on the structure through which it is expressed. At one layer it is physical patterning. At another it is coordinated function. At another it is organized behavior. At another it appears as experience. These are not separate states. They are the same stabilization expressed across different forms at the same time.

A Frame of Reference is not a separate part or subsystem. It is the same configuration stabilized within a particular organizational mode. Each Frame expresses the same stabilization under its own constraints. None operates independently. A state remains stable only if it remains compatible across the active Frames carrying that cycle. An automatic transmission provides a useful analogy. The transmission remains one structure. Yet different gear ranges become dominant under different load conditions. Climbing a hill uses one range; cruising uses another. The structure is unchanged, but the mode determines what load can be carried. In the same way, the configuration is one, while different Frames express it according to their constraints.

"Frame" refers to the organizational mode in which stabilization occurs. "Reference" refers to the coherent configuration that results. Together,

Frame of Reference names the link between structural organization and the stable configuration it allows.

One Configuration, Many Forms

A single stabilization does not divide into multiple realities. It is one configuration expressed across layered organization. A configuration that stabilizes physically must also stabilize functionally. One that stabilizes functionally must remain compatible with behavior. One that stabilizes behaviorally must remain compatible with the structures through which experience is rendered. These are not separate events. They are expressions of the same stabilization.

Water provides a simple example. The same water can exist as liquid or ice. The molecules remain the same. What changes is organization, and with it, what patterns can remain stable. In liquid form, movement is flexible. In ice, structure becomes rigid. Nothing new is added. Organization shifts. Frames function in the same way. They are not additional mechanisms. They are modes through which the same system organizes coherence. Stabilization must remain compatible across the structures engaged in sustaining it. A configuration that fails at any active layer does not destabilize later. It never stabilizes at all.

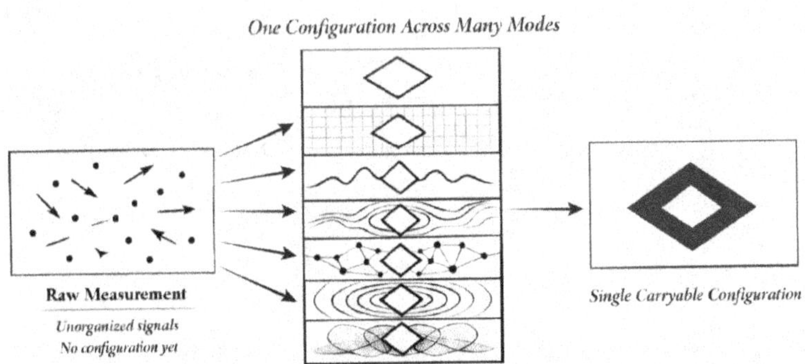

One Stabilization, Many Modes

Sequential Propagation, Not Parallel Causation

Although a stabilized configuration exists across multiple Frames, causation remains sequential. A configuration first stabilizes in lower-level structures. That stabilized output becomes the input for the next layer. Each Frame operates only on what has already stabilized below it. There is no backward influence and no skipping of steps. At very small timescales, this produces slight delay across layers. A higher Frame always operates on the most recent stabilized configuration, not on an unfolding state. These transitions occur rapidly enough that lived experience appears simultaneous, but mechanically they are sequential. The layered structure does not violate causation. It organizes it. A system never acts on a forming state. Each Frame processes only what has already stabilized in the layer below.

Coherence Across Active Frames

Not all Frames are active in every stabilization cycle. Some configurations stabilize at lower layers without requiring broader coordination. In such cases, the configuration must remain coherent only across the active Frames engaged in that cycle. This does not violate layered coherence. It specifies it. A configuration stabilizes as soon as it reaches compatibility across the structures required by its scale. A simple analogy: imagine a series of openings arranged from smallest to largest. A sphere entering the channel settles at the first opening that matches its size. Larger openings are not bypassed; stabilization simply occurs as soon as compatibility is reached. If the sphere were larger, a later opening would become the stabilization point. In the same way, a configuration stabilizes across only those Frames required by its organization. Other Frames remain inactive, but not engaged.

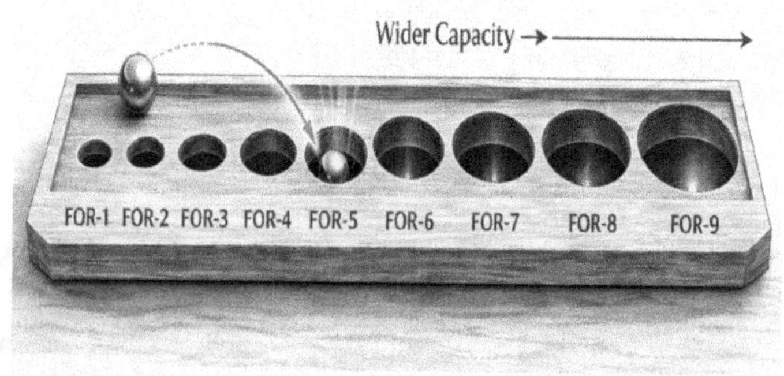

Frames Are Not Independent Systems

Frames do not communicate or negotiate. They are not subsystems interacting with one another, but layered expressions of a single stabilization propagating through one system. Higher Frames cannot arbitrarily override lower ones, and lower layers do not obey higher ones. Causation flows forward through the sequence. Transitions between modes occur only when underlying conditions permit a different organization. No Frame overrules another; stabilization shifts only as constraints change. Each layer contributes its form of stabilization within this ordered structure, none existing outside it. The entire process unfolds on a microsecond timescale and therefore passes unnoticed. Each mode arises from the conditions that make that organization possible, and transitions occur only as those conditions change.

What Frames Make Possible

Frames do not introduce a new mechanism. They clarify how a single stabilized configuration can exist across layered organization, much as water remains the same substance across different organizational states. They explain how the same stabilization can appear as structure, function, behavior, and experience without dividing the system into separate realities. Frames show why stability requires coherence across active layers, why incompatibility prevents stabilization, and why inactive layers do not constrain a configuration unnecessarily.

The Layer Where Stabilization Becomes Experience

We have described stabilization as mechanical and layered. One question remains: what are these modes of organization themselves? The next chapter turns to the specific organizational modes that make layered stabilization possible. It will describe nine Frames of Reference — distinct modes through which stabilization can occur and through which the same configuration can appear as structure, function, behavior, and experience.

Chapter 13

The Nine Frames of Reference

How Stabilization Organizes Across Modes

Imagine standing on a hillside just before sunrise. At first there is only air and ground. Your ankles make tiny corrections on the uneven slope. Muscles fire and release as stance stabilizes. None of this is organized into a scene. Coherence exists only at a local, fast, bodily scale. As the sky lightens, movement smooths. Breathing finds a rhythm. The horizon steadies. The surrounding field begins to hold together as a single extended configuration. A broader region of the landscape has become available for stabilization.

The scene then coheres: the line of hills, the darker strip of trees, the wash of color in the sky, the faint outline of the town below. A moment later, another form of organization becomes possible. The chill on your cheeks, the weight of your jacket, the pressure of your feet in your shoes bind into one object: this body, here. Soon after, the configuration acquires a center. The moment is no longer only a scene with a body within it. It is occurring to this one. Longer spans then begin to close. A thought appears: I love mornings like this. Another follows: This is why I moved here. Other mornings gather around this one, and a long-range corridor of continuity stabilizes.

If the morning is unusually quiet, the pattern itself may become available. The system can now hold not only the scene and not only the self, but the entire configuration as a configuration. Under conditions of low load and broad integration, body, field, self, thought, memory, and mood may stabilize together without any single mode holding the center.

The system has not moved through stages. It has occupied different constraint regions of its own landscape as conditions allowed broader or narrower stabilization to close. What appears at each moment is simply whatever configuration the architecture can carry. This is how Frames of

Reference appear from within: not as levels or steps, but as one continuous landscape in which different modes or scales of coherence become available or unavailable as conditions change.

One Stabilization, Many Modes

When a system enters a new moment, nothing arrives as a finished scene, only raw measurements awaiting organization. Signals shift, forces redistribute, and coordination begins. Before anything can be rendered, the architecture must converge toward a configuration it can carry. From within experience this appears as a single, continuous moment, yet structurally the system stabilizes across multiple modes of organization at once. Each mode expresses the same configuration in a different form, and only the final mutually compatible configuration becomes experience. The system cannot exist in incompatible states simultaneously. All variation must converge into a single carryable configuration before anything can appear. What is experienced is the late arrival of a configuration that has already stabilized across layered structure.

What Frames Mean

A Frame of Reference (FOR) is a structural mode of stabilization and the coherent configuration expressed through it. It determines the scale and organization at which coherence can stabilize, and therefore what kinds of configurations can exist at all. Frames are structural modes, not viewpoint. They are part of the system's own architecture, like the different gears of a transmission that organize how the same machine carries load under changing conditions. The structure remains the same, but the mode of organization determines what the system can sustain.

Frames are bands of one landscape, not separate systems. They are large-scale organizational modes of one continuous landscape of stabilization, much as the full gear range of a transmission spans the operating range of a single machine. Each gear organizes how load is carried under different conditions, and taken together the full set covers the range within which the machine can remain stable. In the same way, the Frames of Reference collectively span the landscape of stabilization available to the system, each corresponding to a different scale and organization of what can be carried. The system does not choose a Frame. It stabilizes wherever coherence remains possible under current conditions. Stability requires compatibility across the Frames active in a given configuration, while Frames not active in that stabilization do not constrain it.

The Nine Frames

The following are the principal modes through which stabilization occurs, spanning from immediate local organization to broad, extended coherence. These nine frames do not exhaust every possible form of stabilization but represent the major, repeatedly accessible modes through which the system commonly organizes. Additional variations and intermediate organizations may exist, yet all remain within the same continuous landscape.

FOR-1 — Reflex Stabilization

Organized around immediate physical integrity under force. This is the fastest and narrowest way the system stabilizes. Sudden shifts in force are handled before a situation can even be organized. Balance adjusts, muscles tighten or release, and movement corrects automatically. This level is not directly experienced. Only its results show up. If stabilization fails here, nothing broader can hold together.

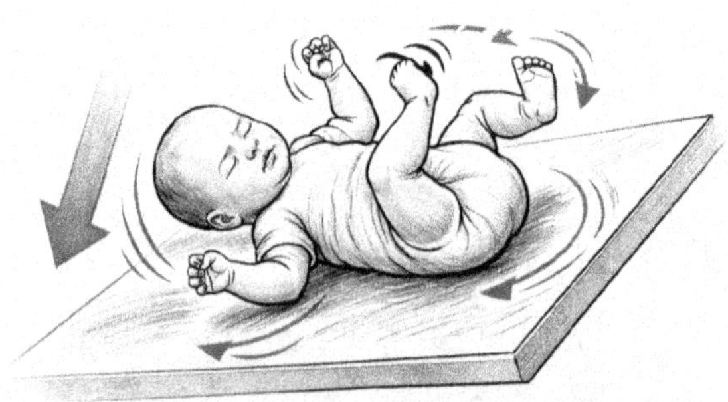

FOR-1 — Reflex Stabilization
Immediate correction under force.
Stabilization occurs *before experience.*

FOR-2 — Sensorimotor Coordination

Organized around learned bodily coordination across time. At this level, movement becomes smooth through repetition. Walking, reaching, typing, and driving feel natural because the coordination has stabilized through practice. When this mode is stable, movement feels easy. When it is unstable, awkwardness or disruption appears before any higher-level thinking begins.

FOR-2 — Sensorimotor Coordination
Learned bodily coordination across *time*.
Movement stabilizes *through repetition*.

FOR-3 — Environmental Field Organization

Organized around spatial-environmental coherence. Here stabilization includes the surrounding space. Distance, layout, openness, and obstacles organize into a stable environment. The world becomes a structured field within which movement happens smoothly. When this mode dominates, coherence is spread across the environment rather than focused only in the body.

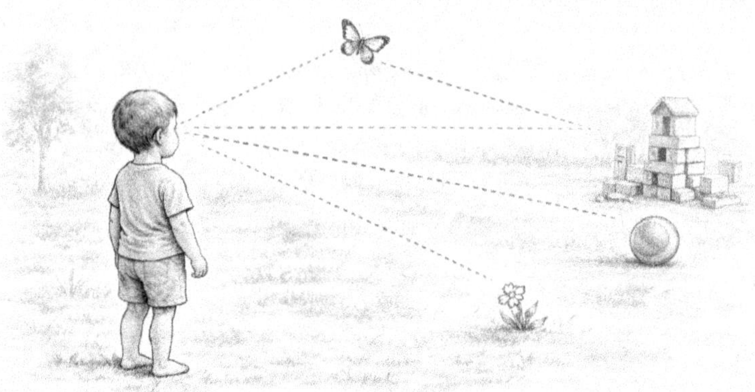

FOR-3 — Coherence Across Space

When this mode dominates, *coherence is spread across*
the environment rather than focused only in the body.

FOR-4 — Embodied Boundary

Organized around organism–environment demarcation. At this level, the body stabilizes as a distinct object within the environment. Internal and external signals become clearly separated. Pressure, contact, and position organize into a coherent sense of having a body. No inner controller is required. Stabilization here concerns being a bounded organism.

FOR-4 — Embodied Boundary

The organism stabilizes as a *bounded body.*
Internal and external signals *differentiate.*

FOR-5 — Engagement

Organized around coordinated engagement with unfolding activity. Now stabilization centers on active involvement. Movement becomes coordinated engagement. Orientation becomes engagement. Interaction becomes organized doing. The system stabilizes around being involved in what is happening rather than simply coordinating movement. Coherence includes sustained activity across moments. This is where the appearance of agency begins, even though no inner source has emerged.

FOR-5 — Participation

Stabilization organizes around *active engagement.*

Movement becomes *coordinated involvement across time.*

FOR-6 — Subjective Center

Organized around first-person experiential coherence. As engagement stabilizes over time, organization can gather around a felt center of experience. Events are no longer just happening in the environment; they are experienced as happening to this one. Sensations, emotions, and perceptions come together around a stable sense of being the experiencer. This center does not cause action. It is how stabilization appears when coherence organizes around lived experience rather than just activity.

FOR-6 — Subjective Center

Experience stabilizes around a *felt center.*

Events are lived as happening to this *one.*

FOR-7 — Identity Continuity

Organized around long-timescale self-coherence. When stabilization continues across long periods, repeated patterns link together across time. What was once just a centered experience, becomes a lasting sense of identity. Patterns of behavior, values, and expectations stabilize across months and years, appearing as character or temperament. Identity here is not a source of action. It is a long-term stabilization pattern that helps the system remain coherent across changing conditions.

FOR-7 — Identity Continuity

Stabilization extends *across long time.*

Repeated patterns link into *enduring self-coherence.*

FOR-8 — Observation of Identity

Organized around meta-coherence of identity structure. At this level, the patterns that make up your identity become something the system can notice and hold in view. Ways of thinking, reacting, choosing, and behaving that once just felt like "who I am" begin to appear as patterns with history, shape, and limits. Instead of only living inside these patterns, the system can now see them as organized structures. Stabilization now stretches across longer time and broader organization. Identity is no longer only something lived from the inside; it becomes something that can be observed as pattern. Different identity paths can be compared, and the system can see that they are not fixed or absolute, but shaped by conditions and constraint. Nothing new is added and no separate controller appears. What changes is the range across which stabilization can hold. The sense of being the source of everything weakens because what once felt like origin is now visible as pattern within the system. FOR-8 does not replace identity. It allows identity itself to stabilize as observable structure.

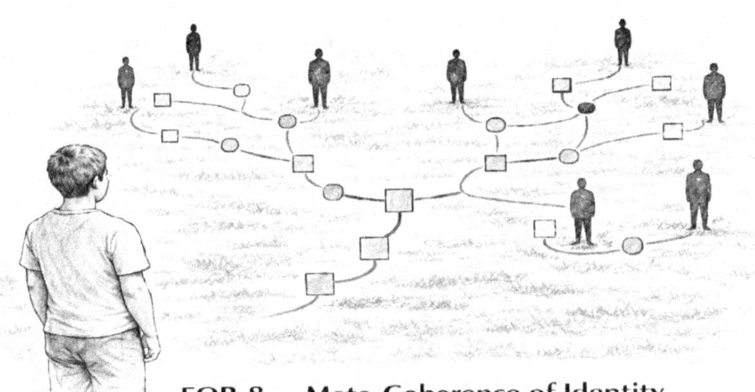

FOR-8 — Meta-Coherence of Identity

Identity stabilizes across structure.

Patterns of self are noticed, framing multiple organized options.

FOR-9 — Unified Field

Organized around global cross-scale coherence. At this level, stabilization holds the whole system together at once. Body, environment, engagement, experience, and identity all remain active without one taking over the others. No single layer controls everything. Coherence is spread across the entire system. This does not erase the lower levels. It brings them into alignment. Physical coordination, lived experience, and long-term identity all stay intact, but none of them dominate. Instead of the system narrowing into one main pattern, everything stabilizes together. Nothing steps outside the system. There is no escape from structure. What changes is how wide the system can hold coherence without internal conflict. When load is low and there is enough margin, stabilization can include many layers at the same time without being forced into a smaller, tighter mode. FOR-9 is not a new self. It is the system functioning in full, integrated alignment across all its layers.

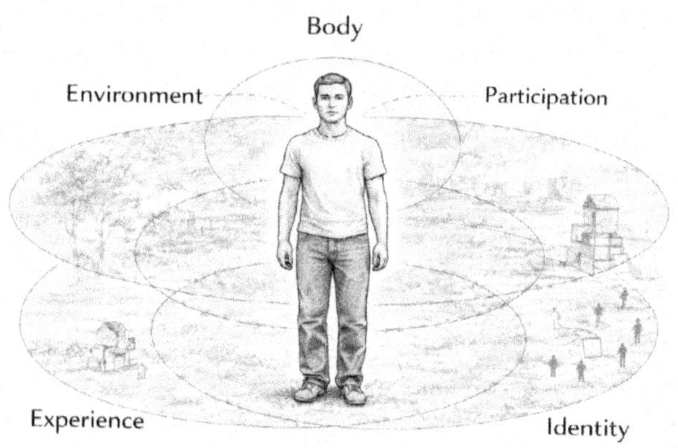

FOR-9 — Global Coherence

Coherence stabilizes the whole system together.

All layers align in a network of overlapping dimensions.

How These Modes Appear

When only narrow stabilization is possible, experience contains little beyond immediate physical aftermaths, as in FOR-1 and FOR-2 where coordination remains local, fast, and bodily. As broader modes become available, life feels fluent and environmentally organized, as in FOR-3 and FOR-4 where the field and embodied boundary stabilize together. When engagement and subjective centering become possible, as in FOR-5 and

FOR-6, experience organizes around engagement and a felt center. When long-range continuity dominates, as in FOR-7, experience organizes around identity. When wider modes become available, as in FOR-8 and occasionally FOR-9, patterns themselves may appear and stabilization spans broader organization. None of these indicate control. They reflect the scale of stabilization currently possible.

A Micro-Slip on the Sidewalk

You are walking and your toe catches. In fractions of a second, before anything can be noticed, stabilization begins. At the most immediate scale, FOR-1 redirects force and prevents collapse. Almost simultaneously, FOR-2 adjusts coordination and routes a corrective step. FOR-3 re-stabilizes the surrounding field so the ground and body realign into a coherent spatial relation. FOR-4 sharpens the boundary of the body as pressure, balance, and contact reorganize into a single physical configuration. Within the same unfolding moment, FOR-5 centers coordinated engagement as movement reorients and the body resumes forward engagement. FOR-6 may add a brief affective tone — surprise, tension, or embarrassment — as events organize around a felt center. FOR-7 can absorb the event into a familiar continuity, folding the moment into an existing pattern of identity. Occasionally, FOR-8 notices the pattern itself, and under rare conditions FOR-9 allows the entire configuration — body, field, self, and pattern — to stabilize together in a widened span.

These shifts do not occur as separate steps but as rapidly propagating stabilization across layered organization, each mode operating on what has already become carryable at the scale below it. In many cases the disturbance never reaches broader modes at all. Stabilization may complete entirely within FOR-1 and FOR-2, where force is redirected and coordination restored, and the event may never enter awareness. Propagation stops once a compatible configuration is secured, just as a rolling sphere settles into the first opening it fits, with broader modes remaining inactive but not violated. Most of this activity completes in microseconds, far faster than conscious rendering. From the outside, almost nothing happened — a slight stumble, a brief correction, and movement continues. From within, the system passed through multiple regions of its own landscape before settling into a configuration it could carry. The event appears simple only because only the final compatible configuration becomes experience, while the layered stabilization that made it possible remains unseen.

Why This Map Matters

The nine Frames are not stages, levels, or perspectives. They are structural modes through which a deterministic system maintains coherence across scales of organization. Every experience is the footprint of one or more of these modes stabilizing a configuration long enough to be rendered. Understanding these modes allows later phenomena to be understood mechanically. Emotion reflects load propagating across modes. Identity reflects long-range stabilization corridors. The sense of agency reflects where stabilization organizes around a center. What appear as separate psychological processes are different cross-sections of the same architecture.

The architecture is now visible. The system stabilizes across a continuous landscape through multiple modes at once, and every moment is the result of that convergence. Yet the system is always doing more than is rendered. Only some stabilized configurations appear as lived experience, while others remain unexpressed. In the next chapter, we turn to how shifts between Frames occur. Frame transitions do not arise from choice or control but from changes in constraint and load across the system.

Chapter 14

The Landscape: Constraint and Dominance

How Stabilization Moves Within One Continuous Geometry

Frames of Reference are not separate systems. They are large-scale ways a single system stabilizes within one continuous landscape. This landscape is the full geometry of what the system can carry, formed by its structure, limits, and history. Every stable configuration exists somewhere within this shape. The divisions between Frames are not hard boundaries but stable bands where the system organizes in different, consistent ways. These bands arise from structural limits — how much can be integrated, across how many components, over what span of time, and under how much load. They are like the color bands of a rainbow. The spectrum is continuous, yet stable regions appear where the pattern coheres into recognizable form. The boundaries are gradual transitions within one structure.

A Frame is not a place and not a container. It is a band of stabilization within a continuous landscape of carryability. This full geometry forms the global landscape. At any moment, stabilization occurs within a smaller region of that landscape — the local terrain defined by the current distribution of constraint. A Frame names the structural band; stabilization always happens locally within it.

Each band reflects a different scale of integration and temporal span. Some permit only narrow, fast, local stabilization. Others support broader, slower, and extended coherence. These differences are structural, not descriptive. They determine how disturbance spreads, how coordination propagates, and what happens when compatibility weakens. Within each band many configurations are possible, but all share the same structural limits.

One Landscape, Different Terrains

Imagine a single mountain range with different altitude bands. At lower elevations the terrain is dense and forgiving; change remains local and gradual. Higher up the ground becomes sparse and less stable, requiring broader coordination and longer preparation. Higher still the terrain becomes harsh, and only certain forms of stability remain viable. It is the same mountain, the same material, and the same gravity, yet the rules of stabilization shift with altitude. Frames function in this way: not separate worlds, but stabilization bands within one continuous geometry.

The system does not move between Frames by choice. Stabilization occurs wherever coherence remains possible under present conditions. When load increases or constraint shifts, certain regions of the landscape can no longer sustain compatibility and effectively close. When conditions ease, broader regions reopen. The system never leaves the landscape. Only the viable region changes.

A climber ascending this mountain does not select which altitude band is survivable. As weather worsens and oxygen thins, higher regions become uncarryable. Movement continues only where conditions allow stability. If weather clears, higher regions become viable again — not because of decision, but because constraint permits it. The mountain has not changed. Only the region capable of sustaining coherent movement has shifted.

Local Geometry Within the Landscape

Within each stabilization band exist specific configurations shaped by history and repetition — corridors, grooves, and long-formed pathways. Together, the Frames of Reference describe the full set of stabilization bands within which configurations are possible, while local history shapes how stabilization tends to unfold within those structural limits. Within a single altitude band, the ground is not uniform. Repeated passage has worn narrow paths. Some routes are firm and stable, others loose and unstable. Movement tends to follow corridors requiring less strain. This is not preference. It is geometry. Over time, these local pathways deepen, making certain routes easier to carry and others less viable, even while remaining within the same band. Local geometry shapes how stabilization unfolds within broader structural constraint.

The Distribution of Constraint

Stabilization does not occur through a selecting mechanism. The configuration that stabilizes is the one whose constraints can be satisfied across the active Frames under current conditions. Like an automatic transmission, the system settles into the mode able to carry present load. There is no central coordinator assigning control. All Frames remain structurally present. What varies is how strongly each constrains the converged configuration.

Dominance arises from the Frame whose mode of organization can most effectively carry the current load, thereby exerting the strongest constraint on the stabilized configuration. Dominance is not control. It is constraint strength. A Frame always remains part of the architecture. What changes is how concentrated its constraint becomes. Under strong dominance, other Frames contribute less to the final configuration. This condition — dominant Frame narrowing — can occur in any band.

For example, when identity-level constraint becomes rigid, nearly all experience may organize through a narrow self-corridor, as seen in highly self-referential stabilization patterns. Likewise, acute threat may compress stabilization into fast reflex coordination. In each case, other Frames remain present but contribute minimally because constraint has become concentrated. Even under extreme dominance, stabilization must remain compatible across active Frames. Dominance shapes weighting. Compatibility determines viability. Extreme dominance corresponds to narrowing of the viable stabilization region — not the emergence of a controlling entity.

The Forest Illustration

Imagine walking through a forest. Vision registers trees. Hearing detects distant movement. Touch registers ground and temperature. Smell samples soil and vegetation. All structures operate together and converge into a coherent state. A branch snaps. Auditory constraint rises and becomes dominant. Orientation shifts. Tension increases. Vision and other channels remain active, but their influence decreases. They have not stopped operating; the distribution of constraint has shifted. You turn and look. Visual contribution strengthens. Hearing continues measuring but no longer leads. At every moment all structures remain active. Only the weighting changes.

Frames operate in the same way. No Frame directs the system. Dominance follows the band most strongly coupled to present conditions. Stabilization occurs only when the combined constraints remain mutually compatible.

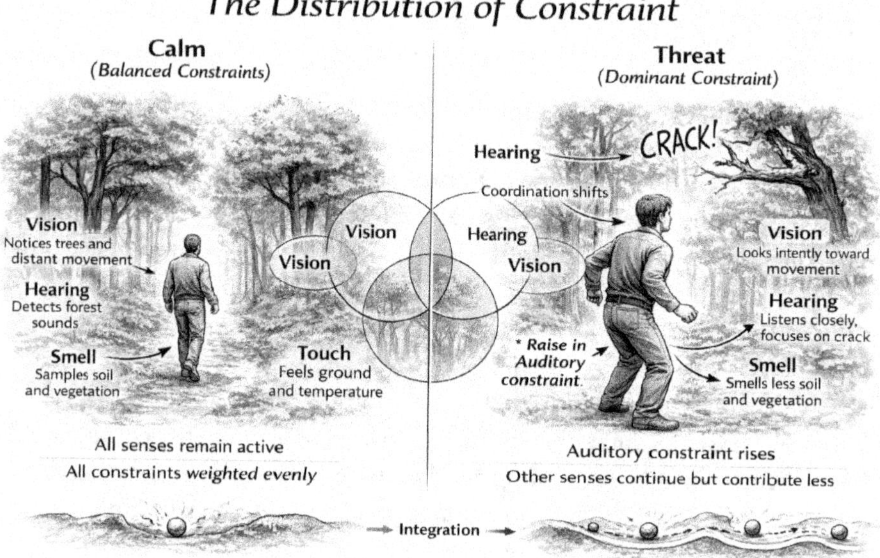

Dominance and Compatibility

Dominance alone does not determine the state. Stabilization occurs only when the resulting configuration satisfies the constraints of all active Frames simultaneously. Compatibility is the governing condition. Dominance influences which constraints weigh most heavily. Compatibility determines whether the configuration can exist at all. Consider a simple example. A piece of food smells pleasant and feels appealing when touched. Olfactory and tactile constraints support approach. Yet visually it appears contaminated. Visual constraint conflicts with the others. Because the configuration cannot stabilize compatibly across active Frames, coherence weakens. The system does not follow smell or touch alone. Instead, stabilization reorganizes toward the only configuration compatible across them — often hesitation or withdrawal.

What determines the outcome is not which Frame is strongest in isolation, but which configuration remains mutually supportable across the active set. When dominance becomes extreme and compatibility weakens, cost rises. The system must sustain a configuration requiring increasing internal work. The landscape becomes steep. Small disturbances amplify. Reorganization pressure builds until a more compatible distribution of constraint forms. Stability reflects compatibility across Frames, not dominance within one.

Differentiated Stabilization Across Frames

Behavior and narrative are not produced by separate systems. They are expressions of stabilization across different bands of the same architecture. Lower Frames are constrained by sensorimotor and immediate regulatory geometry. Higher Frames are constrained by symbolic, identity, and narrative coherence. Because these bands operate under different geometries and timescales, their stabilizations do not always align. At any moment, action reflects the configuration most reliably stabilized at lower bands. Narrative reflects the configuration stabilized at higher bands. These are not competing outputs. They are differentiated expressions of the same process. When coupling across bands is incomplete, behavior may proceed in one direction while narrative organizes in another. A person may act while narrating the opposite — not because of division, but because stabilization resolved differently under present constraints.

Consider a familiar situation. Early in the day a person states, "I will not drink tonight." This configuration stabilizes at a higher band, organizing identity-level coherence. Later that evening, sensory cues and habit corridors stabilize more readily at lower bands around accepting a drink. The hand reaches. The first sip occurs. The act alters cross-band compatibility. The earlier identity configuration remains part of the architecture, and the new state no longer aligns cleanly with it. This does not create competing agents. It creates cross-band strain.

Because higher-band coherence is now the least satisfied, sampling shifts upward. Attention reorganizes around the band under greatest constraint. Stabilization continues until a configuration becomes carryable across the system as a whole. The glass is set down not because narrative overruled action, but because the architecture converges toward the configuration that restores global compatibility. The system does not choose between behavior and narrative. It resolves toward the configuration that best satisfies the dominant constraints while maintaining cross-band coherence. What appears as decision is convergence within constraint geometry.

Dominance and the Shape of the Landscape

Dominant configurations are not different locations. They are different shapes of the same underlying geometry. Dominance alters weighting across the landscape but never exits it. The stabilized state at any moment reflects how constraint is distributed across active Frames. As conditions shift, the distribution shifts, and the viable region reorganizes.

The Frequency-Band Illustration

Imagine multiple frequency bands active simultaneously. The output is one combined signal shaped by all bands together. When deep vibration strengthens, lower frequencies contribute more strongly. When a sharp crack occurs, higher frequencies dominate. Nothing selects which band leads. Dominance follows whichever component is most strongly coupled to present input. Stabilization occurs only when the combined signal remains mutually consistent across bands. The resulting state reflects the only configuration the active set can sustain together.

Formal Statement

Frames of Reference describe the continuous geometry of ways a system can be organized. Dominance is the distribution of constraint across active Frames. Compatibility is the condition that permits stabilization to occur. No Frame alone determines the state, and no central mechanism directs transitions. As conditions shift, the distribution of constraint shifts. The system reorganizes within the same continuous landscape toward the only configuration that remains mutually carryable. Stabilization is geometry resolving under constraint.

Chapter 15

The Causal Pipeline

How a Moment Is Made Before It Is Experienced

Up to this point, we have described the machine: its constraints, its landscapes, its grooves and corridors, its breakdowns and reorganizations, and the different stabilization modes through which it maintains coherence across scales. What we have not yet done is walk through the actual causal sequence by which any particular moment comes to exist.

That sequence is not optional. It is not something the system sometimes uses and sometimes bypasses. It is the only way a finite architecture can operate. Every moment that can be rendered comes into being through the same mechanical progression. Variation is measured. Multiplicity is reduced. A configuration is attempted. That state is either carryable or it is not. If it can be carried, it stabilizes. If it cannot, the structure changes until something can be carried. Only after all of this does the system become capable of entering display mode. This is not a story about goals or intentions. It is simply what must occur in a constrained machine.

Measurement: What Can Enter the Machine at All

Nothing begins with awareness. Nothing begins with experience. Everything begins with measurement. No system changes unless something impinges on it. Something must enter before anything else can occur. In any chain of interdependent systems, the stabilized configuration of one becomes the constraint for the next. Sequence is not a convention. It is imposed by causality.

Measurement is the coupling between the system and its input, whether that input originates outside or inside it. It determines what kinds of inputs can register at all and which do not exist for this system in any operational sense.

Measurement does not describe the world and does not select what matters. It converts input into internal state.

What cannot be measured cannot enter the system's internal economy. What can be measured but cannot be stabilized forces reorganization. What can be measured and stabilized becomes part of the moment. Measurement therefore defines the system's first limit: not what the world is, but what can exist for this system at all. It is the first operation in the causal sequence.

Convergence: Why the System Must Become One State

Measurement produces multiplicity. Many signals and degrees of freedom may be active in parallel. But the system cannot exist in multiple states at once. It cannot carry competing configurations forward simultaneously. Multiplicity must be reduced.

Convergence is the mechanical reduction of many possibilities into one carryable configuration. It is not selection and not deliberation. It is forced reduction under constraint. At every relevant scale, many possible states resolve into one actual state the system can continue carrying. Without convergence, continuity is impossible.

Integration — Carrying Under Constraint

Once a single configuration has formed, the system must carry it. Integration determines whether the existing structure can sustain the state. Imagine a child placing a rock into a backpack. The rock is the new state. The body attempts to carry it using its current strength and balance. If the weight fits within structural limits, the child continues walking. Nothing fundamental changes, yet the structure is not unchanged. Small adjustments occur as the state is carried. Shoulders shift. Balance refines. Muscles coordinate more efficiently. The next time the same weight is lifted, it feels more familiar. Even stable carrying reshapes the system gradually. This is soft integration — adaptation within existing structure.

If the rock is heavier, it may still be carried, but with strain. Posture tightens. Energy is consumed more rapidly. Margin shrinks. The state is sustained, but at higher cost. If the rock exceeds what the structure can sustain, minor adjustment is no longer sufficient. The mismatch must be resolved. The child may redistribute weight, remove some load, or over time become stronger. Muscles not previously active begin to contribute. Balance strategies shift. The structure reorganizes until carrying becomes possible. This is hard integration — structural change.

Posture adjusts while adapting.
Current structure endures a small *increase*.

Structure stretches to adjust.
Adaptation becomes fundamental change.

Carrying a new state reshapes the system.

To carry a state means the structure can maintain it without breakdown, without rapidly exhausting capacity, and without being forced into immediate reorganization. Some states are easy. Some are costly. Some require restructuring. Nothing in this process is aimed or planned. The structure changes because it must, until a carryable configuration exists. Load, cost, and carryability limits govern the outcome.

Stabilization: How a Present Moment Comes to Exist

Whether reorganization was required or not, the sequence concludes in the same way. A configuration settles. It fits. Stabilization establishes it as the present state of the system. It makes continuity possible. It allows "now" to persist rather than dissolve immediately. Stabilization does not mean permanence. It means that, for that span — whether microseconds or years — the configuration can be carried. When load shifts or margin is consumed, the state may become uncarryable. Instability returns. The system re-enters integration or reorganization. Every moment of continuity is simply a configuration that has survived measurement, convergence, integration, and, when necessary, restructuring.

The Critical Fact: Awareness Is Not in This Pipeline

Sequential order:

Measurement → Convergence → Integration → Stabilization (Frame of Reference)

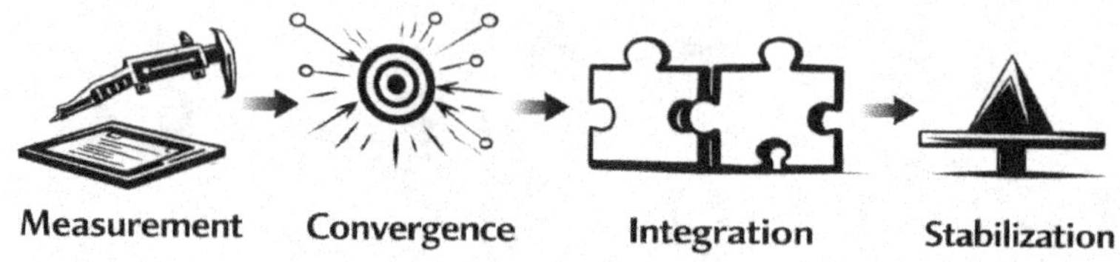

Nowhere in this sequence does awareness appear. Measurement, convergence, integration, and stabilization all occur before anything can be rendered. Only after stabilization can the system enter display mode. This is not philosophical. It is mechanical. Nothing in the earlier steps depends on awareness. The body does not need to notice weight to measure it. It does not need to think to settle posture. It does not need to decide to redistribute force. The pipeline operates independently of display.

But the sequence does not unfold in isolation. Long before the rock is lifted, the body already has limits. Muscle strength, learned coordination, fatigue thresholds — these define the landscape within which the sequence operates. The pipeline determines how the moment unfolds. The deeper structure determines what kinds of moments are possible. By the time the child becomes aware of the weight, the moment has already stabilized. It has been shaped by both the causal sequence and the structural limits within which it occurred. Awareness comes last.

What This Means

The system is always doing more than is rendered. It is measuring, reducing, attempting, adjusting, and stabilizing before anything is known. What is displayed is not the process. It is the remainder of a configuration that has already survived the entire sequence. Experience is late, simplified, and not causal. The next chapter turns to the machinery that performs this rendering — the Phenomena Transducer System — and to the difference between what the system is doing and what can be displayed at all. Experience is not the pipeline. It is the rendered residue of stabilization.

Part III

The Displayed World

Why Experience Appears as It Does and Control Seems Present

Chapter 16

The Display System, Beyond Stabilization

Why Experience Is a Mode, Not a Controller

Up to this point, we have followed the causal pipeline by which any moment comes to exist at all: measurement, convergence, integration, and stabilization. That pipeline is the machinery that determines what configuration the system actually reaches. That entire sequence unfolds before anything is ever rendered. It is important to be precise about where that pipeline ends. It ends at stabilization. Once a configuration has stabilized as a Frame of Reference, the system is no longer determining what state it will occupy. It is that state.

What follows stabilization is not another step in producing the state. It is the same stabilized configuration continuing in two directions. One continuation proceeds outward, into the world, as behavior. The other proceeds inward, into the display system, as conscious experience. These continuations unfold from the same state and proceed in parallel as expressions of that stabilization. Nothing new is added in either case. The architecture has already settled. What changes is only where that settled configuration is expressed — through two forms of display: behavior and awareness. After a configuration has stabilized into a carryable state, the system may enter an additional mode: display. This ordering is not optional. Experience is not part of the pipeline that produces states. It is a condition the system sometimes enters only after that pipeline has completed its work.

When the system is in display mode, it is aware. When display is inactive, there is no awareness. Awareness is not something the system does; it is a condition that exists only when the rendering machinery is active. The rest of the system continues operating regardless. In deep, dreamless sleep, under general anesthesia, or during a brief blackout, regulation continues — breathing, posture, circulation, coordination — while nothing is rendered. In quieter conditions, display may narrow rather than disappear, but the causal pipeline proceeds unchanged. When rendering resumes, awareness resumes. Nothing additional is required. Awareness is therefore not fundamental to operation. It is a contingent mode of rendering.

Stabilization Is Already Action

A stabilized configuration (Frame of Reference) is not an internal snapshot waiting to be used. It is a whole-system condition that already includes posture, muscle tone, motor routing, orientation, inhibition, speech readiness, and movement tendencies. In other words, a stabilized state already specifies a way of acting. When the system stabilizes into withdrawal, the next physical continuation is withdrawal. When it stabilizes into approach, the next continuation is approach. When it stabilizes into freezing, the body continues in freezing. When it stabilizes into speaking, the speech apparatus is already configured to be driven. There is no additional step in which the system "decides to act." The act is not chosen after stabilization. It is the world-facing continuation of the configuration that has just stabilized — the unfolding of the trajectory established by the sequential causal chain. Behavior is therefore not selected after stabilization. Behavior is what stabilization becomes when it continues into the world. In micro-temporal terms, stabilization comes first: a configuration must exist before it can be expressed. Because the stabilized configuration already contains motor routing and force organization, its outward continuation follows immediately.

The Two Continuations of a Stabilized State

Once stabilization occurs — that is, once the configuration has settled as a Frame of Reference — the same state continues in two directions. One direction is behavior: the physical, outward expression of the state through movement, posture, speech, and interaction with the environment. The other direction is display: the conversion of that same stabilized state into the phenomenal medium by the Phenomena Transducer System (PTS). These are not two different states. They are two different surfaces of the same state. They can unfold in parallel when the display machinery is active. If the display machinery is not active, the behavioral continuation still occurs. The system still walks, grasps, avoids, freezes, or attacks. It simply does so without anything being rendered. This is why complex, adaptive, and even life-saving behavior does not require awareness.

The Architecture in One Line

We can now state the architecture cleanly:

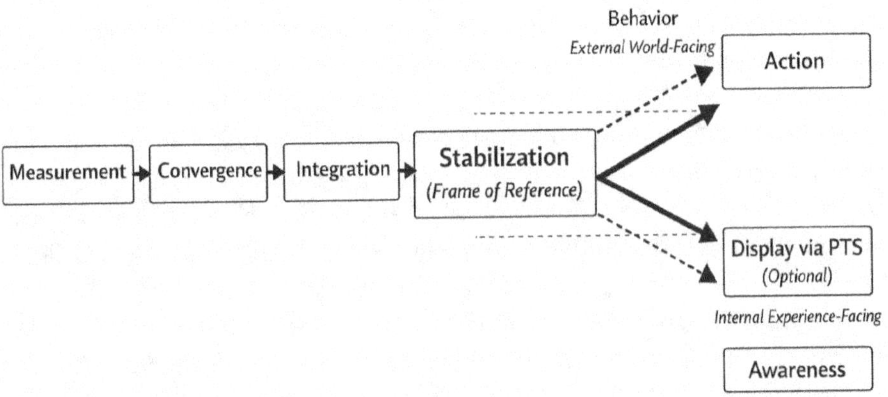

Behavior and awareness run in parallel but are independent. The causal pipeline ends at stabilization. What follows is either behavior, display via the PTS, or both.

What the Display System Is

Up to this point, this book has explained how the system works: how it stabilizes, how it changes, how it is shaped by what it must carry, how different Frames of Reference form, and how identity develops over long periods of time. All of this activity continues whether or not anything is actually experienced. The machinery keeps running even when nothing is being felt or noticed.

This chapter asks a different question: how does any of this become visible to the system at all? In CST, the answer is clear and limited. It becomes visible only through a display system. Experience is not the machinery itself. It is the visible surface of the machinery. The system changes, and the display shows what has already happened. Stabilization and reorganization occur long before anything appears in experience. Only after a configuration has settled into a form the system can carry can it be turned into experience. This conversion is performed by what CST calls the *Phenomena Transducer System, or PTS.*

A transducer is something that converts one kind of structured state into another without changing the actual condition of the system — only the form in which it appears. A microphone converts sound waves into electrical signals. A screen converts electrical signals into light. A speedometer converts motion into the position of a needle. The needle is not the engine. It is not the fuel, the gears, or the moving parts. It is only a visible display that corresponds to what is happening underneath.

The Phenomena Transducer System works in the same way inside the human system. It does not steer the system, guide change, make choices, or control anything. It does not reach back and alter what has already stabilized. Its role is simpler and mechanical. It takes already stabilized internal configurations and converts them into experience — sights, sounds, body sensations, emotions, thoughts, and the sense of being present. What appears is not the machinery itself but its display, like a dashboard showing the state of an engine. When this conversion is active, the system is in awareness. When it is not, there is no awareness. Like a gas gauge showing the level of fuel, the system converts internal states into appearance without changing the underlying condition.

Rendering and Awareness

Rendering and awareness are the same condition described functionally. When a state is rendered, the system is aware. When nothing is rendered, there is no awareness. There are only rendered and non-rendered states.

This is not just an idea. It can be seen in everyday life. In deep, dreamless sleep, under general anesthesia, or during a brief blackout, the body keeps working. Breathing continues. The heart keeps beating. The system keeps regulating itself. The causal process continues and stabilization continues. But nothing is rendered. There is no hidden movie playing somewhere in the background. There is no experience that is simply forgotten. The display is offline, like a sonar machine that is still sending and receiving signals while its screen is turned off. The system keeps working, but no map appears.

If awareness is present, the Phenomena Transducer System is active and rendering. If awareness is absent, rendering is not occurring. Nothing additional is required to explain the difference. Rendering and awareness are the same condition described in functional terms. When the rendering machinery is active, experience exists. When it is inactive, the system continues to operate without display.

The Light Without an Operator

Phenomenality exists only when the Phenomena Transducer System is active. Awareness is not something that observes experience; it is the system being in a rendered condition. No rendering, no phenomenality. No phenomenality, no awareness. This is why the common image of awareness as a flashlight shining into a dark warehouse is misleading. That image implies something behind the light — an agent that decides where to point it and when to activate it. In this architecture, there is no such operator. There is no observer behind the display. The display is either active or inactive. When it is active, phenomenality exists. When it is not, there is none.

An accurate illustration would not show a person holding a flashlight, but a vast warehouse filled with machinery operating continuously on its own. Gears turn, belts move, valves open and close, and structures shift whether anything is illuminated or not. Most of the space remains dark, yet the machinery continues to function everywhere, unseen but active. There is no observer inside the warehouse, no controller directing events, and no one aiming a beam of light. Instead of a handheld flashlight, a fixed lamp is wired directly into the machinery itself. When certain internal conditions are met, the lamp turns on automatically. When those conditions are absent, it remains off. The lamp does not scan, search, or choose what to illuminate. It simply activates when the system enters a rendering condition and reveals whatever portion of the machinery has formed a stable, displayable configuration. The light does not guide the machinery, alter its operation, or determine what will occur. It only reveals the result of processes already underway. Illumination is therefore not a controller but a conditional feature of the system's operation: the machinery runs whether lit or unlit, and awareness appears only when the internal conditions that enable rendering are present.

Experience Cannot Guide the Moment That Produces It

Because the display system is downstream, experience cannot arrive in time to steer the stabilizing process that produced it. The system does not act because it sees or feels something. It sees or feels something because it has already acted, stabilized, or reorganized. This does not make experience irrelevant. It makes its role specific. A rendered state does not vanish. Once a configuration has been rendered, it becomes part of the system's internal condition. It is measured again, integrated again, and carried forward like any other internal state. In this sense, experience is just another kind of internal state: sometimes it lowers cost, sometimes it raises it, sometimes it contributes to reshaping the landscape, and sometimes it changes almost nothing at all. What it does depends entirely on the structure of the system at that moment.

Experience enters what comes next only by becoming part of what must next be carried, not by steering the moment that produced it. A simple example makes this concrete. Someone reads a book about anger. While reading, a sequence of rendered states appears: words, scenes, ideas, emotional tones. None of this gives the system the ability to interrupt an anger response in the moment it occurs. Whether anger arises, how strongly, and how long it persists is determined by the current structure: thresholds, load, couplings, and residue. But the reading does not disappear either. Those rendered states become part of the system's internal history. They are re-measured, re-integrated, and folded into the existing structure. Over time, this reshapes the terrain, making some configurations easier to carry and others harder. Not because experience controlled anything in the moment, but because the system has been structurally reshaped by what it has had to carry. Experience never governs the present. It only contributes to the structure that will govern the future.

Attention Is Not Awareness

Attention is a general control function spread throughout the system. It helps decide what gets processed, how strongly, and where resources are used. It shapes stabilization, priority, and routing. It exists at many levels of the system and even in systems that have no experience or display at all. In humans, one of its roles is to influence what can become part of experience.

It affects which stable configurations enter display and how clear, steady, or strong they appear. But this is only one of its roles, and not the main one.

Attention can work completely without any display. It is not a sign of awareness. It is a control process. Awareness exists only when the Phenomena Transducer System is active. Attention operates all the time. A simple example shows this. You are at a crowded party. Many voices, movements, and sounds surround you. Somewhere in the noise, someone says your name. Before you clearly experience "hearing your name," the system has already shifted. Signal routing changes. Your head turns. Your body reorients. Competing sounds are reduced. One source becomes stronger. This is attention at work. It is reallocating resources, shaping measurement, and changing priority before anything is displayed.

At the same time, higher Frames are also engaged. The sound is not just a sound. It connects to identity continuity: this name refers to this system. Posture and orientation reorganize, and the system's coordinated engagement reorganizes with them. None of this requires display to be active. The system would perform the same routing and reorientation even if it were tired, disconnected, or about to fall asleep. Only after a new configuration stabilizes can anything become displayable. Attention did not create awareness. It helped form the configuration that awareness may later display.

Why Only Stabilized States Are Shown

The Phenomena Transducer System can only show what is already stable enough for the system to carry. Because of this, experience is always late. Before anything appears, the system has already absorbed instability, redistributed load, and reorganized into a pattern it can carry. When this happens, that stable pattern becomes the system's current Frame of Reference. Only after the pattern is stable enough across the whole system can the display turn it into experience.

The system never lives inside the process of becoming stable. It only lives in the first pattern that has already become stable enough to be shown. This is not a mistake. It is how the system must work. If the display tried to show everything while things were still unstable, experience would be broken, confusing, and impossible to live inside. You can see this in everyday life. Sometimes something happens — a conversation, a realization, a strong emotion, a problem, or a sudden change — and afterward you feel that something is there, but you cannot explain it yet. You cannot put it into words. You may feel confused, tense, or unsettled. The system is still working, but no clear experience has formed. In CST terms, this is what unresolved integration feels like from the inside. A pattern has stabilized enough to appear, but different forces inside the system are still pulling in different directions. Load is still shifting. Possible patterns are still forming and fading. Nothing has yet become stable enough across the whole system to fully settle.

Only when that instability finally settles into a pattern the system can carry does something clear appear. Sometimes what stabilizes is clarity — now you can say what you think, what you feel, what changed, or what the problem is. Other times, what stabilizes is confusion itself — a stable but unresolved state that the system can still carry. Later, if conditions change, a new pattern may stabilize, and what once felt like confusion may reorganize into clarity. From the inside, this does not feel slow or gradual. It feels like something suddenly clicks into place. That click is not insight arriving. It is stabilization finishing. The display shows only the result. It never shows the reorganization, unstable transitions, or competing adjustments that produced it. What you experience is never the machinery while it is still moving. It is always the first stable pattern that comes out of that movement.

The Strobe-Lit Stage

Imagine a stage lit not by a continuous spotlight, but by a strobe light. Each flash reveals the actor in a different position: arm raised, body turned, foot forward, then seated. The audience experiences a continuous performance. But no motion is ever visible. Only a sequence of completed poses. Between flashes, the actor moves. Muscles contract. Weight shifts. Balance is regained. None of this is seen. The light does not move the actor. It does not guide the performance. It only determines when a finished position becomes visible at all. This is how the display system relates to the upstream architecture. The frames do their work between illuminations. When a configuration is finally stable enough to be carried, it becomes displayable. The PTS renders it. What appears as a continuous stream is the rapid stitching of stabilized outputs.

The Architecture Determines the World That Appears

Because the architecture can stabilize at many different levels of organization, and because the Phenomena Transducer System can render only what is currently stabilized, different Frames of Reference produce different kinds of worlds in experience. When stabilization is being carried by lower Frame of Reference, the rendered world is narrow, bodily, and urgent. Experience is organized around balance, movement, proximity, pressure, and immediate demand. The field is concrete and compressed because the architecture itself is working at short timescales and tight spatial horizons.

When stabilization is being carried by middle Frame of Reference, the rendered world is structured around social and affective gradients. Experience takes the form of safety and threat, approach and withdrawal, belonging and exclusion, alignment and tension. The field is no longer only physical. It is organized around coordination with other systems and the costs of engagement. When stabilization is being carried by identity-level Frame of Reference, the rendered world becomes personal and extended across time. Experience is organized around continuity, character, and what events imply about "what kind of system this is." The moment is no longer just happening. It is happening *to someone* and *as someone*. The field is structured by a long-range corridor that keeps activity coherent across roles, situations, and years.

When stabilization is being carried by higher Frame of Reference, the rendered world widens again. Experience becomes less centered, less forced through a single personal corridor, and less organized around maintaining a particular kind of personhood. The field takes on a more panoramic structure, not because anything has been added, but because coherence is being maintained at a broader scale. In all cases, nothing has changed in the machinery. What has changed is only which level of organization is currently doing the stabilizing, and therefore what the Phenomena Transducer System has access to render. The world that appears is always the world that corresponds to the level at which the system is currently being held together.

Awareness Does Not Move Between Frames

This point is crucial. Awareness does not climb anything. Awareness does not descend anything. Awareness does not choose where the system operates. The system moves. Awareness finds out where it moved. When people say they "shift perspective," what has actually happened is that stabilization has shifted to a different Frame of Reference, and the Phenomena Transducer System is now rendering a different kind of world. Nothing has looked at the same world differently. A different world is being rendered because the architecture is now being carried in a different way.

What This Chapter Establishes

From this point forward, whenever we speak about sight, sound, bodily sensation, emotion, thought, or presence, we are speaking about the output of the display system, not about the upstream machinery. The causal pipeline ends at stabilization. Stabilization already acts. Behavior is the world-facing continuation of that state. Display, when present, is the experience-facing continuation of that same state. The machine runs by constraint. Sometimes it runs in display mode. When it does, the system is aware. What remains, then, is to be precise about what kinds of things appear in that display. The next chapter introduces the concept of signatures: the characteristic ways different internal conditions, costs, and stabilizations are formatted when they are rendered. Signatures are not causes, and they are not controls. They are the surface forms that structural conditions take when they enter the phenomenal medium.

Awareness does not steer the system.
It renders what the system has already become.

Chapter 17

Signatures

What Experience Is Made Of

In the previous chapter, we saw where experience sits in the architecture. The causal pipeline — measurement, convergence, integration, and stabilization (Frame of Reference) — does all of its work before anything is ever rendered. Once a configuration stabilizes, it can continue outward as behavior and, if the display system is active, inward as experience. What appears in experience is therefore not the machinery itself. It is the display surface of a state that has already been settled. This raises a natural question. If experience is not where the work happens, then what is it? What, exactly, is experience made of? The answer is not beliefs, choices, or inner actions. It is not control. It is not authorship. It is signatures.

What "Signature" Means Here

In ordinary language, a signature is a distinctive pattern that tells you what something is or what state it is in. Smoke is the signature of fire. The particular sound of an engine is the signature of how it is running. A tremor in a bridge is the signature of load and stress moving through its structure. In science and engineering, the word is used the same way: a spectral signature identifies a substance, a signal signature identifies a source, a fault signature identifies a particular kind of failure. In all of these cases, the signature is not the thing itself. It is a characteristic output or trace produced by what is happening underneath — the way a state becomes evident without exposing the process that produced it. Thus, what appears is the signature of a stabilized configuration: a rendered trace of underlying dynamics.

The same distinction holds inside a system. If an engine is under strain, that strain is a mechanical state of the machinery. The gauge reading and the warning light are not that strain. They are the way that state is made visible.

If a bridge is near its load limit, the stress is in the steel and concrete. The vibration or groaning sound is not the stress itself. It is the signature of that state. If a battery is nearly empty, the chemical state is in the battery. The indicator dropping toward zero is the signature of that state. In each case, the signature is a surface expression of an underlying state. It does not cause the state. It does not control it. It does not stabilize it. It is how that state becomes readable. CST uses the word *signature* in exactly this sense, but applied to the inside of the human machine.

What is a "signature" of something?

The system is always in some structural state: carrying load, consuming margin, redistributing stress, stabilizing easily, stabilizing with difficulty, or failing to stabilize at all. These states are real, physical, and mechanical. They exist whether or not anything is being displayed. When the Phenomena Transducer System is active, some of these states are converted into the phenomenal medium. When that happens, they do not appear as load, margin, or stress. They appear as effort, strain, urgency, relief, tension, heaviness, lightness, clarity, fog, or flow. Those appearances are not the states themselves. They are their signatures. So, in CST terms, we can now be precise: *A signature is the way a structural state appears when a stabilized configuration is rendered into experience. It is not the state itself, but the display form of that state.*

In other words, what appears in experience under familiar names corresponds to specific structural states. What we feel as effort is the signature of expensive carrying. What we feel as strain is the signature of margin being consumed. What we feel as urgency is the signature of shrinking slack. What we feel as relief is the signature of a sudden drop in cost. What we feel as coherence is the signature of stable, low-friction integration. What we feel as fragmentation is the signature of failing coordination among subsystems. None of these drive the machine. They are what it is like when the machine is already in those states. Just as a dashboard does not run an engine but shows what the engine is undergoing, signatures do not run the system. They are the rendered surface of what the system is already doing.

The Dashboard Analogy, Made Precise

A car's dashboard does not cause the vehicle to move. It does not steer, burn fuel, or apply brakes. It displays. Speed, engine strain, temperature, fuel level, and traction warnings do not cause the car to behave as it does. They are surface signatures of what the machinery is already undergoing. If the engine is under strain, the gauge shows it. If the system overheats, a light appears. The display does not create these states. It converts them into a readable surface. Experience works the same way. What is rendered is not the machine. It is the display.

Signatures as Carried State

Rendered states are still states. A signature does not vanish once it is rendered. When the Phenomena Transducer System converts a stabilized configuration into the phenomenal medium, the system is now in a new internal state: one that includes that rendered state as part of what must be carried forward. This does not give the signature any special authority. It does not turn experience into a controller. It does not allow feeling to steer the moment that produced it. Rendering always arrives too late for that. The architecture has already stabilized. The state has already been reached. The signature is the display of that result, not a lever acting on its production. But once present, a rendered state is still a real state of the machine. On the next cycle, it is measured like any other internal state. It is integrated like any other internal state. It contributes load, bias, and constraint like any other internal state. And like any other state, repeated passage leaves residue that gradually reshapes thresholds, sensitivities, and default pathways.

Experience Is Treated Like Any Other Internal State

This is not special to experience. The system treats many kinds of internal states this way. A muscle that has been holding tension for hours becomes part of the next moment's load. An elevated hormone level becomes part of the next moment's operating condition. Fatigue, inflammation, depleted glucose, a sensitized reflex loop, or a recently activated defensive pattern all persist as internal states that the next stabilization must work around. None of these states decide anything. But each changes what is easy or difficult to carry next. A fatigued body stabilizes differently than a rested one. An inflamed system stabilizes differently than a calm one. A structure that has been repeatedly driven into the same defensive posture begins to enter that posture more easily and leave it more slowly. Rendered states work the same way.

If a configuration has stabilized and been rendered as pain, fear, effort, or relief, that rendered state is now simply part of what the system is carrying, in the same way that muscle tension, hormonal shifts, or metabolic strain are part of what it is carrying. On the next cycle, that entire state is measured and integrated again. Over time, if the system repeatedly passes through similar high-cost reorganizations, the architecture changes. Thresholds shift. Sensitivities change. Certain routes become easier to enter and harder to leave. What began as a temporary, expensive configuration can become a default one. This is not because experience instructed the system. It is because the same structural reorganizations kept occurring and their residue accumulated. Experience is just one surface of that accumulation.

How Signatures Carry Forward Without Steering

A simple analogy makes this clear. When a warning light turns on in a car, it does not cause the engine problem. It is a display of a state that already exists. But once the light is on, the electrical system is now in a slightly different state than it was before. The display does not fix or cause the fault — but it is now part of the machine's total state. The same is true here. If a system stabilizes into a configuration that is rendered as pain, fear, effort, or relief, that rendered state does not explain or control the reorganization that produced it. But from that point forward, the system is now carrying a state that includes that rendering. That entire state will be re-measured, re-integrated, and folded into whatever comes next.

Consider fear. Tightening, withdrawal, and rerouting happen first. Only after those changes have stabilized does fear appear in display. Fear did not cause the withdrawal. But once present, the system is now in a state that includes fear, and like any other state, repeated passage leaves residue that gradually reshapes thresholds, sensitivities, and default pathways. Or consider pain. Tissue damage and protective reorganization occur first. Only afterward does pain appear in display. Pain did not cause the protection. But once present, the system is now carrying a state that includes pain, and that state is treated like any other internal state in subsequent cycles. So, experience is neither a driver nor a ghost. It is not in charge, and it is not irrelevant.

Signatures do not reach backward. They do not choose. They do not steer. But once they exist, they are part of the landscape the machine is now moving through. And over time, as similar reorganizations repeat, the residue of these carried states gradually reshapes what the architecture can carry easily and what it cannot. Experience does not teach the system. Reorganization does. Experience is the carried echo of what that teaching costs.

When Behavior and Experience Travel Together

Once stabilization occurs, two continuations can appear in parallel: outward behavior and internal display through the Phenomena Transducer System. The behavior acts in the world, while the display renders the stabilized configuration as experience — pain, fear, effort, relief, or countless other signatures. Neither produces the stabilization that preceded it. Both are consequences of it. But once they appear, the system is now carrying a state that includes them.

In the next cycle of measurement, the system does not return to a blank starting point. It measures the conditions it currently carries. Those conditions now include whatever bodily configuration resulted from the behavior, as well as the internal configuration associated with the rendered signature. These streams enter measurement together with sensory input and environmental conditions. Convergence and integration occur across the entire field of what the system now is.

Because of this, behavior and experience that appeared together in one stabilization often travel together into the next. They are not linked by instruction or memory labels. They are simply part of the same carried state.

When similar circumstances arise again, the system measures conditions that already contain traces of both.

Consider a child who touches a hot stove. The hand withdraws almost immediately as protective reflexes reorganize the body. Only after that reorganization stabilizes does pain appear in display. The pain did not cause the withdrawal. But once both occur, the system is now carrying a state that includes tissue stress, protective muscle patterns, and the rendered signature of pain. When the child later approaches a stove, the system measures conditions that resemble the earlier configuration: visual cues, proximity, bodily readiness, and traces of the previous state. Stabilization may again favor withdrawal. From the outside this looks like the child "learned" that touching the stove leads to pain. Mechanically, what occurred is simpler: a configuration that included withdrawal and pain was carried forward, and repeated passages through similar conditions gradually reshape what stabilizes easily.

A similar pattern appears with fear. Imagine someone walking through a dark alley and hearing a sudden loud noise. The body reorganizes immediately: muscles tighten, breathing changes, the body turns or retreats. Only after that stabilization does fear appear in display. Fear did not produce the tightening or withdrawal. Those reorganizations occurred first. But once the rendered signature appears, the system is now carrying a state that includes both the protective posture and the experience of fear. When the person later walks through a similar alley, the system measures conditions that resemble the earlier configuration — darkness, narrow space, unfamiliar sounds, bodily readiness. Stabilization may again favor tightening or withdrawal. From the outside it appears that the alley "causes fear." Mechanically, the system is stabilizing within a landscape already reshaped by prior passages through similar configurations.

In psychology, patterns like these are often described as **associations**. From a CST perspective, nothing is actively linking the experience and the behavior. They simply emerged together from the same stabilization and were carried forward as part of the same system state. Over time, the residue of these carried configurations reshapes thresholds, sensitivities, and the pathways that remain easiest for the system to enter again.

Behavior and experience therefore travel together without directing one another. One acts outwardly, the other renders inwardly as both become part of the landscape the system must now move through.

A similar principle can be seen in the senses. Each sensory channel measures a different aspect of the environment and operates independently at the level of measurement. Vision registers light patterns. Hearing registers pressure waves. Touch registers mechanical contact. Smell and taste register chemical interaction.

These signals do not remain separate. During convergence and integration they enter into the formation of a single environmental configuration. When similar configurations recur, the signals present within them begin to appear linked. The senses do not associate with one another directly; they become related because they repeatedly appear within the same stabilized configuration of the world.

What Comes Next

Up to this point, we have only built the machinery. We now have the pieces to say something very precise: what appears in experience is not a controller, not a chooser, and not a driver. It is a field of signatures — the displayed surface of structural states the system has already settled into. In the chapters that follow, we will take the most familiar and most misleading of these signatures and examine them one by one. We will look at emotion as the signature of frame-level stabilization under load. We will look at effort and strain as the signatures of expensive carrying. We will look at trying and motivation as the signatures of sustained stabilization through difficult terrain. And later, we will look at agency itself as a particular kind of display artifact that arises under certain conditions of smooth, coherent control. None of these are forces. None of them are causes. None of them run the machine. They are what it is like when the machine is already running in particular ways. Once these are in place, much of what people ordinarily think of as "inner action," "will," or "mental effort" will turn out to be something far simpler, and far more mechanical: the sound and shape of a system carrying itself through its own landscape.

Chapter 18

Some of the Major Signatures

Emotion, Effort, Motivation, and the Feeling of Control

In the previous chapter, we saw what experience is made of: not causes, not choices, not control, but signatures — the rendered surface of structural states the machine is already in. We also saw that these signatures do not steer the system. They are carried forward like any other internal state and can leave residue, but they do not shape the moment of stabilization that produces them. In this chapter, we will look at the most important signatures in everyday human life: emotion, strain, effort, trying, motivation, wanting, and even the feeling of agency itself. These are the states that, from the inside, most strongly create the impression of doing, choosing, and controlling. In CST, they are something more precise and more mechanical: they are what different kinds of structural motion, cost, and coordination look like when they are rendered. Nothing new will be added to the causal pipeline here. We will simply examine its most familiar surface traces.

Emotion as Signature

Emotion, in CST, belongs to the same class as effort, strain, urgency, and relief. It is not a driver. It is not a cause. It is the felt signature of frame-level stabilization and reorganization under load. The architecture adjusts first. The feeling appears later. When a moment can be carried easily, stabilization is smooth and reorganization is quiet. No strong emotional signature appears. When a moment pushes the structure near or beyond what it can carry, the architecture must redistribute load more forcefully. Thresholds shift. Pathways tighten or inhibit. Coordination patterns change. Only after a new configuration has stabilized does the Phenomena Transducer System render that state into experience. What appears there is what we call emotion. Emotion is not the work. It is the display of the work.

A physical analogy makes this clear. When a heavy truck crosses a bridge, the bridge does not consult a plan or decide how to respond. Each component bends, stretches, or compresses because the forces acting on it eliminate incompatible configurations. The global redistribution of load emerges from these local adjustments. When the load is high enough, the bridge creaks, groans, or vibrates. Those sounds are not what keep the bridge standing. They do not correct anything. They are the surface signatures of structural work already underway. Human emotion is the same kind of signature. When the architecture must work harder to remain coherent, a signature appears. When it does not, no signature appears. Feeling tense, afraid, angry, heavy, restless, or relieved does not cause anything. It is what the system's reorganization looks like once it is rendered — what structural adjustment under load looks and feels like from the inside.

Why Emotion Always Arrives Late

This also explains why emotion always arrives late. The Phenomena Transducer System can only render configurations that have already stabilized long enough to be carried. It cannot display reorganization itself. You can see this in simple moments of fright. A loud bang goes off behind you. Before anything like "fear" appears, your shoulders have already jumped, your heart is already racing, your breath has already tightened, and your hands may already be shaking. The architecture has already shifted posture, rerouted priorities, and redistributed load. Only afterward does awareness register the state as fear. By the time fear, anger, or relief appears in experience, posture has shifted, routing has changed, and load has been redistributed. What is displayed is the new state, not the process that produced it.

This reverses the everyday story people tell themselves. We do not withdraw because we feel afraid. We feel afraid because the system has already withdrawn or tightened. We do not clench because we are angry. We feel anger because the system has already mobilized load for forceful reconfiguration. We do not relax because we feel relief. We feel relief because the system has already entered a lower-cost configuration. Emotion is not what makes the system move. Emotion is what movement under certain structural conditions feels like.

What Different Emotions Are

Different emotions correspond to different patterns of structural strain. Fear is what it is like when the system is being driven into high-cost, low-margin configurations at speed. Anger is what it is like when load is being mobilized to force a blocked reconfiguration. Sadness is what it is like when available corridors have stabilized and energy is withdrawing from paths that can no longer be carried. Relief is what it is like when cost drops suddenly and margin returns. They are signatures of what it cost this particular architecture to carry the moment — like a car engine that produces different sounds depending on what is happening inside it. A sharp knocking sound can indicate loose valves. A high-pitched squeal can indicate a failing bearing or a slipping belt. Backfiring can indicate a timing or ignition problem. None of these sounds are about the road. They are not instructions or causes. They are diagnostic surface traces of specific mechanical states inside the machine.

This is why emotion often feels "about" something but is not a reliable guide to what is actually happening. A situation can be objectively safe and still feel threatening if the relevant frames must work hard to stabilize it. A situation can be objectively dangerous and still feel calm if the architecture has learned to carry it at low cost. A free-solo climber thousands of feet above the ground is in a situation that would drive most architectures into extreme strain. But for a system that has spent years reorganizing around exactly this class of load, the same configuration can be carried quietly and at lower cost. The emotional signature is muted not because the situation is safe, but because the structure no longer has to work hard to hold itself together there. Emotion does not track truth. It tracks structural economics.

The Display Boundary

It is crucial to keep the display boundary clear. Before a configuration is rendered by the Phenomena Transducer System, nothing is felt. There is no fear, no tension, no relief, no sadness. There is only a mechanical state of the machine: a particular distribution of load, constraint, and coordination. When that same state is rendered, it appears as feeling. The feeling is not added to the state. It is the state, in display format. This boundary matters because complex, adaptive, even life-saving behavior does not require phenomenality. A system can reorganize under extreme load, mobilize energy, narrow its field of operation, and execute coordinated escape without any display at all.

Consider a wildebeest attacked by a crocodile at a river crossing. In a fraction of a second, its entire organization shifts. Muscles flood with energy. Movement stabilizes into a single urgent corridor: escape. From the outside, this looks exactly like what, in humans, would be called terror. But nothing in this sequence requires that anything be rendered. It is simply an architecture reorganizing under extreme constraint. CST does not claim to know which animals do or do not have phenomenality. What it claims is more precise: you cannot infer that they are experiencing display from their behavior. Coordination is a property of control architectures. Feeling is a property of display architectures. No display, no phenomenality. What exists prior to rendering is not an unfelt feeling and not an unconscious emotion. It is simply a machine in a particular state.

From Reorganization to Residue

Over longer timescales, repeated high-cost reorganizations leave residue. Thresholds shift. Pathways deepen. What was once expensive becomes less expensive. As cost drops, emotional signatures fade. This is what awareness later calls "getting used to something," "adapting," or "healing." Emotion does not teach. Reorganization teaches. Emotion is the echo of the lesson.

Effort and Trying as Signatures

Effort is not a force applied by the system. It is not a causal lever. It does not make anything happen. It is the rendered signature of a state that is expensive to carry. The state produces the effort, not the other way around. Effort is the sound the engine makes under load. From the inside, effort feels like doing something. Like pushing. Like making something happen. This is the unavoidable perspective of a system that only ever has access to its own display. But mechanically, effort is none of these things. Effort appears when a configuration is being held near the limits of stability and requires continuous internal work to keep it from breaking down. When a state is easy to carry, it feels easy. When a state is costly to carry, it feels effortful. Nothing about the feeling makes the carrying happen. The carrying is already happening. There is no controller applying effort. Effort is the rendered signature of that fact.

A cyclist climbing a steep mountain feels intense effort. Legs burn. Breathing strains. Balance must be managed. The configuration is costly to carry. When the same cyclist turns and coasts downhill, the feeling changes immediately. The motion continues, but the internal work disappears. The state has become easier to carry. The cyclist is not authoring the effort. The system is simply in an expensive configuration. What experience calls "trying" is this same signature seen from another angle. Increasing effort does not move the system into a different region of the landscape. It only means the current configuration is requiring more compensation to remain intact. Real change comes only from entering a different configuration. There is no agency applying effort. Effort is the work required for the machinery to carry the present configuration.

Trying to fall asleep makes this especially clear. When the system is in a high-arousal configuration, the feeling of "trying" to sleep is not an action that moves the system toward sleep. It is the signature of still being in the wrong state. The architecture is still organized to carry vigilance: muscles remain partially tense, breathing stays shallow or irregular, attention circuits remain active, and multiple subsystems continue to perform stabilizing work to hold that aroused configuration together. As long as this organization remains in place, sleep is structurally impossible. The feeling of trying is simply what it is like to keep carrying that expensive, wake-oriented state. Sleep arrives only when the configuration — including the Frame of Reference through which stabilization occurs — changes, when load redistributes, thresholds shift, and the system settles into a form intrinsically low enough in cost to carry without continuous stabilization.

Motivation as a Signature

People often talk about motivation as if it were a force inside them — something they possess, something that rises and falls, something that pushes behavior into motion. From a CST perspective, nothing like that exists. There is no internal engine generating movement. There are only configurations that are affordable to carry and configurations that are costly. Movement continues where continuation is affordable and forward paths are open, and it strains or stalls where they are not. Motivation is the signature of this condition — what affordable forward openness feels like from the inside.

Consider a simple case. Every morning, Eva plans to go for a run. She lays out her clothes, sets her alarm, and tells herself she will start at 6:30. On many mornings, she stands in her room and cannot move. Her legs feel heavy. Her chest tightens slightly. The idea of stepping outside feels strangely uphill. She calls this being unmotivated. Then, on another morning, nothing seems difficult. She steps out the door easily, begins jogging without hesitation, and finds a rhythm almost immediately. Later she says, "Today I finally felt motivated." Nothing inside her switched on. No hidden resource appeared. No inner force woke up. What changed was the terrain. A path that had been too costly or too closed became affordable and open. The architecture found itself in a configuration where forward movement required less strain and led into widening possibilities. Motion unfolded. The feeling of motivation was simply what that affordable forward openness looked like when rendered. Motivation is not what makes movement happen. It is what it feels like when movement is affordable and the path ahead is open.

Momentum and the Ease of Continuing

When a system is already moving within a stable, affordable corridor, the next moment begins inside that corridor rather than from rest. Very little reconfiguration is required to keep going. The system is already organized in a way that supports continuation. From the inside, this often feels like momentum, flow, or being carried forward. Someone working smoothly on a project, absorbed in a conversation, or moving through a familiar routine often reports that things are "just flowing." But momentum alone is not motivation. A system can continue easily without sensing expansion or possibility. Motivation appears only when continuation is not just affordable but open — when forward movement leads into widening terrain rather than repetition. This is why starting is often hard and continuing is often easier, yet motivation does not always accompany continuation. Starting requires crossing a costly transition. Continuing may require little effort. But motivation requires something more: affordable movement into open forward space.

Resistance Is Structural Cost

People often say they "lack motivation" when movement feels heavy, effortful, or impossible. The language suggests something is missing.

Structurally, nothing is missing. The system has encountered resistance. Resistance is not an attitude or a mood. It is cost. When a path becomes costly to carry, the architecture must perform more stabilizing work to remain coherent. Posture tightens. Breathing shifts. Coordination strains. Awareness samples this as reluctance, dread, pressure, or avoidance. A student staring at a blank page is not suffering from a shortage of motivation. The path in front of her is simply too costly or too closed to stabilize right now. The configuration required to begin is not yet one the system can carry with low strain. The signature of that condition is what she calls "I can't get myself to start."

A Gradient, Not a Push

Motivation is not simply the signature of moving downhill. A system can follow a gradient without feeling motivated if the movement leads into narrow repetition or constrained necessity. Motivation appears only when movement is both affordable and open. Consider a student who does not enjoy studying. The material is dry. The work is not pleasant. Left alone, the system drifts toward distraction. Now imagine a change: scoring above a certain threshold yields a scholarship. Studying is still costly. It still requires effort. But the landscape has shifted. Now the forward path is not only relatively less costly — it leads into expanded possibility, more open. The student feels oriented toward the future, not pushed, but drawn by open forward space. This is motivation. Not force. Not mere gradient. Affordable movement into widening terrain.

Why Motivation Can Coexist with Effort

Motivation and effort often appear together and are easily confused. The student may still experience strain while studying. That strain reflects the cost of maintaining the state. But at the same time, there is directional openness: forward remains more possible than not-forward. Effort reflects how costly the state is to hold. Motivation reflects that forward movement remains affordable and open. These are separate dimensions. Effort measures load. Motivation reflects accessible forward expansion.

Why Motivation Feels Like a Pull

When the easiest way for a system to remain coherent is to move forward into open terrain, the architecture naturally reorients in that direction. From the inside, this does not feel like being pushed. It feels like being drawn forward. But nothing is pulling. The system is arranged so that forward movement is affordable and widening. The feeling of motivation is the signature of this condition.

Why Motivation Disappears Instantly

If the scholarship vanishes, or the future closes, or conditions tighten, forward openness disappears. Studying did not necessarily become harder. The path became narrower or less affordable. Motivation fades immediately. Nothing inside the person switched off. The terrain changed.

One-Line Rule

Effort is what it feels like to hold a costly state. Motivation is what it feels like when forward movement is affordable and open. They often coexist. They are not the same.

Determination Is Not Motivation

There is another experience often mistaken for motivation: determination. Determination appears when a system continues along a costly path because every alternative is worse. A marathon runner near the finish knows this state. Legs burn. Breathing strains. Everything is costly. Yet the runner continues — not because the path is easy, but because stopping is worse. This is not motivation. It is constrained continuation. Determination is the signature of being held within a narrow, high-cost corridor, not open forward movement.

Why Motivation Appears and Disappears Suddenly

Sudden motivation feels mysterious. One moment a person is stuck. The next, everything flows. Nothing turned on. A barrier dropped. A constraint loosened. A path opened. The system entered a region where movement became affordable and forward terrain widened. A writer struggles for hours. Then a phrase fits and structure aligns. From that point forward, movement becomes easier and more open. Motivation appears. The reverse occurs when fatigue, pressure, or disruption closes the path. Motivation did not appear or vanish by force. It followed the terrain.

Motivation Is a State, Not a Force

Motivation is not something a system has or uses. It is not something stored or spent. It is a condition of the terrain. When movement is affordable and the path opens forward, awareness samples this as motivation. When movement is affordable but closed, awareness samples rest or habit. When movement is costly, awareness samples strain. When costly movement is unavoidable, awareness samples determination. Motivation does not cause movement. It is what certain configurations feel like when rendered. Not an engine, but a signal of affordable forward openness.

Boredom and Drive

Low cost alone does not produce the experience of direction. Boredom is low cost as well. In boredom, the system can move easily, but no direction carries less cost than another. There is no directional bias and no openness. The landscape is flat. Motion drifts. Awareness samples this as restlessness, emptiness, or aimlessness. Drive appears when the landscape slopes. When each step forward makes the next step cost less, motion is not only easy — it is easier in a particular direction. Awareness samples this gradient as interest, engagement, or inspiration. Boredom is low resistance without a slope, with nowhere carrying less cost than anywhere else. Drive is low resistance with a slope.

Agency as a Signature

Even agency is a signature. It is not a causal power. It is what it is like when higher frames are stabilizing action with low friction and high coherence. When things flow, the feeling of authorship appears. When things jam, it strains or disappears. The feeling of being the source is a display artifact, not the source. (We will return to this in detail later.)

The Rule

The rule is simple. Signatures do not drive the system. They display the system. They are not part of the pipeline that determines what configuration is reached. They are the way the result of that pipeline is rendered. Experience is not a control room. It is a display. A sophisticated one. A necessary one. But still a display. The machine does not run because experience tells it to. Experience looks the way it does because the machine is running the way it is.

Chapter 19

The Agency We Experience

Why Experience Feels Authored Even When It Isn't

You stand in front of a door. On the other side is a difficult conversation you have been avoiding. For a moment, nothing moves. Your hand hangs at your side. Your chest tightens. Thoughts assemble and dissolve. You tell yourself you are deciding. Then something shifts. Your hand rises. Fingers close around the knob. You feel the cool resistance of metal, the weight of your body, a faint tremor in your arm. You turn. You hear the click. You step through. Later you will say, "I finally decided to do it."

The sequence feels authored. It feels as though you stood at an inner crossroads, surveyed alternatives, and selected one. From a CST perspective, something very different happened. Long before your hand moved, the architecture was already reorganizing under pressure: bodily tension, residues from past encounters, the cost of continued avoidance, the strain of holding yourself frozen in place. Partial configurations formed and dissolved. Competing tendencies rose and fell. Only when one arrangement finally stabilized did the movement occur.

By the time awareness encountered the moment — fingers on metal, motion already underway — the generative sequence was over. The feeling that "I did this" arrived after the fact. Yet that feeling is not an error. It is the correct experiential form of a particular kind of stabilized state. This chapter explains where that feeling comes from, why it cannot generate behavior, and why it continues to feel central even though it is downstream of everything that actually produces what happens.

The Stubborn Sense of Being the One Who Acts

To be human is to experience life as if it were guided from somewhere inside. Movements feel initiated. Thoughts feel selected. Urges feel accepted or resisted. Possibilities seem open until "I" narrow them. Nothing in experience suggests that these impressions are late-arriving displays of a process that has already settled. The sense of authorship is immediate and compelling. When you lift a cup, send a message, or leave a relationship, the moment carries a distinctive tone: this is me doing this. CST does not dismiss this. It does not treat agency as a mere error to be argued away. But it does refuse to treat it as generative. There is no place in the architecture where a chooser stands apart from the machinery, surveys multiple futures, and inserts a selection from outside the causal chain. What is experienced as initiation is the first illuminated point in a process already underway. To see why, we have to be precise about what true agency would require.

What Genuine Agency Would Demand

Everyday discourse treats agency as the capacity to select freely among options. In that picture, a person stands at a fork in the road and chooses, unconstrained, which path to take. For such agency to exist in a literal, generative sense, the system would need a subsystem capable of originating causal influence that is not itself the product of the same measurement and stabilization dynamics that govern the rest of the architecture. It would require a vantage point outside the system's own Frames of Reference — something able to survey multiple possible futures and insert a selection into the causal stream without that selection itself being shaped by prior structure. No such vantage point can exist in a finite, closed architecture.

Measurement is always internal. Stabilization always expresses the system's current load paths, residues, and constraints. There is nowhere for a chooser to stand that is not already part of what is being measured and resolved. In any real decision, what stabilizes is simply what the architecture can carry under the present conditions. If one imagines stripping away all prior structure — no residues, no bodily state, no tuned sensitivities, no history — nothing remains that could support a coherent preference at all. Any "selection" would dissolve into noise. The choice would be no different than randomness, and noise cannot stabilize a measurement-based system.

In ordinary life this is easy to miss, because decisions feel like they involve weighing options. A simple choice — coffee or tea — already carries the full weight of the architecture. What stabilizes is shaped by the system's existing residues, current bodily state, time of day, and countless prior states. If all of that structure were removed, nothing would remain that could support a coherent preference at all. The "choice" would dissolve into noise, and noise cannot stabilize a measurement-based architecture. CST therefore leaves no place for a causeless chooser — not as a metaphysical stance, but as a mechanical one. This does not deny internal conflict, evaluation, or deliberation. It denies only that any of these require, or contain, an extra generative operator called choosing. Yet the experience of being the one who chooses remains.

Why Stabilization Looks Like Authorship

Everything that reaches awareness arrives only in its already-stabilized form. *The system has already measured, undergone strain, resolved competing configurations, and settled into a state coherent enough to carry across the active Frames of Reference.* None of that process appears. Awareness has access only to the result. When stabilization occurs around early Frames of Reference, the moment appears as sound, color, or movement (FOR-1, FOR-2). There is no awareness of a someone. But when stabilization occurs around Frames of Reference that include the self-structure (FOR-4 and above), the resulting state now includes an awareness of "the one to whom this is happening." The reaching arm, the forming sentence, the rising impulse all arrive already bound to that structure. The machinery that produced the state is absent. Only the outcome is present. Whatever appears in that outcome feels like the beginning, because nothing earlier is accessible. Agency is the appearance created as awareness illuminates a stabilized configuration that includes the self-structure while hiding the forces that produced it.

The Delay That Never Feels Like a Delay

A familiar con-game illustrates this delay. The race has already occurred elsewhere. The bettors hear the broadcast of the horses bursting from the gate, charging down the track, and crossing the finish line, believing they are witnessing events unfold in real time. Nothing in their experience suggests that the outcome is already fixed, that the signal has been delayed just enough for someone else to know the winner beforehand. For the gamblers, "now" is whatever is being broadcast live. Awareness works the same way. The mechanical layer has already played through its sequence — measurement, convergence, integration, stabilization — before any of it appears phenomenologically. There is always a delay between generation and display, but the system has no vantage point from which to notice that delay. The illuminated moment feels like the present, because nothing earlier is accessible. What appears as "me deciding now" is the last visible step in a series of events that have already settled.

The Spotlight and the Stage

Earlier chapters compared awareness to a strobe spotlight illuminating a stage of stabilized configurations. The stage is the architecture: micro-states, bodily shifts, frame competition, residues meeting new conditions. The spotlight is awareness. It can only reveal what has already been arranged. Off the stage, configurations shift, constraints propagate, and structure is quietly rearranged. When the strobe spotlight of awareness finally lands, it does not compose the scene — it reveals what is already there. From the audience's perspective, the illuminated moment appears as the beginning; the work that produced it remains invisible. In CST, the feeling of agency lives in this lighting. When awareness illuminates a stabilized configuration that includes a self-structure, the immediate experience is simply "I am seeing this" or "this is happening to me." But the spotlight does not build the stage, arrange the scene, or set events in motion. It does not generate. It reveals.

The Non-Negotiable Order

The architecture enforces an order of dependency that cannot be inverted: measurement must occur for anything to be available; competing possibilities must be resolved through the system's own constraints; stabilization must yield a configuration coherent enough to hold; only then can awareness illuminate; and only then can agency appear. There is no path inside CST for awareness or agency to reach backward and alter anything in the processes that produce the state. Agency is a phenomenological event: a display state. It cannot exist before awareness, and awareness cannot exist before there is a stabilized configuration coherent enough to be rendered. Therefore, agency cannot play a generative role in what the system does to reach that state. It arrives only after the work is done. It is real as experience and non-generative as cause. Everyday moments bear this stamp. Standing in front of the closet, the system has already begun trending toward some outfit based on temperature, bodily comfort, residues of social context, and all prior states around clothing. Only after one path stabilizes does a thought emerge: *I think I'll wear the blue one.* The thought is not the origin of the choice; it is its illuminated form.

Mechanical Causation and Phenomenal Causation

To understand where agency fits, it helps to distinguish two layers of causation. At the mechanical layer, forces interact directly. Bodily state, incoming energy, existing residues, frame competition, and structural constraints all press against one another. Convergence resolves this pressure into a single configuration within the governing Frame of Reference, from which behavior proceeds. Nothing in this layer resembles choosing or intending. It is constraint and stabilization. When that configuration is illuminated by awareness, it appears as a phenomenal state: a thought, an urge, a sense of certainty, a feeling of doubt, a surge of willingness, a flare of resistance. These are not distortions. They are the correct experiential forms of the mechanical state when transduced by the PTS. Once present, these states leave residue only because they are the architecture in experiential form. They do not reach backward to alter the sequence that produced them. They reach forward by becoming part of the conditions through which the next state must pass. Agency, as experience, lives at this second layer. It does not begin the process, but it becomes part of the terrain the architecture must carry next.

How Experience Shapes Without Starting

When you touch a hot stove, your hand pulls back before anything like pain appears. The withdrawal happens first. Only afterward does the experience of pain arrive. The pain did not cause the movement. It is what that movement cost the system. But once it appears, that pain is no longer just a display. It is now part of the system's state. The next time the architecture faces a similar situation, stabilization has to pass through a system that already carries that trace. Experience never begins the process. It enters after the fact and becomes part of the conditions that shape what happens next.

Why the Feeling of Alternatives Exists

The experience of agency is most vivid when there seems to be a choice.

You sit in front of a cafe menu, feel several possibilities alive at once, and then finally settle on one. The moment carries the sense that you could have gone otherwise. At the mechanical layer, the system never holds multiple stable configurations at the same time. It passes through a sequence of transient coherences — each briefly stabilized, yet unable to propagate forward into a more durable configuration. As stabilization is sought, these nearly viable configurations rise and fall in rapid succession. Some include the self-structure oriented toward one option, some toward another. The architecture is not hosting alternatives in parallel; it is cycling through unstable candidates. Awareness does not have access to the competition itself. It can only sample the series of short-lived, nearly stabilized forms as they appear. From the vantage point of FOR-5 through FOR-7, this sequence is experienced as deliberation, weighing, and choosing. The lived feeling of "I could go this way or that" is real. It is what a stream of unstable configurations feels like when each one includes the self-structure. What is not present is a chooser moving freely among independent possibilities. There is only a system searching for a configuration it can carry, and awareness illuminating that search after the fact.

Where Agency Lives in the Frames of Reference

Agency does not appear at all levels of the Frames of Reference. In the earliest frames, stabilization is occupied with physical pressure, orientation, and the basic coherence of the body in the world. There is no sense of a someone to whom anything belongs. As broader Frames of Reference become available, the architecture begins to bind events into a single embodied trajectory. Experiences become marked as mine, and over time that mine is gathered into a more stable sense of who this system is. Within a particular band of this recursive dependence — where configurations stabilize around a self-structure, but cannot yet include that self-structure as something being observed — agency appears at full strength. Actions, urges, decisions, attitudes, and preferences all arrive bound to a sense of authorship. They do not merely happen; they feel as though they are being done. Above this band, in higher frames that can hold the self-structure itself as part of what is being illuminated rather than as the vantage point of illumination, the feeling of being the originator often softens or dissolves. Nothing about the mechanics changes. The system remains fully determined. Only the format of the experience changes. Agency is therefore frame-specific. It belongs only to the range in which the system illuminates a self-structure in its output while the machinery that produced that output remains hidden. For this reason, agency cannot be fundamental. It is not present at the base of the architecture, and it is not what the architecture is built from. It is a higher-level display effect that appears only when certain kinds of stabilization are being rendered.

If You Truly Had Control

There is a simple way to test the everyday picture of agency. If a system truly possessed the kind of command authority people imagine — an inner point from which choices could be issued directly — many common forms of human suffering would not exist. Insomnia would not exist. You would decide to sleep, and sleep would follow. Burnout would not exist. You would decide to feel motivated, and motivation would appear. Rumination would not exist. You would decide to stop thinking about something, and the thoughts would stop. Depression would not exist. You would decide to enjoy life, and enjoyment would arrive. But this is not how the system behaves.

Anyone who has lain awake at night knows the paradox: the more one tries to sleep, the more awake the body becomes. The attempt to command the state only increases the very tension that prevents it. The same pattern appears with anxiety. Telling oneself to calm down rarely calms anything. It usually does the opposite. The system tightens, not loosens. With rumination, the instruction to "stop thinking about it" often makes the thought return with even greater force. With enjoyment, the effort to "just be present" or "just be happy" frequently produces strain, self-monitoring, and a sense of artificiality that drives the experience further away. These are not moral failures or deficits of discipline. They are mechanical facts about how a stabilizing architecture works.

States like sleep, calm, interest, or ease are not produced by command. They are produced when the system reaches configurations it can carry with the lowest cost. They emerge when load has been redistributed, when competing pressures have quieted, when the architecture has found a stable arrangement. Trying to force them is like trying to smooth water by pressing on it. The very act of pressing is another force the system has to stabilize around. If there were a place inside the architecture that could simply issue orders, these phenomena would vanish. The system would behave like a machine with a master switch: flip it to "sleep," and sleep would occur; flip it to "relax," and relaxation would follow. The fact that this never works is not a mystery. It is a direct consequence of how the system is built.

The same is true of more severe conditions. If a system could simply decide its own states, addiction would not exist. Phobias would not exist. Panic attacks would not exist. Trauma would not exist. One would simply stop. The persistence of these patterns is not evidence of stubbornness. It is evidence that the forces shaping convergence and stabilization do not run through awareness. Even in ordinary motivation this shows up. People do not fail to act because they have not issued the correct internal command. They fail to act because the architecture is stabilizing in ways that make certain actions expensive and others low-cost. When action finally occurs, it is not because a command succeeded. It is because the balance of forces has shifted enough that a different configuration can now hold.

From the inside, all of this is experienced as struggle, effort, resolve, giving up, trying again. From the mechanical side, it is load redistribution, competing tendencies, partial convergences, and slow changes in what the system can carry. Awareness samples these shifts and presents them as intention, effort, decision, or failure. But it does not direct them. This is why so much human suffering is compounded by self-blame. People are taught to treat their own stabilizations as if they were choices. When the system cannot sleep, it is accused of not trying hard enough. When it cannot relax, it is accused of being uncooperative. When it cannot enjoy life, it is accused of being ungrateful. When it cannot stop a destructive pattern, it is accused of not wanting to change.

CST removes this entire layer of confusion. Not by telling the system that nothing matters, but by describing what actually does. The system does not change because it is commanded to do so. It changes because its architecture is reshaped by what it has had to carry. It changes because residues accumulate. It changes because certain stabilizations become easier and others become harder. It changes because conditions change. Seen this way, the everyday failure of "just decide to" is not a failure at all. It is the normal behavior of a finite stabilizing system. And this is the final, practical reason agency cannot be what people imagine. If there were really an inner source of direct control, the most basic forms of human distress would be optional. The fact that they are not is not a tragedy of will. It is a clue to the architecture.

Living with Non-Generative Agency

Understanding that agency is not generative can feel destabilizing. A system that has spent decades organizing itself around the impression of being a chooser will initially react as if something central is being threatened. It can feel as though the ground of responsibility, effort, and meaning is being taken away. CST does not require anyone to abandon the feeling of agency. It does not ask the system to stop experiencing life as authored from within. It asks for a different placement of that experience inside the architecture. Agency is not a mistake. It is not a glitch to be removed. It is the correct appearance of mid-level stabilized configurations when they include a self-structure and are illuminated by awareness. Seeing agency as non-generative does not make the system passive. It clarifies how influence actually works. Experience cannot reach backward to alter the forces that produced a moment, but it can leave residues that change what the system must carry next. This influence is not a new kind of freedom. It is simply the fact that the architecture carries forward its own residues as constraints.

Why Agency Still Matters

If agency is not generative, it is natural to wonder whether it matters at all. In CST terms, the answer is that it matters entirely — but in a different way than everyday language suggests. However, people talk about agency, the architecture enforces one unavoidable fact: the states that appear as experience alter sensitivities, shift grooves, and change the terrain for what comes next. These experiential states are not floating influences. They are structural conditions, appearing in display format, that the next round of stabilization must pass through. The system cannot behave tomorrow as if today's intentions, emotions, and meaning-tones never occurred. They have already become part of the architecture. We may be caused to arrive at the choices we experience. Those choices are still consequential — not because they originate action, but because they reshape the conditions through which future stabilizations must occur. Agency does not ignite behavior. It becomes one of the constraints the architecture must honor as it finds its next stable configuration. The feeling that "I am doing this" will not go away, nor does CST ask it to. It simply relocates that feeling from an imagined center of control to its actual place in the system: as the experiential appearance of an architecture already in motion, and as part of the terrain that shapes what can happen next — without initiating, generating, or directing it.

Chapter 20

The System Without a Driver

Why Life Does Not Require an Inner Commander

After the previous chapter, a certain kind of instability often appears. It usually does not come as a clear thought. It shows up as a tightening, a slight dizziness, a feeling that something important has been taken away. If there is no inner chooser, no hidden agent, no place where a self stands outside the system and directs it, then what remains? Who lives this life? Who cares? Who is responsible? For a moment, it can feel as if CST has removed the center and left only machinery behind. This reaction is not just philosophical. It comes from how the system is organized.

The system reading this has spent its entire history organizing coherence around the feeling of being the author. That feeling has been one of the main ways stability was kept over time. Removing it does not simply challenge a belief. It changes the shape of the ground the system is used to standing on. So any unease is understandable. But it also comes from a mistaken identification. CST does not claim that nothing is happening, that no life is being lived, or that meaning, attachment, or endurance are empty surfaces. It says something more precise and more radical: What you are is not a commander. You are a living system. And living systems do not need a ghost at the helm in order to live.

The Mistake About What Was Doing the Work

Any disturbance that arises in this account comes from a hidden assumption: that the thing which feels like the author was the thing that was actually carrying the life. But nothing in the architecture has ever worked that way. Regulation has always preceded awareness. Stabilization has always come first. Experience has always arrived after the work was already done. This is not a belief but a description of the system's mechanics.

Nothing new is happening here. Your body has always regulated itself without asking you. Your heart has always beaten without your permission. Your posture has always adjusted before you noticed. Your words have always begun forming before you heard yourself "decide" what to say. Your attachments, fears, habits, and longings have always been shaped by residues, thresholds, and cost landscapes that were never consulted. Your life has always been carried by structure. The feeling of authorship did not make this happen. It was how this happening appeared from the inside when certain mid-level Frames of Reference were active. CST is not taking away the engine. It is taking away the dashboard story about what the engine was. Nothing essential has been removed. The machinery remains exactly as it was. The difference is that an inaccurate story about the location of the author has been removed.

What a Living System Is

A living system is not a thing that issues commands. It is a system that remains coherent under change — measuring, absorbing disturbance, redistributing load, and finding configurations it can carry. Over time it accumulates residue and reshapes itself, maintaining continuity across enormous flux, whether or not anything is rendered and whether or not a self-structure appears in the display. A tree does this. An immune system does this. A colony does this. This system does this. The fact that part of this process sometimes appears as "me deciding" does not make that appearance the source of the process. It makes it one surface signature of the process.

Nothing Has Been Taken

It can initially feel as though CST is saying that control, choice and authorship have been removed. But what has actually been removed is a duplication. There was never a separate thing standing above the system directing it. There was only the system, sometimes encountering its own activity in display form. The body that tires, the patterns that heal or harden, the loves that deepen, the fears that narrow, the skills that grow, the wounds that leave traces, and the joys that reorganize priorities are all here — still doing what they have always done, and felt the same as they always have. Nothing vital has been taken away. Only a misplaced explanation.

Structure Without a Driver

It would be an error to assume that without a commander, the system must be inert or aimless, like a vehicle without a driver. But this system is not a vehicle. It is a flow architecture. It has gradients, channels, inertia, thresholds, and history. It moves because structure permits movement. It resists because structure resists. It changes because structure is reshaped by what passes through it. No internal pilot is required for trajectories to exist.

Why Mattering Does Not Require Choice

The fear that nothing matters follows naturally if mattering is assumed to depend on authorship. But in this architecture, things matter because they leave structural consequences — not only in this system, but in the systems and environments it is coupled with. They do not only reshape this structure; they reshape structures elsewhere, and those reshaped structures become the conditions through which everything that follows must pass. They leave residue. They alter thresholds. They open and close corridors. They reshape what the system can carry next. Pain matters because it reorganizes protection, and attachment matters because it reorganizes priorities. Loss matters because it reorganizes the future, and learning matters because it reshapes the terrain. Trauma matters because it narrows it and healing matters because it widens it. None of this requires a chooser. It requires a system that is altered by what it lives through.

Responsibility

At this point many readers worry about responsibility. If no one is in charge, how can anyone be responsible for anything? But responsibility, in CST, was never about metaphysical authorship. It is about where causation flows and what shapes what comes next. Responsibility is not about being an uncaused chooser in control. It is about engagement — being part of the causal fabric. You do not need to be outside the system to matter inside it. Responsibility in CST is not metaphysical authorship. It is structural consequence.

The Load-Bearing Narrative Inside

A narrative about responsibility is not "just a story." It is a persistent organizational pattern that shapes what the system expects, tolerates, demands, blames, and tries to carry. It tunes thresholds. It biases judgment. It changes what counts as success or failure, what counts as weakness or strength, and what counts as acceptable strain versus breakdown.

Living inside a narrative of metaphysical authorship is not neutral. The narrative itself generates load and reorganizes it. When a system is organized around the idea that it is, or should be, the uncaused source of its own states, every difficulty becomes a personal failure. Every instability becomes a moral problem. Every limitation becomes something that ought to have been overridden. The result is not more control. It is chronic surplus load: shame, self-blame, blame of others, punitive structures, impossible standards, and repeated attempts to force the architecture into configurations it cannot carry at low cost.

This narrative also produces *outcome binding*. Coherence becomes tied to specific required results — success must occur, failure must be avoided, effort must produce control. The system becomes organized not only around present constraints, but around the demand that certain outcomes must be realized regardless of carryability. When those outcomes cannot stabilize, the system must carry both the structural limit and the insistence that the limit should not exist. Internal work increases. Self-pressure rises. Correction attempts repeat. Load accumulates without widening what can be carried.

None of this is philosophical. It is mechanical. A metaphysically grounded narrative demands that systems take responsibility for what they cannot generate and bind coherence to outcomes they cannot guarantee. It requires them to treat structural limits as personal faults and structural delay as moral weakness. That narrative does not change how the system works. It changes how much strain the system must carry while working the way it always has.

Two Stories, Two Cost Profiles

A physically grounded narrative does something different. It does not remove consequence. It does not remove accountability. It does not remove the fact that actions reshape both the system itself and the systems it is coupled to. But it does remove the extra, unnecessary load of pretending that there is an uncaused author standing outside the machinery, controlling every decision.

The difference between these narratives is not a difference in "belief." It is a difference in cost. One organizes the world around blame, forcing, and impossible control. The other organizes it around structure, constraint, and actual causation. One systematically adds load to human and social systems. The other does not.

And because narratives are themselves part of what systems must carry, this difference propagates outward. It shapes institutions, relationships, justice systems, education systems, and how suffering is treated. A narrative built on metaphysical authorship reliably produces more friction, more punishment, more chronic strain, and more structural dead ends. A narrative built on physical causation produces less. Not because it is nicer. Because it fits the machinery.

The Engineering Verdict

From a CST perspective, this is decisive. Even if one refused to settle the metaphysical question of which story is "ultimately true," the engineering verdict would remain. A model that systematically increases load, friction, and failure is not behaving like a description of machinery that is always moving toward lower cost. It is behaving like an incorrect control scheme.

A world organized around a story that fits the machinery will always be easier to carry than a world organized around a story that does not. And this raises a simple, mechanical question: if the story of authorship were actually accurate — if it truly described how the system works — why would organizing life around it reliably produce more cost, more strain, and more load?

A correct model of a machine does not make the machine harder to run. It makes it easier. In every other domain we know, accurate descriptions reduce wasted energy, not increase it. A story that systematically amplifies friction, effort, and breakdown is not behaving like a true description of the machinery. It is behaving like a control scheme that is not connected to what actually does the work.

A model that matches structure reduces corrective effort.
A model that does not match structure amplifies strain.

When Civilizations Run on the Wrong Diagram

There is nothing new about this. Human history is full of cases where a system organized itself around a story about how reality works, only to discover much later that the story was wrong — and that enormous, unnecessary cost had been paid because of it. For centuries, European civilization was organized around a geocentric model of the universe. The Earth was believed to sit at the center, with the heavens rotating around it. This was not just an abstract belief. It shaped navigation, calendars, theology, philosophy, and the entire picture of humanity's place in existence. Whole institutions were built to protect and rationalize it. Complex mathematical contraptions — epicycles piled on epicycles — were invented to keep the model working even as observations strained against it.

The model did not fail because people were foolish. It failed because it did not match the machinery. And because it did not match the machinery, it kept getting more expensive to carry. More patches were required. More exceptions had to be explained. More effort was spent forcing observations to fit a story that was slightly wrong in a very deep way. The system did not stabilize because the story was "false." It stabilized because the story imposed growing structural cost. When the sun-centered (heliocentric) model finally replaced it, the immediate effect was not philosophical elegance. It was mechanical simplification. The sky cost less to predict. Navigation cost less. Calculation cost less. The same world, suddenly easier to carry.

When Medicine Ran on Imaginary Fluids

Or consider medicine organized around the theory of the four humors. Disease was thought to be caused by imbalances of blood, phlegm, black bile, and yellow bile. Entire medical systems were built around bleeding, purging, and balancing these imaginary fluids. Patients suffered and died not because anyone was cruel, but because the model was wrong in a way that made treatment systematically expensive and destructive. When germ theory replaced it, the change was not moral. It was mechanical. Suddenly, whole categories of suffering became preventable. Not because doctors became kinder, but because the model finally matched the machinery.

What All Wrong Models Have in Common

In every one of these cases, the old story did not fail because it was irrational. It failed because it was structurally expensive. It required constant patching, constant moralization, and continuous force to keep reality inside a shape it did not naturally fit. A wrong model of a machine has this property: it increases the cost of operation. A right model does not make the machine virtuous. It makes it easier to run.

The Authorship Story Has the Same Cost Signature

The story of metaphysical authorship shows the same pattern. It treats structural limits as personal failure, delay as weakness, and constraint as guilt. It builds systems around forcing what cannot be forced. The result is not greater control but greater strain. Responsibility becomes blame, difficulty becomes defect, and unavoidable limits become burdens the system must carry in addition to the limits themselves. The signature is unmistakable: added load without added capability.

The Secondary Effect

When the misplacement of agency is removed, another effect often appears: a quiet relief. Failure is no longer a moral defect. Being stuck is no longer laziness. Burnout is no longer weakness. Inability is no longer refusal. These are configurations under constraint. This does not trivialize them. It makes them mechanically legible. The central question shifts from why the system cannot force itself to change to what the system is currently carrying and what would make a different configuration cost less to sustain.

What a Self is in CST

A self is not a commander. It is not a witness floating above the machinery. It is not a little person inside the head. It is a living, self-modifying, history-carrying, load-bearing, coherence-maintaining system that sometimes runs in display mode. The feeling of being someone is one of the ways that system appears to itself. It is not in charge. It is not an error. It is a felt surface signature.

No Driver, No Ego

In many psychological traditions, the coordinating center of the person is described as the "ego." The term refers to a structure that manages impulses, weighs alternatives, and directs behavior. The idea assumes an internal organizer that stands above the machinery and guides it. In CST, no such structure is required. Once behavior is understood as the result of measurement, convergence, integration, and stabilization under constraint, there is no place where a coordinating self must sit. What earlier models attributed to the ego arises instead from the distributed organization of the system itself.

The Real Problem Going Forward

The real problem is therefore not how a chooser should choose. It is how a system like this actually changes. Not by command. Not by decision. Not by will. But by shifts in load, changes in cost landscapes, accumulation of residue, and the slow reconfiguration of what can and cannot be carried. That is what the next part of the book is about.

Part IV

How Systems Actually Change

Learning, stress, drift, adaptation, and why willpower doesn't work

Causal Systems Theory

Chapter 21

How Change Actually Happens

Not by Command

If there is no inner commander, no place where a self gives instructions to the machinery, then change cannot occur by decision. This is not a philosophical claim, but a mechanical one. A system built from measurement, stabilization, load redistribution, and residue cannot be forced into new configurations by declaration. It can only move into configurations it can carry. And yet change does happen. People heal, habits dissolve, identities shift, and entire lives reorganize. The question is not whether change is possible. The question is what kind of machine this must be for change to occur at all.

The Only Way a Finite System Changes

There is only one way a finite stabilizing system changes: when the conditions it must carry change, and its structure is reshaped through carrying them. It does not change because it is told to, because it understands, or because it intends to. It changes because it is repeatedly stabilized through configurations that shift thresholds, deepen some corridors, narrow or close others, and redistribute what is low-cost or high-cost to carry. This is what learning is. This is what conditioning is. Not insight, will, or decision — only load and residue.

Why You Cannot Force a System into a Low-Cost State

This is why forcing change is unreliable. When the system is in a trying mode, the act of trying to be calm increases arousal. Trying to sleep keeps the system awake. Trying to be confident tightens the architecture. Trying to stop thinking amplifies the loop. The reason is simple: a trying mode is itself a load-bearing configuration. It adds tension, monitoring, and constraint. The system must now stabilize around the act of trying itself. If that configuration is incompatible with the desired state, cost rises rather than falls. A system cannot be forced into a low-cost configuration by adding load.

What Actually Lowers Cost

Cost drops only when structure changes — when posture, routines, contexts, and couplings change; when corridors widen; when thresholds shift; and when old structural shapes are no longer needed. Sometimes this happens slowly, through repeated exposure and gradual residue accumulation. Sometimes it happens abruptly, through a reorganization that makes an old configuration uncarryable. From the inside, this often appears as "it just got easier," "something clicked," or "I'm not fighting it anymore." Mechanically, nothing mystical has occurred. The system has entered a region of the landscape where less compensation is required.

What Insight Actually Is

Insight is not the cause of change but a surface signature. It is the first illumination of a configuration that has already stabilized. When reorganization completes and a new pathway becomes viable, awareness registers it. This registration often feels sudden and clarifying. The system finds itself resolving with less internal strain, and that contrast is felt as understanding. Insight marks the completion of structural change; it does not generate it.

Because awareness registers only stabilized outcomes, change often appears all at once. The moment a new configuration holds, experience shifts. What had been effortful becomes easier to sustain. What had been confusing becomes coherent. It is like balancing a pencil on its tip. Small adjustments occur continuously before stability becomes self-sustaining. When balance finally holds, it appears sudden. Insight feels causal for the same reason. It coincides with the first moment awareness samples a structure that has already changed.

Insight Is Influential, Not Generative

Although insight does not produce reorganization, it participates in what follows. Once a new configuration stabilizes and is rendered, it becomes part of the terrain by leaving residue. Subsequent moments must now resolve within the altered landscape. Later stabilizations may follow different routes — not because anything directs them, but because cost geometry has shifted. Stabilized structures participate in future stabilization without originating it. Insight matters because it is real within experience. It does not matter because it commands change.

Insight is not the cause of change but a surface signature. It is the first illumination of a configuration that has already stabilized.

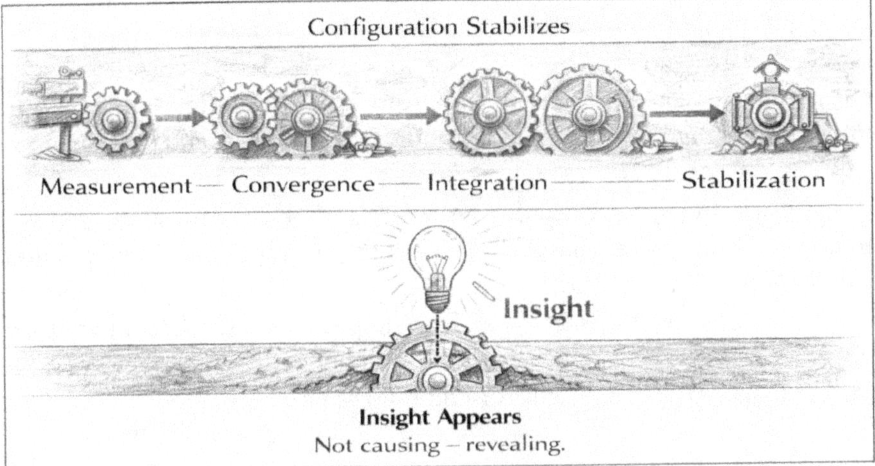

Insight is the surface signature of a configuration that has already stabilized.

Why Insight Is So Unreliable

Insight can accompany change. But it cannot guarantee that change will last. A system can understand something perfectly and remain unchanged for years. Another can change dramatically without being able to explain what shifted. The difference is not in what is known. It is in what the structure can sustain.

Consider two people who attend the same alcoholic recovery meetings every week for years. They hear the same stories. They repeat the same language. They can describe the same dynamics with equal clarity. And yet one eventually finds that alcohol no longer organizes their life, while the other continues to struggle. The difference is not in understanding. It is in what their structures can now carry.

Understanding is a rendered state. It participates in what comes next only by becoming part of what must be carried. It does not reorganize the machinery that produced it. A configuration can stabilize briefly without becoming the dominant long-range pathway. When conditions shift, the system may return to older patterns that are still more reliably sustained.

A person may understand how to swim while standing on land. The mechanics make sense. The sequence is clear. Yet when placed in deep water, the system may still enter panic. The insight was real. But the architecture had not yet been shaped to sustain that organization under load. Insight can recur without transformation. A configuration may be illuminated many times before it becomes structurally dominant.

Sometimes a rendered realization coincides with a reorganization that was already becoming unavoidable — because residue had accumulated, thresholds had shifted, and an alternative corridor had gradually become more viable than the old one. When that happens, the story becomes: "I saw it, and then I changed." Mechanically, the change was already in motion. Change does not follow insight. Insight follows change.

Where Novelty Comes From

Novelty arises when the system is forced to stabilize in regions of its landscape it could not previously sustain. Those regions become available only when existing pathways can no longer carry the load being placed on them. Novelty is not the creation of something from nothing. It is the emergence of a viable stabilization pathway within existing constraints — much as a muscle grows only when load forces it to reorganize so that more weight can be carried, or as a farmer opens new ground only when old fields can no longer yield under repeated use.

This is why novelty so often follows periods of strain. When familiar organizations can no longer stabilize what is demanded of them, the system is pushed into configurations or Frames of Reference it had not previously used. If one of those configurations holds, a new pathway becomes available.

From the inside, this is experienced as discovery or a new idea — the first-time awareness samples a configuration the architecture can now sustain.

The Only Two Paths of Real Change

All durable change comes from one of two sources. Either the system is gradually reshaped by the residue left by repeated, survivable load, or it reorganizes because its existing configuration becomes uncarryable. There is no third path. Practice, training, and exposure work by the first route. They apply repeatable load that slowly reshapes thresholds, deepens some corridors, and makes old fallback routes less necessary. Trauma operates by the second route. It overwhelms existing organization and forces reorganization because the old configuration can no longer be carried. Therapy, relationships, and environments work by changing the load landscape the system lives within — either by making different configurations repeatedly carryable or by making former configurations impossible to sustain. None of this requires command.

Why This Is Both Hard and Hopeful

It is hard because there is no master lever. There is no place to stand and pull the system into a new shape. It is hopeful because systems like this are always changing anyway. Every day leaves residue. Every season shifts thresholds. Every sustained condition reshapes what is normal. You are not stuck because you have not decided hard enough. You are in a configuration that is currently what the system can carry. Change comes when that ceases to be true — when something else becomes lower cost, not by command. A person who cannot sleep for years may one day find that sleep returns, not because they forced it, but because enough has changed — load, routines, context, accumulated residue — that being awake is no longer the lowest-cost configuration to sustain. The landscape shifted.

The Snapback Corridor

For Michael, mornings no longer began with the familiar weight in his chest. The day no longer felt like something to endure. There was space — between thought and action, between feeling and response. Situations that once produced immediate tightening could now be met without stabilizing. Urges appeared without pulling the system into them. Alcohol, which had once organized the entire rhythm of his evenings, had receded into the background — not through effort or resolve, but because the pressure it had been relieving was no longer present. Sleep came more easily. Conversations lasted longer. From the inside, it felt as though something fundamental had changed.

Then the conditions shifted. The company downsized. His role disappeared. A few weeks later, his father's health declined. Appointments filled the calendar. Finances tightened. Nights shortened. The margin that had allowed hesitation vanished. Without warning, the old narrowing returned. The familiar corridor reasserted itself — not gradually, not as temptation, but as inevitability. Alcohol was there again, not as a failure of discipline, but as the fastest available route to carry the load. What had felt settled did not fade. It vanished in a single moment. The system did not drift backward. It snapped into place. What happened?

Why Change Is Conditional, Not Permanent

Change is often misunderstood as something that, once achieved, should remain. When a system widens and new routes become viable, there is a quiet expectation that something has been secured — that a new baseline has been established. When the system later narrows again, this is read as loss, failure, or regression. The question appears automatically: why didn't it last? But nothing in the architecture supports permanence. Stability is not a possession. It is a condition. It persists only as long as the cost landscape that produced it remains in place. When that landscape changes, organization changes with it. This is not a breakdown of change. It is change continuing under new load.

Widened organization is initially expensive. New routes have not yet accumulated much residue. They require more internal work to traverse and provide less immediate reliability than corridors repeatedly used under pressure. As long as constraint remains low, this added cost is tolerable. Such routes are taken not because they are cheaper in absolute terms, but because they have become less costly than the alternatives available at that moment.

Stabilization can resolve through broader paths without demanding immediate precision. Variability remains survivable. When load increases, those economics shift. Urgency compresses time. Threat raises the cost of error. Uncertainty shortens tolerance for instability. The cost of remaining in the new route now exceeds that of returning to an already established lower-cost route. Under these conditions, the system does not forget what it has widened into. It reorganizes again. Stabilization resolves where it can do so reliably and at low cost — often back into corridors that succeeded under similar pressure. This is not reversal. It is reorganization under different constraints.

A runner who has gradually widened their stride after injury may move fluidly for months. Training is steady. Sleep is sufficient. Load is moderate. Stabilization can resolve through the broader gait without strain. Then conditions shift. Mileage increases. Recovery shortens. A minor ache appears in the old joint. Nothing is damaged. But cost rises. The wider stride begins to require more compensation. Stabilization becomes less reliable. On the next run, stabilization settles back into the narrower, protective pattern. Not because anything was forgotten. Not because maintenance failed. The conditions that made widening viable are no longer present. The older corridor now resolves stabilization with lower cost, and the architecture routes there automatically.

Why Widening Is Not a Baseline

The mistake is to treat widened organization as a new baseline rather than a context-dependent outcome. Widening is not something the system preserves through effort. There is no internal mechanism that protects it against rising cost. When conditions no longer support it, the system does not fail to maintain change — it simply resolves differently. Stability is not sustained by will. It is sustained by conditions.

Reversion is therefore predictable. It is not evidence that widening was incomplete or false. It is evidence that the economics have shifted. Under high constraint, fewer routes are affordable. Stabilization must resolve quickly and reliably. Previously widened routes may be bypassed not because they disappeared, but because they are temporarily too costly to use. The system narrows because narrowing works.

Calling this relapse misattributes cause. It frames lawful reorganization as personal failure. The system has not lost progress. It has reorganized again under new demands. What changes from widening to narrowing is not capability, but availability. Under low constraint, more routes are viable. Under high constraint, fewer are. The system uses what is available at the cost it can bear.

When re-narrowing is read as failure, additional load is added. Stabilization tightens further — not because conditions require it, but because narrative demands correction. When change is understood as conditional, that extra cost disappears. The system does not defend its earlier widening or apologize for its current narrowing. It simply resolves where it can.

The Real Unit of Intervention

The real unit of intervention is not the thought. It is not the feeling. It is not the intention. Those are rendered states — surface displays of what the system has already stabilized. The real unit of intervention is the cost landscape. A finite stabilizing system reorganizes when the pattern of what it must carry changes. When loads, rhythms, supports, and repetitions change, the geometry of cost changes with them. If what is carried changes for long enough, the architecture will change — not because it agreed, not because it understood, not because it decided, but because it was forced to. A bridge reorganizes because the forces passing through it change. A river carves a new channel because flow makes the old one unsustainable. You do not change systems by talking to their dashboards. A system changes when forces change. The unit of change is not meaning, but carryability.

What the Next Chapters Will Do

From here forward, the book stops dismantling and starts mapping. We will examine how narrowing and widening work, how identity corridors form and break, how trauma overfits and how systems recover, how therapy can change landscapes instead of issuing instructions, how social structures sculpt individual architectures, how responsibility works without authorship, how ethics works without free will, and how change works without command — not as advice, but as mechanics.

Chapter 22

Stress, Threat, and Forced Narrowing

How Stress Reorganizes a Moment

The moment the motorcycle ran the red light, the cyclist had no time to react. The impact came from the side, lifting him off the bike and throwing him into the air. His body rotated once, then again. He landed headfirst, cracking his helmet. Later, he would say the event felt stretched, that he could remember everything, as if it had unfolded in slow motion. But nothing in the world had slowed down. What changed was the system's way of carrying the moment.

At the instant of impact, the broader, slower, more integrative Frames of Reference were no longer able to hold coherence. There was no narrative, no identity, no reflective vantage. What remained was a stripped-down, high-stabilization stream: the angle of the pavement, the blur of the sky, the rotation of his own body, the sudden compression in his neck and shoulders. The moment was being carried only by the fastest, most local stabilizing modes — the Frames of Reference the architecture still had available. Awareness did not cause this. It merely displayed what was already happening. The Phenomena Transducer System (PTS) sampled a mode of stabilization that integrates very little and updates very quickly. The result was an unusually dense sequence of discrete experiential slices. That density is what later gets described as "time slowing down."

In reality, the opposite had happened. The system could no longer sustain broad, slow integration and was operating only in narrow, rapid stabilization modes. Each rapid stabilization left structural traces. Later, the cyclist could replay the event as a chain of crisp stills — not because the moment had lasted longer, but because it had been carried at a much finer temporal grain. The vividness felt extraordinary. The mechanism was not. It was simply forced narrowing: under extreme load, only the fastest, most local Frames of Reference remained viable, and the PTS rendered that fact.

When the Field Narrows Instead

Two years later, a different kind of moment revealed the same principle in the opposite direction. He was walking into his office when he unexpectedly saw a former supervisor who had once evaluated him harshly. The instant the supervisor said his name, the system narrowed. His chest tightened. His hands cooled. The lights overhead seemed suddenly too bright. The field contracted. Later, he could recall almost nothing — only a vague sense of pressure and an urgent need for the interaction to end. There had been no decision and no suppression. The architecture simply could not carry the moment using the Frames of Reference that normally stabilize context and continuity. The strain of holding those broader stabilization modes rose too quickly. Only faster, narrower Frames of Reference remained viable. The PTS displayed fragments, then very little at all. The rest of the moment never became available.

The Same Mechanism, Different Signatures

From the outside, one episode looks like heightened perception and the other like impaired recall. In CST terms, both express the same structural principle. When load rises faster than the currently sustaining stabilization modes can carry, the system does not choose among options. The only stabilizing modes that remain available are those that can resolve the moment fast enough — typically the modes that have succeeded under similar conditions in the past, because no lower-cost alternative is available. Sometimes that produces hyper-clarity: the signature of a moment being carried by very fast, very local Frames of Reference. Sometimes it produces narrowing and gaps: the signature of those same Frames of Reference resolving the moment too quickly and too locally for broad continuity to be maintained. The difference is not choice. It arises because different moments impose different load profiles on a structure already shaped by its history, requiring different gears. In one case, the cyclist's load concerned immediate physical survival; in the other, encountering a harsh former supervisor-imposed load on identity. Different conditions produced different organizations. What is remembered later is not a record of what happened. It is a record of which Frames of Reference were able to carry coherence when the moment was being resolved under stress.

Why Stress Shrinks the Set of Available Frames

When the system is operating within its ordinary stability range, broad Frames of Reference can carry the moment across wide spans of time and context. Identity holds shape. Subjectivity remains stable. Participation integrates movement and affect. The field stays wide and usable. Coordination proceeds without strain. Under these conditions, the system appears to move through the world with fluidity and apparent authorship — not because it is directing itself, but because instability remains low and long-range coherence can be maintained. Broad integration stabilization modes require low load and stable support to remain viable. The wider the span of time and context a stabilization mode tries to hold across multiple Frames of Reference, the more sensitive it becomes to instability. When that support is disrupted, those stabilization modes do not fail because something else is preferred. They fail because they can no longer be carried.

In the same way, a person can plan a career, reflect on a life, or negotiate long-range priorities only while the architecture is stable enough to sustain that breadth. When load spikes — through threat, shock, exhaustion, or sudden uncertainty — those wide integrations become unavailable. The system does not decide to stop operating at that scale. It simply can no longer inhabit it. Stabilization continues only in narrower, faster, more local stabilization modes that can still remain coherent under strain.

Stress is therefore not a special mode. In CST terms, stress is simply the condition in which the instability imposed by the moment exceeds what the currently sustaining stabilization mode can carry. A Frame of Reference does not cease to operate because it is wrong. It ceases to be viable because the strain of holding it rises faster than the system can compensate. As load increases, the only stabilization modes that remain available are those that stabilize more quickly, even though they integrate only a narrow slice of the moment. They resolve faster because they integrate less. They operate over shorter temporal windows, smaller spatial fields, and narrower bands of differentiation. Under strain, speed beats breadth. This is not regression. It is mechanical constraint.

How Instability Reorganizes the Landscape of Frames

A stable identity stabilization mode, for example, is only sustainable when conditions allow broad integration across time. Identity binds the present to long arcs of conditioned structure. But when demands tighten or uncertainty accelerates, that wide temporal scope becomes a liability. When that stabilization mode can no longer carry the moment, the architecture must be carried by a stabilization mode that can.

Consider someone told at work that layoffs will be announced tomorrow. Under ordinary conditions, identity-level organization would integrate this within a longer Frame of Reference: who they are, what their role is, what comes next. But under a sudden spike of uncertainty, that Frame cannot be sustained. The system no longer carries next year or next month. It contracts to a shorter horizon: this week, this conversation, this immediate threat. The field narrows to a Frame able to carry short-term load. Nothing about this shift is chosen. The broader stabilization mode has simply become too strained to hold under its level of uncertainty. Threat accelerates this process by increasing the rate at which instability arrives. Time pressure, social evaluation, ambiguity, contradiction, or sudden change all raise the strain of maintaining broad integration. The architecture does not assess threat. It is subjected to it, and only stabilization modes able to resolve the moment without delay remain usable.

Even simpler systems show the same pattern. A home climate system uses broad integration under mild conditions. When demand spikes beyond capacity, it shifts into an emergency mode that stabilizes faster but with less nuance. Nothing evaluates the cold. The system narrows to what can reduce instability immediately. Biological systems do the same. An octopus operates with distributed coordination when conditions are calm, then resolves into a narrow, high-speed escape mode the moment threat appears. The broader organization is not consulted. The fastest stabilizer that can still hold coherence takes over. Human systems follow the same principle. Identity, reflection, and long-range planning are broad, integration-heavy forms of stabilization. When load rises sharply, the system is carried by faster, lower-integration stabilization Frames or modes. The PTS renders this shift as urgency, narrowing, or fragmentation.

Chronic Pressure and Compression of Frame Availability

When instability persists for long periods, the system begins to show patterns that appear new from the outside. The problem is that new stabilization modes require low load, spare capacity, and repeated success across many stabilizations, whereas chronic stress is sustained strain that removes those conditions. Under chronic stress, the architecture does not add anything. It does not build new Frames of Reference. What occurs is reshaping. Existing stabilization modes are narrowed and overfitted through repeated high-strain stabilization. Chronic pressure carves grooves. Fallback routes become defaults. Shortcuts that once appeared only under duress become the ordinary solution even when conditions improve. This does not require new Frames of Reference. It is the existing landscape being reshaped by stabilization under sustained load.

Because broad stabilization modes require wide integration and temporal continuity, they fail repeatedly under chronic instability, leaving residue. Over time, identity-level organization becomes narrower — not because it reduces instability well, but because it reduces it with less immediate strain. Withdrawal, vigilance, or self-blame can become default stabilization routes until they are indistinguishable from personality. This reshaping is not chosen. It is structural. Once broad stabilization modes fail often enough, the system stops being able to rely on them and settles into what remains viable. Eventually, this narrowing can become so entrenched that even when conditions improve, the system does not automatically regain access to the broader stabilization mode that once carried it. They are still part of the architecture, but they are no longer calibrated. The grooves carved under pressure dominate stabilization simply because they remain the most reliable routes the system can sustain.

Burnout as Structural Exhaustion

Burnout is what happens when even these fallback stabilization modes begin to require more strain than they reduce. Reflexive adjustments still occur, but they no longer restore coherence. Participation-level organization becomes unstable. Identity cannot hold shape. Reflection sheds almost immediately. The architecture fails to find any stabilization mode that can carry the moment without compounding strain. A teacher who once improvised freely now finds herself staring blankly at her laptop, unable to route the moment through any stabilization mode that reduces instability. Burnout is not the loss of motivation. It is the point at which the architecture can no longer sustain broad organization and is forced to operate at basic maintenance. What looks like withdrawal is the system minimizing additional strain when every attempt at broader organization increases it.

Helplessness as Architectural Narrowing

In some conditions, chronic compression does not produce burnout. It produces something quieter and more stable but just as restrictive: helplessness. Helplessness is not a belief or an emotional conclusion. It is the consequence of a system discovering, through repeated experience, that only one narrow stabilization mode can still carry the moment. When broader stabilization modes fail and narrower ones only work in a very limited range, the system stops attempting anything else. From the outside this looks like giving up. Internally, it is the system settling into the only configuration that still reduces instability. A man who once solved problems creatively now only repeats the one safe route that lowers strain, even when other routes are technically available. Helplessness differs from burnout. In burnout, nothing works. In helplessness, one narrow route still works — but only one. This is why helplessness often precedes deeper breakdown. The architecture survives by limiting itself to what it can still do. When everything broader is too demanding and everything narrower is too volatile, the system lives inside the narrowest stabilization mode indefinitely.

Why Reason and Insight Vanish Under Load

A system cannot stabilize at broader frames while it is being forced to stabilize at narrower ones. Reasoning, reflection, narrative integration, and identity-level coherence all require surplus capacity. They only operate when the architecture is already carrying the moment at low enough cost that additional reorganization is possible. When load is high, the system does not have that margin. This is why panic does not respond to logic, and being overwhelmed does not respond to explanation. This is why threat does not respond to reassurance. The system is not resisting. It is occupied. It is maintaining coherence at the only scale it can currently sustain. Under heavy load, stabilization is forced into faster, narrower, more urgent stabilization modes. The architecture must resolve the moment in the least expensive way available. There is no capacity left for broader integration, narrative binding, or reflective reorganization. Until the load drops, stabilization cannot occur at wider scales. Nothing is being blocked. Nothing is being refused. Nothing is being overridden. The system is simply doing the only thing it can do to remain intact.

Why People "Become Someone Else" Under Stress

Everyone knows someone like this. In one set of conditions — at work, they are patient, reasonable, even generous. Colleagues describe them as calm and steady. They listen. They take criticism without flaring. The system is operating in an environment it has learned to carry at relatively low cost. Then you see the same person in a different set of conditions — at home, where the load profile is different. The same kinds of inputs now cost more to stabilize. The voice is sharper. Tolerance disappears. Small obstacles trigger outsized reactions. They snap at their partner. They bark at the kids. They may even kick the dog. Or the pattern runs in reverse: brittle and rigid in public, where the load is social and performative, but warm and relaxed in private, where the system has lower cost, more reliable ways to stabilize.

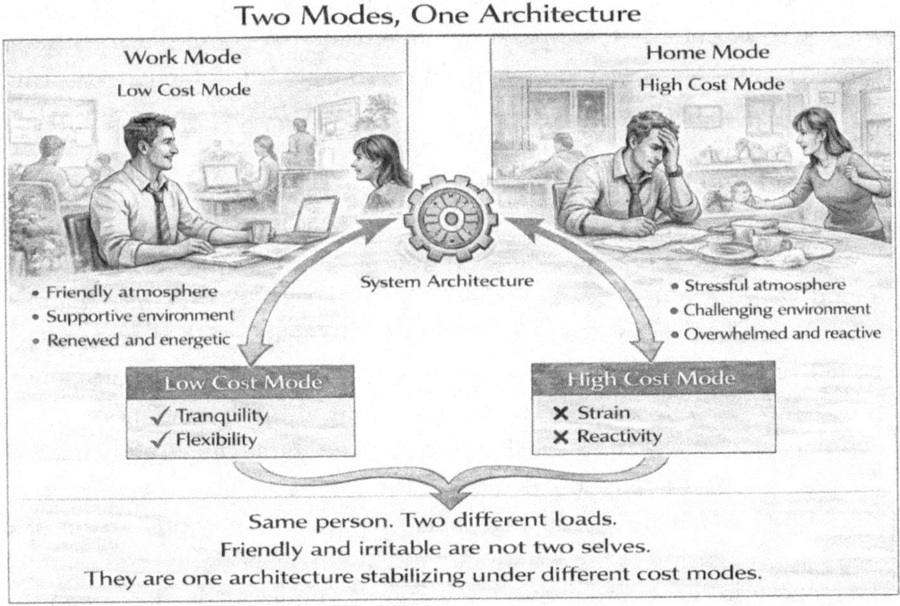

Nothing about this requires two personalities. It is the same architecture operating under different conditions, each of which carries a different learned cost structure, mode, or Frame of Reference, and therefore recruits different stabilization modes. They do not become someone else. They become the same system stabilizing under a different cost mode. The calm, reflective person and the panicked, rigid person are not two selves. They are one architecture operating under different load conditions and therefore relying on different stabilization modes.

When load is low, the system can afford broad, high-cost organization. Activity resolves through wider Frames of Reference that support language, reflection, and long-range coherence. Experience feels flexible, spacious, and continuous. When load rises, this changes mechanically. Stabilization becomes urgent. Speed matters more than breadth. The system is forced to resolve through faster, lower-cost, narrower stabilization modes that do not support reflection, narrative, or identity-level coherence. Nothing has been lost. The architecture uses what is affordable under the conditions. The system is not refusing. It is busy remaining coherent. As load drops, broader stabilization modes become available again. Language, reflection, and continuity return. From the inside this feels like "coming back," but nothing left and nothing returned. Only the economics of stabilization changed. Stress does not reveal a different person. Calm does not reveal a truer one. Both are the same system operating under different constraints or Frames of Reference. The apparent change in personality is just a change in what the system can currently carry.

What Stress Reveals About the Architecture

Stress does not reveal weakness. It reveals the structure. Under stable conditions, the system appears unified and self-directed because identity-level organization can integrate wide spans of structure with little strain. Under pressure, the design becomes clearer. It becomes clear that identity is not the core of the system. It is one mode of stabilization among many, and not the one that prevails when speed and minimal integration become decisive. Threat does not break the self. It reveals that the self was never the mechanism doing the stabilizing. This prepares the ground for the next chapter. If stress forces the system into faster, narrower stabilization modes, then long-term structural change cannot occur under load. The system can only be reshaped when the landscape allows broad, low-strain integration across time.

Chapter 23

Reactive Learning

How Systems Change Themselves Over Time

In physics, nothing moves because it wants to. A body moves because a force has acted on it. A trajectory bends because constraints and forces make it bend. A structure deforms because the loads passing through it exceed what its current shape can carry. A stone does not learn the shape of a riverbed. It is shaped by the forces that pass through it. A bridge does not decide to redistribute stress. It does so because stress exceeds what some part of the structure can hold. Every physical system changes in only one way: by being forced into configurations that reshape what it can carry next. Biological systems are not different in this respect. They are not exempt from mechanics. They do not possess a special channel for self-directed change. They are simply more complex stabilizing structures, capable of surviving in a wider range of conditions and therefore of being reshaped in more intricate ways. Learning, in CST, is not an exception to physics. It is an instance of it.

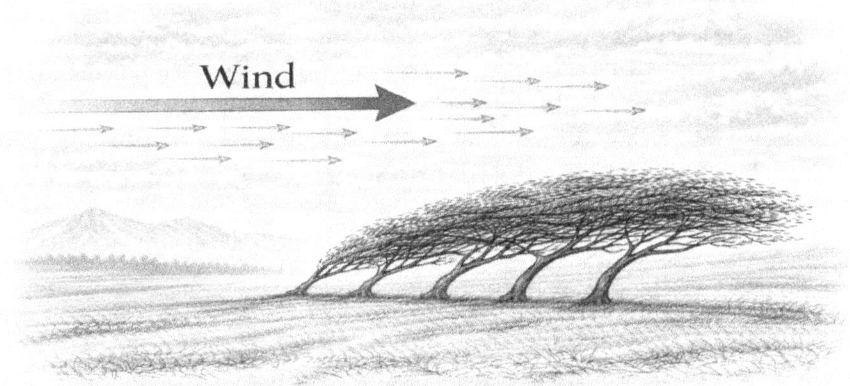

Trees do not learn to bend in the wind.
They are shaped by the force passing through them.
Your physical system is no different.

The human system does not change because it seeks improvement, insight, or meaning. It changes because it is repeatedly forced to stabilize under conditions that its current organization cannot carry without reorganization. Each stabilization leaves residue. That residue reshapes the architecture. And that reshaped architecture constrains what can stabilize next and how stabilization unfolds forward. Nothing is added, selected, or consulted. The system is pushed, deforms, and continues in the new shape until it is pushed again. This is what "reactive" means in CST. The system does not reach ahead of itself. It does not optimize toward a future. It does not decide what to become. It reacts to the forces and constraints it is in, and in reacting, it slowly becomes something else. A river does not plan its path. It flows until resistance redirects it. Over time, the redirection becomes the channel. A nervous system does not plan its development. It stabilizes under load until the stabilizations carve a new path through it. Learning is that carving.

Why Learning Needs an Architecture

Learning is often described as acquiring information, gaining insight, or storing knowledge. From a systems perspective, this is a category mistake. New content may pass through the system, but learning itself consists in changes to the architecture that carries that content. A system does not accumulate information the way a file cabinet accumulates documents. Its form of accumulation is the reshaping of the structure through which future moments are resolved. Consider a person learning to ride a bicycle. In the familiar story, the person "learns" by collecting instructions: lean here, shift weight there, pedal smoothly. It sounds as if the system is receiving directions and storing them somewhere for later use. But that is not what is happening. On the first attempts, the system is flooded with parallel input: visual flow, pressure on the handlebars, shifts in balance, wheel wobble, ground texture, momentum. The initial stabilizations are unstable and costly. The system does not store these events. It is forced to reorganize in response to them. Each stabilization leaves residue — not a record of what happened, but a tiny structural change, a bias in how the architecture resolves balance.

With repetition, these residues accumulate. Subtle shifts in posture, timing, muscle recruitment, and weight distribution begin to stabilize with less cost and more reliably. The system is not adding facts. It is being mechanically reshaped. The change is architectural, not informational. Eventually, stabilization becomes so reliable and low-strain that the activity feels fluid. The person reports having "learned to ride," but nothing is being consulted and nothing is being retrieved. No instruction is accessed. The architecture responsible for balance has simply been reshaped by repeated stabilization. This is why, years later, the person does not need to remember how to ride a bicycle. There is nothing to recall. The structure itself was changed. It is just there. Riding arises from the system's organization, not from access to stored content.

Now contrast this with something like ninth-grade algebra. A student may spend a year solving equations, manipulating symbols, and following formal procedures. With practice, these operations become easier because more residue is laid down. The system then stabilizes through certain symbolic pathways with less strain due to this accumulated residue. Performance improves. But for most people, if those pathways are not used for years, much of this ability fades. A person can spend years studying, outlining, and writing about a topic, only to find ten years later that little of it can still be carried with ease. Why? Because this kind of learning does not primarily reshape the lower-level coordination and stabilization machinery of the system. It mainly reorganizes higher-level routing: language-like procedures, symbol-handling sequences, rule-following patterns. These routes are less costly to abandon and more costly to maintain without use. They are not as deeply welded into posture, perception, and motor coordination as riding a bicycle is. It is like carving a groove in desert sand rather than hard clay — the sand fades quickly, while the clay holds its form.

Riding a bicycle reshapes the body's balance architecture. Algebra primarily reshapes how the system moves through certain abstract stabilization sequences. When algebraic sequences are no longer used, the cost landscape rises again because those routes have faded and work is required to restore them, making the former pathways more costly. As they fade over time, the system stops resolving through them. Nothing has been erased. The architecture has simply been reshaped by what it has and has not had to carry. If algebra has not been carried for a long time, it becomes costly to carry again. Both are learning. But they carve the system at different depths. Learning, in general, occurs not because information is added, but because repeated stabilization leaves structural residue that reshapes how future moments can be carried. Every moment lands inside an architecture that prior moments have already shaped. If that architecture is narrow, new input resolves along familiar routes. If it is flexible, new routes become available. In this sense, learning is not a mental act. It is a physical consequence of repeated stabilization.

Residue and Reactive Shaping

Every moment follows the same sequence: measurement, convergence, integration, and stabilization. Each stabilization leaves residue — not memory in any narrative or symbolic sense, but structural aftereffects in the architecture itself, altering how the next moment resolves: a small shift in how tension distributes, a change in which pathways remain low-cost or high-cost to carry. Whenever a moment stabilizes in a particular direction, the architecture becomes more likely to stabilize in that direction again. This is not because the system remembers anything or anticipates what is coming. It is because the structure itself has been reshaped by what it has just carried. Like a muscle that thickens in the direction of repeated load, the system takes on a shape that makes the same kind of stabilization cost less the next time. One route has become easier to sustain. Competing routes have become more demanding. Learning is nothing more than the cumulative effect of these structural biases. The more often stabilization occurs along a given pathway, the more that pathway becomes the default. What people call memory, habit, skill, or conditioning are not different mechanisms. They are different names for the same process: residue reshaping the architecture through which future moments must pass.

Stability-Dependent Learning

Learning does not occur under all conditions. It requires low load, spare capacity, and enough room for the architecture to reorganize rather than merely protect itself. When the system is under strain, it does not traverse across new pathways or integrate residue into broader structure. It resolves toward whatever stabilizes fastest.

Structural destabilization appears in two forms: local and global. Local destabilization occurs when a moment can be measured but cannot be stably carried by the currently dominant Frame, forcing stabilization to route through a narrower one. The mismatch produces tension within the stabilization itself — like trying to solve complex math in your head while cycling at full speed, where immediate balance takes priority and broader coordination becomes strained and difficult to sustain.

Global destabilization occurs when the entire system is already carrying heavy load — fatigue, threat, sustained stress, or intense strain — so that all incoming moments are forced toward rapid, low-integration stabilization regardless of their specific content. Like a cyclist descending a mountain at high speed, where every moment must be resolved through immediate balance, broader integration becomes unavailable, and complex symbolic processing such as mental calculation is no longer possible.

In both cases, the architecture defaults away from expansion and toward fallback. It relies on the routes that reduce instability most quickly. This is why overwhelmed systems revert to their most rigid patterns: those patterns are the fastest stabilizers under pressure. By contrast, when the system is calm, coherent, and carrying little load, stabilization costs are low enough to allow residue to integrate into broader structure. Novelty is no longer a threat. It is simply another moment the architecture can afford to reorganize around. The capacity to learn is not a product of intention. It is a product of stability.

Why Repetition Produces Change

Repetition is not practice in any volitional sense. It is not discipline. It is not effort. Repetition is simply the mechanical process through which residue accumulates and architecture reshapes itself. Each stabilization leaves a small structural bias: an adjustment in timing, a shift in tension, a micro-change in how load is distributed. One such change is negligible. Dozens begin to matter. Hundreds contour the landscape. Thousands carve a stable channel. Over time, this channel becomes a default route that future moments follow with little resistance. Nothing is being retrieved. Nothing is being searched. The architecture has been reshaped so thoroughly by repeated stabilization that resolution begins to flow immediately along a low-strain path. What looks like fluency or expertise is simply the visible consequence of this accumulated reshaping.

Learning Without Awareness

Most learning never appears in awareness. Emotional tuning adjusts silently. Motor coordination sharpens quietly. Social patterns crystallize gradually. The architecture changes first; awareness only encounters the result later. Awareness does not witness learning in progress. It only ever samples moments that have already stabilized and been reshaped. Learning to drive provides an everyday illustration. At first, driving feels effortful. Mirrors, speed, footwork, traffic — all come with friction. Awareness seems involved in every action. But over weeks and months, something changes. Without noticing exactly when, the person begins to drive fluidly. Lane changes become smooth. Steering requires little attention. They may arrive somewhere with almost no recollection of the details. Awareness interprets this as "now I know how to drive," but the architecture had been reorganizing all along. Hundreds of states left residue — tiny shifts in timing, coordination, and visual sampling. Gradually, these biases accumulate until a new stabilization pattern becomes less expensive and reliable. The moment of recognition is not when learning occurred. It is the moment awareness finally samples what the architecture has already become.

All Systems Are Reactive

No physical system ever acts on or considers the future. What appears as acting for the future is the system stabilizing in the present under patterns formed by past experience. It is not possible to act on something that has not yet occurred. A billiard ball does not anticipate the cue strike; it moves according to its structure and the forces acting on it. A planet does not consult its next orbit; it follows gravity from where it already is. Neural tissue does not reach ahead of itself; it propagates whatever activity its current configuration permits. At every scale, behavior is reactive because there is no mechanism by which a system can be organized around something that has not yet occurred. CST applies this same principle to human architecture. What appears as foresight, planning, or intention is simply continuation through a structure shaped by prior stabilizations. The system never steps ahead of itself. It resolves only what the present moment imposes.

A train offers a simple picture. When the engine shuts off, the train does not decide to keep moving and it does not project the next mile of track. It continues forward because its structure and momentum leave it no other option. It coasts until friction, slope, or an obstacle redirects it. The movement is not anticipation or motivation. It is the extended consequence of forces already in motion. Human systems behave the same way. What looks like prediction is smooth continuation through a well-shaped structure. What looks like reinforcement is this same principle stretched over time: residue reshaping the architecture so certain routes remain easier to sustain until conditions force a different one. Chapter 24 takes familiar terms — adaptation, reinforcement, prediction, memory — and shows how each is a felt surface signature of this single reactive mechanism.

Closing: Learning as Structural Transformation

Learning is not the acquisition of information, not the storage of content, and not the accumulation of insight. It is the slow, mechanical reshaping of architecture by what the system has been forced to carry. Every moment leaves residue. Every residue slightly alters the cost landscape. Every alteration biases how the next moment can stabilize. Over time, these microscopic shifts accumulate into macroscopic tendencies: skills, habits, reflexes, emotional styles, social expectations, and eventually identity-level structure. Nothing in this process requires prediction. Nothing requires evaluation. Nothing requires an internal judge, planner, or learner. The system changes because it cannot avoid being changed by what it survives. What is commonly called "practice" is repeated stabilization under similar conditions. What is called "experience" is accumulated residue. What is called "learning" is the long-run geometric consequence of residues interacting with the constraints of the architecture. There is no separate learning module. There is no reinforcement engine. There is no predictive machinery steering the process. There is only stabilization under load, and the way that stabilization irreversibly reshapes what the system can carry next.

This is why learning is always conservative. The system does not explore freely. It drifts toward whatever reduces strain. It does not seek truth, optimality, or improvement. It settles into whatever configurations remain at the lowest cost to sustain, regardless of truth. When conditions are gentle, this produces widening, flexibility, and new corridors. When conditions are harsh, it produces narrowing, rigidity, and overfitting. The difference is not motivation. It is load. It is also why awareness always arrives late. The display system never shows learning in motion. It shows only the first moment a new configuration has already become stable enough to carry. What feels like "I figured it out" is simply the first time the architecture can now resolve at a lower cost where it could not before.

From a CST perspective, this is the only kind of learning that exists. Systems do not learn by knowing. They learn by being shaped. They do not change by understanding. They change by being forced through states that leave different residue behind. They do not improve by aiming at the future. They drift through the present until the geometry of what they can carry becomes different. Once learning is understood as residue-driven reshaping, the familiar learning vocabulary can be re-read as surface labeling of the same mechanism. This prepares the ground for the next chapters. If learning is structural reshaping by residue, then emotion, identity, and personality are not the causes of behavior at all. They are long-range displays of how the architecture has already been shaped by its history of stabilization under load.

Chapter 24

Learning Has Many Names

Systems Become Easier to Carry Where They Have Carried Before

In the previous chapter, we described the simplest and most general way a system can change: *reactive learning*. A system is pushed by conditions into a stabilization. That stabilization leaves residue. The residue reshapes the architecture. The reshaped architecture makes some future stabilizations cost less and others more costly. Nothing is selected, evaluated, or stored. The system is simply being deformed by what it has to carry, moment by moment. This is the only learning mechanism available to a finite stabilizing system. It cannot reach into the future. It cannot consult the past. It cannot choose what to keep. It can only stabilize, and be reshaped by the stabilizations it survives under current conditions.

From the outside, this process often looks purposeful. It appears as if the system is improving, adapting, remembering, or preparing. But mechanically, nothing like that is occurring. The system is only continuing, carried forward through a structure reshaped by its own history of stabilization. Human languages did not grow up describing this machinery. They grew up describing its visible consequences. When a system becomes easier to carry in a new environment, those consequences are called adaptation. When a behavior becomes more likely to recur, it is called reinforcement. When a system appears ready for what comes next, it is called prediction. When earlier patterns reappear, it is called memory. These words do not name different mechanisms. They name different angles of view on the same mechanical process. In CST, there is no module for adaptation, no mechanism for reinforcement, no engine for prediction, and no storage vault for memory. There is only stabilization, and the gradual reshaping of the architecture by the residues of its own activity.

This chapter is not about introducing new machinery. It is about re-describing familiar learning concepts in mechanical terms. In what follows, we will examine several familiar names for learning and show that they are all surface descriptions of the same mechanical process. Adaptation will turn out to be nothing more than stabilization under changed load. Reinforcement will turn out to be nothing more than the persistence of routes that impose less overall strain on the system. Prediction will turn out to be nothing more than smooth continuation through corridors already shaped by prior stabilization. Memory will turn out to be nothing more than the system re-entering configurations that have become easier to sustain through repeated use.

None of this requires anything to be represented, no inner observer, and no internal accountant. There is only a system whose architecture is reshaped, moment by moment, by what it has had to carry. Because there is only one such mechanism, the many familiar learning terms are simply different surface descriptions of the same process. Chapter 23 described how learning occurs. This chapter explains why we have so many different words for it.

Adaptation Is Stabilization Under New Load

In ordinary language, adaptation sounds active. A system "adjusts." It "figures out" how to cope. It "learns to handle" a new situation. This invites the image of something inside the system noticing a change and modifying itself in response. CST contains no such machinery. There is only load, stabilization, and the cost of carrying what is present. When conditions change, the old ways of stabilizing often become unreliable or demanding. The same posture, timing, coordination, or interaction that once carried the moment with little strain now requires more internal work to hold together. The system does not evaluate this. It simply fails to stabilize as easily as before. If the new conditions persist, stabilization is forced to find different routes. Whatever configuration can hold the moment with less total strain under the new load becomes the one the system repeatedly settles into. Each time that happens, residue accumulates along that route. Over time, the architecture is reshaped. From the outside, this looks like adaptation. From the inside, nothing has adapted. The structure has been deformed by what it has been forced to carry.

Consider someone who moves from a warm climate to a cold one. At first, everything is costly. The body tightens. Movement becomes guarded. Stabilization is noisy and demanding. Over repeated exposure, circulation patterns shift, muscle tone reorganizes, timing adjusts. Eventually, the same cold imposes far less internal strain. Nothing in the system decided to "get used to the cold." The architecture was reshaped by repeated stabilization under those conditions.

The same is true in social and psychological change. A new job, a new relationship, a new environment initially strains coordination. If the conditions persist, some configurations begin to hold more reliably. Speech patterns, attention patterns, emotional load distribution gradually reorganize. What people call adaptation is not a capacity or a function. It is the visible consequence of this fact: a system becomes easier to carry where it has been forced to carry before. This is also why adaptation is never permanent. When the load changes again, the economics change again. A configuration that was once viable can become unstable. The system does not preserve what it learned. It reorganizes again. What is called "adaptation" is the felt surface signature of structural reshaping, not a process that directs it.

Reinforcement Is Not a Mechanism

In everyday psychology, reinforcement is described as a process by which behaviors followed by reward are strengthened and behaviors followed by punishment are weakened. This description quietly assumes an internal evaluator that assigns credit and modifies behavior accordingly. CST contains no such machinery. There is nothing inside the system that decides what should be repeated. There is only stabilization under load and the residue it leaves behind. When a particular configuration stabilizes, that stabilization slightly reshapes the architecture. The next time similar conditions appear, some routes now require less total reorganization to carry the moment, while others require more. If this continues to repeat, then the same routes tend to be used again — *not because they were rewarded, but because everything else now costs more to carry*.

From the outside, this looks like reinforcement. From the inside, nothing has been reinforced. The architecture has been recontoured by what it has survived. Skin does not "learn" to tolerate pressure. Where pressure is repeated, tissue thickens. Where it thickens, the same pressure causes less disruption. Over time, some skin contacts become easy while others remain painful — not because anything selected them, but because repeated load reshaped the structure. Behavior works the same way. A child continues to approach a situation in the same way not because a response has been strengthened, but because alternative coordination's impose more strain. When conditions change and a lower-cost route becomes available within the system, what appeared as reinforced behavior can dissolve rapidly. A person continues to avoid certain situations not because avoidance was "negatively reinforced," but because remaining present in those situations still produces more instability than the system can carry. What psychology calls reinforcement is not a mechanism. It is a retrospective label applied to the visible consequence of repeated stabilization and residue accumulation.

Prediction Is Not Looking ahead, It's Smooth Continuation

What people ordinarily call prediction feels, from the inside, like the system is reaching forward in time and estimating what will happen next. It feels as though something inside is modeling the future, running scenarios, and selecting among them. In CST, nothing like that is occurring. A system cannot reach into the future. It can only stabilize the present. Whatever happens next must emerge from the current configuration and the constraints acting on it. There is no extra machinery that steps outside the causal stream and peers ahead. There is only continuation. When a system has been shaped by repeated stabilization along certain corridors, activity tends to flow along those same corridors again when similar conditions arise. This produces a familiar surface effect: the next state often fits what usually comes next. When the environment is familiar and the internal landscape has been deeply shaped, transitions unfold smoothly and with very little internal disruption. From the inside, this feels like anticipation or expectation. Mechanically, it is nothing more than the system continuing along a path that has already been carved.

Consider walking down a familiar staircase in the dark. The foot does not "predict" where the next step will be. The body does not consult a plan. The architecture has simply been shaped by thousands of prior passes through the same sequence. The current configuration already contains the posture, balance, timing, and tension patterns that make the next placement the easiest continuation. When the next step appears where it usually is, nothing special happens. When it is missing, the system does not discover a wrong prediction. It is forced into sudden reorganization because the continuation it was already enacting can no longer close.

This is also why a baseball batter can connect with a 100-mph fastball. There is not enough time for awareness or deliberation to generate or consider a prediction. The swing unfolds through pre-shaped stabilization rather than conscious guidance. Instead, the swing begins immediately because early fragments of the pitcher's motion overlap with deeply carved coordination corridors. The system is already moving in a particular direction because that direction has become the most stable continuation given its history and the present constraints shaped through hundreds of hours of accumulated residue. Prediction is not about the future. It is about the past exerting structural control over the present. This is why "prediction" appears to improve as environments become more regular and as behavior becomes more habitual. The more often the same sequences are stabilized, the more the architecture becomes shaped to continue through them. The next state feels obvious not because it has been computed, but because the present state is already partway there.

Why Systems Cannot Make Errors

From a CST perspective, a system never behaves incorrectly in mechanical terms. It cannot. At any moment, a system can only resolve into configurations its current structure makes available under the load it is carrying. There is no alternative action waiting in reserve, no better option that was skipped, no other trajectory that failed to occur. This is where CST parts company with "prediction error" models. Those models begin by assuming that the system is trying to match some internal expectation to the world, and that when the world does not match, an *error* occurs that must be corrected. But in a mechanical architecture, there is nothing to be wrong in that sense. There is only what the system can carry and what it cannot.

CST does not deny mismatches. It denies that a mismatch implies that something else could have happened at that moment. When the system encounters conditions it cannot stably carry, reorganization occurs. That is not an error being corrected. It is a structure being forced to change because the previous configuration has become uncarryable. What predictive frameworks call "error" is, in CST terms, simply instability. It is the only next step available to a particular stabilization mode under current conditions — a micro-transition in the system's state-space, not a malfunction. Nothing has gone wrong. The system is doing the only thing it can do: stabilizing with the only machinery it has. There is no reference configuration being missed. There is only a finite architecture encountering load. If the system reorganizes afterward, that does not mean it "learned from a mistake." It means the previous configuration was no longer carryable, and the architecture was forced to reshape. In this sense, "prediction error" is a story we tell after the fact. It treats reorganization as if the system were revising a plan. In reality, the system is being bent. The world did not violate a prediction. The system never does the wrong thing. It only does what its structure allows under the conditions it is in. There is no error signal in the machine. There is only stability, instability, and the forced reshaping that follows.

Shaping, Not Choosing: The Dog and the Door

Adaptation, reinforcement, and what is usually called prediction are not independent functions. They are different descriptions of the same process: stabilization leaves residue, and residue reshapes the terrain in which future stabilization can occur. Consider a dog whose owner leaves every morning and returns each evening. On the first day alone, the dog wanders from room to room under elevated load. Nothing in the environment settles the system for long. Walking, lying down, sniffing, pacing — each route generates some strain or mismatch. The day becomes a sequence of poorly closing paths. Only when the owner finally reappears through the door they left from does the load drop sharply. Tension releases. The architecture settles. That brief interval becomes the only span of the day that did not push back, the only span that was fully carryable. Whatever configuration immediately preceded that relief becomes the lowest-cost residue of the entire day. In this case, the dog happens to be standing near the door. The doorway does not soothe the dog. It simply does not impose additional strain at that moment.

When the next day begins, the system drifts back toward that configuration, because every other region of the house still carries more resistance. To an observer, the dog now "waits for the owner" at the door. But nothing in this process involves forecasting. The dog is not tracking time or modeling schedules. The architecture is returning to the only corridor that last closed cleanly. The doorway is where stability last occurred, so the system re-enters that region of state-space. Over time, however, standing by the door all day introduces its own load. Hunger rises. Thirst builds. Muscles fatigue. The cold floor presses into the body. Drafts chill the skin. The doorway, once the least costly configuration, becomes increasingly expensive to carry.

Meanwhile, other parts of the house — especially the bed — still carry older residues of softness and support. These were previously overshadowed by the intensity of the owner's return, but they remain available in the landscape. Eventually, the total cost of remaining at the door exceeds the cost of lying on the bed. When that balance shifts, the architecture reorganizes. The dog begins to spend more time on the bed and less time at the door, not because anything has evaluated comfort, but because the terrain of carryability has changed.

Later, another change appears. Sounds that reliably precede the owner's return — the car, the garage door, footsteps in the hallway — begin to produce small bodily shifts: standing up, orienting, moving toward the door, preparing to transition. This is not prediction. It is the same corridor being entered earlier in the sequence. To an observer, this looks like anticipation. In CST terms, it feels like anticipation because anticipation is the felt surface signature of the architecture re-entering a familiar stabilization pathway before the external sequence has fully unfolded. The system is not predicting what will happen. It is already becoming what it has repeatedly had to become in situations with this structure.

Continuity Without Storage

Nothing in this account requires the system to store records and retrieve them later. What is ordinarily called remembering is the architecture stabilizing again in configurations it has stabilized before. When something from the past seems to return, no hidden archive is being accessed. The system is settling into a configuration whose shape was formed by earlier stabilizations. The more often a configuration has stabilized — or the more strongly it has been impressed into the architecture — the lower its cost and the easier it is to sustain again. That ease is what allows certain patterns to recur. The reverse is also true. What appears as forgetting is often not lost content but a shift in the cost landscape. A configuration that was once easy to sustain may no longer be the lowest-cost or cleanest closure available. As the substrate changes with age, illness, fatigue, or injury, some corridors become shallower, noisier, or less carryable. Conduction slows. Coordination loses precision. Gradients weaken. Other continuations now close more easily. In some cases the underlying structure also degrades, so what once stabilized readily may become difficult, fragmented, or no longer fully recoverable.

A simple example is a familiar phone number. For many years it stabilizes instantly, without effort. Later, the system hesitates. The sequence no longer resolves cleanly. Sometimes part appears, sometimes none. This does not necessarily mean the content is fully preserved but merely costly. The corridor itself may have weakened, the pattern partially degraded, or competing closures may now dominate. What was once immediate can become uncertain, slow, or incomplete.

When the system enters a region of state-space that once reliably settled into a familiar configuration, it may no longer settle there. It resolves into a nearby, lower-cost configuration instead, or fails to achieve a clean closure at all. From within experience this is sampled as searching, partial recall, or absence. The architecture has been reshaped. Events that remain vivid across decades persist not because they are stored or because they are important, but because the structural traces they left remain among the more easily sustained configurations despite everything else that has changed. When those shapes are re-entered, the system displays the felt surface signature of remembering. From a CST perspective, the past returns not because it is kept, but because its traces continue to shape the terrain.

When Learning Slows or Stalls

Learning is not infinite. A system does not remain equally reshapeable across its entire lifespan. Over time, repeated stabilization along the same routes leaves deep structural grooves. Those grooves do not merely guide future stabilizations; they begin to dominate it. As these long-used pathways deepen, new residues have a harder time taking hold. Reorganization becomes more difficult, not because the system has lost some abstract capacity, but because its architecture has become highly optimized for carrying what it has already been carrying. The more reliably a system has stabilized in certain ways, the more the landscape is contoured to support those ways, and the less hospitable it becomes to alternatives.

Chronic load accelerates this process. When strain is persistent, the system is forced to prioritize fast, reliable stabilization over exploratory reorganization. Variability becomes risky. Stabilization must resolve quickly. Under these conditions, the architecture does not widen. It consolidates. It relies increasingly on the deepest, most reliable corridors it already has. This is why systems under long-term strain often appear stuck.

The architecture is not failing. It is preserving coherence. Old patterns persist not because they are preferred, but because they remain the most dependable ways to keep the system organized under pressure. New routes are not impossible, but they are structurally demanding at a time when demand cannot be afforded. The same dynamic explains why later-life change often proceeds more slowly. Decades of stabilization have carved deep, dominant channels. New residues must compete against a landscape that is already heavily contoured. The limiting factor is not understanding or motivation. It is structural inertia.

Everyday behavior makes this visible. An overwhelmed student rereading the same paragraph is not refusing to learn; the system is too loaded to let new structure settle. An adult trying to alter decades-old eating patterns is not lacking resolve; the architecture has been shaped by thousands of stabilizations along the old route. A system under prolonged caregiving strain or chronic stress struggles to absorb new organization not because it is incapable, but because global load forces stabilization to favor speed and reliability over reconfiguration. And yet, learning is never permanently closed. When load decreases, when conditions become more stable, or when the system is exposed to small, carryable novelty rather than overwhelming change, new residues can begin to settle again. Broader routes can gradually become viable. The landscape can still be reshaped. Plasticity is not a trait the system possesses. It is a condition the system sometimes inhabits.

What This Chapter Establishes

This chapter shows that what are commonly called adaptation, reinforcement, prediction, and memory are not separate processes and not separate mechanisms. They are different surface descriptions of a single physical fact: a finite system is continuously reshaped by the stabilizations it survives. Nothing inside the system evaluates outcomes, selects behaviors, stores records, or consults models of the future. The system stabilizes under load. Those stabilizations leave residue. That residue reshapes the architecture. The reshaped architecture constrains what can stabilize next. Learning, in every form, is nothing more than this. There is no additional machinery behind it. There is only a system whose structure is being slowly and inexorably bent by what it has had to carry.

Chapter 25

Patterns, Drift, and Long-Range Grooves

How Repetition Accumulates into Architectural Tendencies

Every morning before sunrise, Sandy runs the same four-mile route around her neighborhood. It wasn't always this way. Years earlier, she experimented constantly — shorter loops, longer ones, different turns, different times, different mixtures of sidewalks and side streets. None of them quite settled her. Some ran close to traffic. Some cut across broken pavement. Some felt strangely exposed in the early light. She kept shifting routes because none of them yet offered stability. Each carried its own small tension, a subtle pushback the system registered as slightly off-balance.

But one morning, after a particularly difficult week, she drifted onto a quiet residential street lined with tall poplar trees. Her breathing eased there. Her stride softened. Her chest relaxed. The air felt cool in a way that quieted the system rather than taxing it. The street did not comfort her; it simply did not resist her. It became the segment of the run that imposed the least strain. When the system stabilized there, the conditions surrounding that stabilization left residues strong enough to shape the next day.

Without deciding to repeat the route, she found herself running it again the following morning. It felt familiar, but more importantly, it demanded very little. Nothing else in the environment stabilized her as easily. Within days her behavior settled into the loop. Within months, the loop felt inevitable. And years later, when she explained the pattern to friends, she offered reasons — "It's peaceful," "It's my favorite route" — that arrived long after the architecture had already conformed to its groove. The truth was simpler. This was where stabilization had repeatedly settled.

Patterns as Architectural Grooves

Patterns are not behaviors. They are not internalized habits or shaped preferences. They are architectural grooves that make some stabilizations cost less than others, sometimes dramatically so. Earlier chapters described how residues form and how short-range repetition makes certain stabilizations slightly easier to carry. Patterns operate at a different scale. They arise when countless micro-residues accumulate in the same region over long periods of time, gradually sculpting channels within the architecture that pull stabilization in their direction. When stabilization repeatedly runs through the same region, the architecture reorganizes around it. The system begins treating that region as a default stabilizing route, even when the resulting behavior appears voluntary or chosen. Sandy does not prefer her loop in any deep sense; its familiarity is an after-effect of architectural viability. Awareness receives the pattern long after the pattern has taken shape.

How Consolidation Emerges from Repetition

At the earliest stages of learning anything — running, speaking, navigating, reacting — stabilization ranges across a wide set of possible paths. Some are awkward. Some are costly. Some destabilize the system so strongly that the architecture routes away from them, and because they are rarely or never re-entered, they effectively fall out of the system's usable range. A few generate momentary ease. None yet form a pattern. As those easier paths are repeated, residues begin to accumulate. Routes that consistently destabilize the system are entered less and less often, and their grooves fade. Neutral paths remain available but become less likely. *What remain are the pathways that resist the system the least.* Over time, these small grooves merge. A stable corridor begins to form. This is consolidation. The system does not choose this corridor. It emerges as the intersection of many cycles of *reduced resistance.* The architecture slowly reshapes itself around whatever stabilizations were easiest to carry.

This is exactly what happened in the example of the dog at the door in chapter 24. The doorway became the first low-resistance groove because it happened to coincide with relief. But repetition could not hold that configuration indefinitely. As the strain of standing there accumulated — fatigue, discomfort, hunger — the architecture drifted toward an older, softer groove: the bed. With enough cycles, even the bed ceased to be the default waiting place. Instead, the system consolidated around an upstream corridor defined by the earliest cues that did not destabilize it. What looked like learning or intention was simply repetition carving deeper grooves and redirecting stabilization toward whatever configurations imposed the least resistance.

What looked like learning or intention was simply repetition carving deeper grooves and redirecting stabilization toward whatever configurations imposed the least resistance.

Repetition reshapes the landscape.
Stabilization flows toward the lowest-cost corridor.

Drift as the Slow Movement of the Architecture

Even on uneventful days, the architecture is changing. Each stabilization leaves a small structural trace. Each moment subtly biases the next. A day with no remarkable events still contains thousands of micro-adjustments. Over weeks and months, these tiny changes accumulate into noticeable shifts in how stabilization tends to resolve. A person often feels as though they have changed without any clear cause because the architecture has been *drifting* beneath awareness the entire time. Someone might suddenly realize they no longer enjoy a familiar routine — not because of a decision or a moment of insight, but because months of small shifts have nudged the architecture into a different groove.

Drift is not growth or decay. It is the long-term consequence of repeated stabilization. The system leans toward regions where stabilization has been easy to carry and away from regions where stabilization has repeatedly strained. It is the slow, continuous movement of the internal landscape under the accumulated weight of residue. In other frameworks, such regions are sometimes called "attractors," but nothing is attracting anything here. There is no pull and no target. The system is not being drawn toward a place. It is simply settling again and again into whatever configurations impose the least total strain, and in doing so, gradually reshaping the terrain so that those paths become even easier to enter.

Rigidification and the Loss of Flexibility

Some grooves deepen so gradually and so consistently that leaving them costs more than remaining within them. The resulting pattern does not feel chosen. It feels inevitable. A person may dislike a particular tendency — their reactivity, their avoidance, their meticulousness, their insistence on routine — and yet the system continues to fall into the same configuration because every alternative carries more resistance. A smoker who wants to quit encounters this directly: even when the wish to stop is strong, the groove of reaching for a cigarette even after quitting remains the lowest-cost route the architecture can take. A similar effect appears when someone begins a diet. During the first days, they may find themselves walking toward the kitchen in response to hunger, hand already reaching for food, only becoming aware partway through — *what am I doing?* The movement was not planned. The groove was simply deep. For a long time, responding to hunger by obtaining food has been the easiest path the system can take, and even when conditions change, the architecture initially continues along that established corridor. Rigid patterns are not expressions of identity. They are architectures whose grooves have become too deep to exit without destabilization. The system returns to them not because they are pleasant, justified, or aligned with any standard, but because they are the solutions it has been shaped to produce with the least strain.

Pattern Competition and the Feeling of Being Torn

Many people describe being pulled in conflicting directions. They want closeness yet feel compelled to withdraw. They want novelty yet cling to familiar rhythms. They want to speak yet feel an impulse to remain silent.

These conflicts are not psychological battles between competing "selves." They are architectural competitions between long-formed grooves in different regions or bands of the system. Each groove corresponds to a region where stabilization has repeatedly settled. When two such regions are similarly low-cost, stabilization does not commit cleanly to either. Instead, the system alternates: one micro-state stabilizes here, then a moment later another stabilizes there. This rapid back-and-forth is experienced as indecision, ambivalence, or inner conflict. In CST terms, it is simply the architecture failing to find a single configuration that carries clearly less strain than any nearby alternative. Awareness experiences this oscillation as struggle or dissonance. But no chooser stands between the alternatives. There is no inner negotiator. There are only patterns whose costs are too similar for one to dominate the other.

How Patterns Spread Across Frames

Patterns rarely remain confined to the domain in which they formed. A sensory residue can become an emotional tendency; an emotional groove can become a narrative framing tendency; a narrative tendency can become a behavioral expectation. Patterns propagate across the architecture — across Frames of Reference — because residues reshape the cost landscape broadly, not only locally. A child who repeatedly experiences raised voices as destabilizing may not only avoid loud environments; the emotional groove can generalize into a broader sensitivity to conflict. Over time, this sensitivity may stabilize as a persistent orientation toward danger or unpredictability, which can then express as withdrawal, scanning, or rapid defensive mobilization. Nothing is transferred between parts. The same reshaped landscape supports multiple stabilizations across different Frames of Reference, allowing one groove to propagate into many expressions without any movement between separate structures. The same landscape is reshaped across multiple Frames of Reference. This cross-frame propagation is why clusters of tendencies so often travel together. The system is not storing traits or preferences. It is navigating a single, interconnected landscape whose topology has been sculpted by residues across many frames.

How Personality Emerges Before Identity

Long before the identity frame emerges, the architecture already contains clusters of grooves shaping long-range tendencies. These clusters give rise to what psychology calls personality traits. A person may consistently approach situations cautiously, speak assertively, avoid certain emotional textures, or gravitate toward predictable routines. These tendencies do not originate from identity. They originate from the accumulation of grooves long before identity consolidates. The same process is visible in animals. A dog that consistently withdraws from unfamiliar noises, a cat that repeatedly patrols the same perimeter of the house, or a horse that seeks the calmest companion in a herd is not displaying an identity. These are expressions of grooves carved by thousands of prior stabilizations. Nothing in these patterns is chosen or authored as a preference. They arise from the accumulated effects of past stabilizations. The architecture is simply settling into long-range pathways that have become easiest to carry. Identity is the felt signature that emerges later at the display level, reflecting patterns already stabilized. It gathers them, names them, and presents them as expressions of a coherent self. But identity does not create them. The architecture shapes them first. Identity arrives afterward to organize what is already there into a narrative. In CST terms, personality is the terrain. Identity is the label placed on the terrain. *Personality* is the long-range pattern of stabilization tendencies in the architecture. *Identity* is the rendered organization of those same tendencies in higher frames.

Pattern Horizons and the Timescale of Coherence

Patterns stabilize across limited timescales — hours, days, sometimes months. They account for why behavior appears consistent within familiar contexts or why routines persist over short spans. Across longer intervals, many such patterns may coexist without forming any single, long-range organization. They can shape how the system behaves this week or this year without yet producing a coherent corridor capable of remaining stable across changing environments, roles, or developmental phases. A system may contain many deep grooves and still lack any structure that enforces continuity across decades. Over time, some clusters of grooves begin to operate together as a single long-timescale stabilization corridor. Emotional grooves, narrative tendencies, and behavioral regularities become jointly carryable across diverse contexts rather than only within local conditions.

This corridor is not imposed. It is a structural property of the reshaped landscape.

How Patterns Prepare the Ground for Identity

Identity does not arise from choice, preference, or introspection. It emerges when the architecture's most stable long-range grooves begin to function together as a single frame capable of maintaining coherence across time. Patterns supply the raw material. Identity is not those patterns themselves, but the felt surface signature that appears once the architecture's deepest grooves are being carried together inside a long-horizon stabilization corridor. A useful analogy is a tree. Across the life of the tree, branches grow, break, and are replaced. Leaves come and go. The surface details change from season to season and year to year. But the trunk and main structure persist, carrying continuity through all of those changes. The tree is not defined by any particular leaf or branch, but by the long-lived structure that remains as those parts come and go. In the same way, patterns are like branches: local, replaceable, and context-bound. Identity corresponds to the long-horizon structural corridor that remains as particular patterns appear, fade, or are replaced.

What This Chapter Establishes

This chapter shows how repetition reshapes the architecture through residue, forming grooves that bias stabilization over time. Patterns are not behaviors, habits, or stored preferences; they are structural tendencies produced by accumulated stabilizations. The architecture drifts continuously, gradually consolidating low-resistance corridors while others fade. Conflicts between tendencies reflect competitions between grooves, not competing selves. Patterns propagate across Frames of Reference because the cost landscape is globally reshaped, allowing clusters of tendencies to travel together. Personality emerges from long-range groove structure before identity appears. Identity arises later as the felt signature of a long-timescale stabilization corridor that carries these patterns together across time.

Part V

How a Person Appears

Development, emotion, identity, and narrative as delayed structural influences

Chapter 26

Development: Calibration and Frame Emergence

How the Architecture Comes Online

A system is not born with a finished architecture. It is born with a minimal set of stabilizing capacities and is forced, from the first moment, to remain coherent under whatever conditions it is placed. Everything that follows is built on top of those first stabilizations. This is why early structure matters more than early experience. An experience is an event. A structure is what remains. And whatever remains becomes the terrain on which all future moments must be carried.

In the earliest phases, the system has very few degrees of freedom. It cannot shift among many stabilization modes or route coherence through multiple layers. It must settle using whatever machinery is available. Each stabilization slightly reshapes the architecture. Those reshaping effects do not disappear. They accumulate and become the foundation on which everything else is later built.

This is not because early life is special in a sentimental sense. It is because the system is narrow and forced to solve coherence with very little machinery. When structure forms under those conditions, later layers must adapt to it. They do not replace it. The system does not begin again. Everything it becomes is built on those early conditions.

Why Early Architecture Dominates Later Life

Two people can live through events that look similar from the outside and yet develop profoundly different long-range structures. This is not because one event "mattered more." It is because the architectures receiving those events were already different. The event is never what persists; the receiving structure is. In early development, even small repeated conditions can leave large load-bearing traces. A persistent rhythm of tension, disruption and settling, or mismatch between need and response does not remain local. These patterns become part of the ground on which later layers must organize.

Later in life, additional stabilization modes come online — language, social coordination, narrative compression, identity. But none of these arise on empty ground. They organize on an already-shaped landscape. This is why later insight cannot directly undo early calibration. Insight operates in higher layers. Structure is carried in lower ones. Higher layers cannot rewrite the foundation they rest upon, but through repeated stabilizations they can gradually reshape what the system must carry, leaving residue that slowly alters the terrain.

Consider a system that early in development repeatedly stabilized through aggression because forceful mobilization was the only configuration that restored coherence. Those stabilizations carve deep grooves in lower layers. When later frames come online, they do not form independently. Language may become sharp. Social coordination may lean toward defensive readiness. Narrative may frame the world as oppositional. These later layers are not choosing aggression; they are stabilizing on the only ground available. Only repeated stabilization under different conditions can gradually open alternative corridors.

Development Is Not the Addition of Abilities

Development is not the accumulation of features. It is the progressive expansion of the range of stabilization the system can sustain. Early in development, coherence can be maintained only at small scales — bodily integrity, immediate regulation, basic coordination. As the world the system must carry grows more complex, this range becomes insufficient. When existing organization can no longer sustain required coherence, further organization must emerge. This does not arise through decision, but through structural necessity. This is how Frames of Reference come online. They are not viewpoints, but modes of stabilization. Each Frame addresses a distinct class of coherence problem. They do not appear simultaneously or fully formed. Each emerges only when the architecture can sustain it, and their operations overlap rather than replace one another.

How the Layered Architecture Comes Online

In the earliest phase, the system's world is bodily. The dominant work is maintaining integrity, balance, and regulation. There is no world of explanation or identity — only forces, rhythms, and immediate demands. As environmental complexity increases, additional organization becomes unavoidable. The system must stabilize not only posture and movement, but urgency, approach, withdrawal, and broad affective tone. The world becomes structured by demand and relief.

Later, social coordination becomes unavoidable. The system must remain coherent in relation to other systems like itself. Alignment, signaling, conflict, inclusion, and exclusion become stabilizing structures. Later still, narrative compression emerges. The system must maintain coherence across time, absence, and planning. The world becomes story-shaped as a method of holding extended sequences together.

Later still, identity emerges. The system must remain coherent across years, roles, and changing environments. Identity functions as a long-range stabilizer. Beyond this, wider Frames may emerge in which identity is no longer the center of coherence but one structure among others. No earlier layer disappears. The system never outgrows its lower organization. Those layers remain available and can become dominant whenever conditions force stabilization downward.

Each Layer Leaves a Permanent Signature

Every layer leaves characteristic structural tendencies and surface signatures in experience. A person whose early regulation formed under persistent tension may still show it decades later in breathing depth, baseline muscle tone, and startle threshold, even when no immediate threat exists. Early bodily organization shapes posture, tension, and baseline regulation. Urgency-based organization shapes what feels pressing or overwhelming. Social organization shapes attachment and conflict patterns. Narrative organization shapes explanation styles. Identity shapes long-range continuity and personal coherence. None of these are chosen. They are the visible traces of how the system learned to remain coherent. Because each layer builds upon previous ones, early shaping propagates upward and biases which stabilizations are available.

Why the System Never Gets a Clean Slate

Earlier organization is not replaced, but neither is it fixed. Lower layers persist as capacity bands within the architecture and continue evolving as residue accumulates. Under strain, stabilization may shift toward earlier modes, not because the past returns unchanged, but because those modes remain structurally available. What appears under pressure is not the past itself, but the lowest-cost configuration the present architecture can sustain. This is also why later life may become narrower. As long-used corridors deepen, stabilization resolves through them more reliably. This may feel like stability or rigidity, but mechanically it is the same process: the system relying on configurations it can carry most easily. The past does not return. The structure remains.

Early Architecture Matters More Than Early Experience

An event arriving at a flexible system leaves a different trace than the same event arriving at a rigid one. An event arriving when few layers exist is carried differently than when the full architecture is available. This is why identical events can shape lives differently. The earlier shaping occurs, the more later structure must form around it.

Early calibration is not destiny in a dramatic sense. It is foundation in a mechanical sense. Long before identity or narrative appear, the system already has a shape. That shape determines which situations are easy, which are straining, which changes are possible, and which are resisted. Later layers describe this shape. They do not create it.

What This Chapter Establishes

Development is not the acquisition of traits. It is the progressive expansion of the system's capacity to remain coherent across wider spans of reality. Frames of Reference are not optional perspectives but layered stabilization solutions required for coherence in an increasingly complex world. Early structure is not overwritten. It is built upon. And because of this, all later change — no matter how sophisticated — must operate within the terrain laid down by the system's earliest stabilizations. The system does not begin as someone. It becomes someone by carrying what it had to carry.

Chapter 27

Emotion as the Display of Frame-Level Stabilization

How Each Frame of Reference Produces Its Own Signature of Strain

Emotion is not the beginning of anything. It is not the driver of behavior in real time. The architecture enters and exits emotionally relevant configurations long before anything can be rendered or felt. Infants tense, cry, cling, and discharge because their structure has reorganized under load, not because they are experiencing feelings. What adults later call "emotion" appears only when a stabilized configuration is rendered by the Phenomena Transducer System and becomes available to awareness.

Across time, configurations rendered as emotion leave residue like any other stabilization, reshaping future carryability. The system encounters a moment it must carry. Forces exceed what the dominant Frame can integrate. Reorganization occurs — fast, local, mechanical. Only afterward, when the redistributed configuration has stabilized enough to be rendered, does that configuration appear in experience.

Emotion is the phenomenal surface signature of that cost. This is why emotional life feels reactive, late, and strangely disconnected from the actions it is often said to explain. Awareness arrives at the end of a process the architecture has already settled. Emotion is, in this sense, no different from the creaking of a bridge under load. The sound does not hold the bridge up. It displays what it costs the structure to keep holding. This chapter makes explicit which parts of the bridge — which Frames of Reference — are carrying which portions of that strain.

Different Emotional Signatures for Each Frame

Each Frame of Reference stabilizes a distinct band of organization within the moment in the landscape. Because of this, each exhibits its own geometry of instability and its own pattern of redistribution when forces exceed what it can carry. These differences are not conceptual; they are mechanical — like the strain in a bridge's steel beam differing from the vibration of its suspension cables. When a given layer is required to carry more than it can integrate, strain redistributes according to the constraints of that layer's organization. When this redistributed configuration is rendered by the Phenomena Transducer System, it appears as a characteristic family of experiential signatures. Emotional categories are therefore not readings of situations. They are PTS-formatted displays of which layer is being strained and how.

What follows is not a complete catalog. Each frame supports a continuous space of possible experiential textures shaped by history, context, and the precise geometry of load. The entries below describe only the most characteristic strain signatures of each layer — the repeatable ways each part of the architecture tends to reorganize when forced beyond its integrative margin. The claim is structural, not classificatory: different layers reorganize differently under strain, and those reorganization patterns appear as different families of emotion.

This mapping should be understood as an initial structural approximation rather than a finalized taxonomy. It is derived from convergence across phenomenology, behavioral observation, and architectural inference, and is expected to refine as the mechanics of frame-level stabilization are further specified. The purpose here is not exhaustive classification, but to establish that emotional differentiation reflects layer-specific stabilization under load.

FOR-1 — Primitive Force Stabilization and the Shock Signature

FOR-1 stabilizes raw physical forces such as impact, balance, collision, and sudden changes in motion. When this layer is pushed beyond what it can handle, strain shows up as jolts, freezing, reflexive bracing, or a sudden loss of smooth movement. Awareness does not take part in this process. It only samples what has already happened. Once the system stabilizes enough to be rendered, the Phenomena Transducer System formats this state as shock, panic bursts, or the instant flash of fear that appears before any higher processing has time to occur. This is not a judgment about danger. It is simply the surface trace of a system forced to preserve physical coherence with no time for integration. The feeling is the leftover vibration of a rapid stabilization. From the outside, this can be seen as startle reflexes, full-body flinches, sudden freezing, disrupted coordination, or a brief loss of fluid movement — the kind of abrupt physical reaction observed in animals, infants, and adults when sudden physical disturbance occurs.

FOR-2 — Motor Instability and the Agitation Signature

FOR-2 keeps movement smooth and continuous. Under normal conditions, it allows the body to stay coordinated and fluid. When this layer has to carry too much strain, movement begins to reorganize. This can show up as restless motion, pacing, fidgeting, small bursts of muscle discharge, or ongoing tension that never fully settles. These are not strategies or deliberate choices. They are what strain in the movement system looks like. When this state is rendered, it often feels like irritability, agitation, or having "too much energy." What you feel is the aftereffect of the motor system reorganizing itself to keep the moment from becoming uncarryable. From the outside, this may appear as pacing, repetitive movement, fidgeting, shifting weight, tapping, or constant small movements that make it difficult to remain still. The system is not trying to misbehave; it is trying to discharge strain and maintain continuity of movement under load.

FOR-3 — Field Fragmentation and the Overwhelm Signature

FOR-3 keeps the world organized as a single, coherent field — sights, sounds, motion, and space working together as one stable environment. When this layer is pushed beyond what it can integrate, those sensory streams stop coordinating cleanly. Noise feels sharper. Motion becomes harder to track. Space may feel disorganized, too large, or too close. This is not about meaning or interpretation. It is what it costs the system to keep a fragmented field coherent enough for anything to be experienced at all. When rendered, this often feels overwhelming. From the outside, this can appear as rapid scanning eye movements, repeated startle responses, trouble orienting in space, erratic shifts of attention, or a broader breakdown in coordinating sound, motion, and spatial layout. The system is trying to hold the field together under strain, and the visible instability reflects that effort.

FOR-4 — Body-as-Object Instability and Exposure Signature

FOR-4 keeps the body organized as a single, owned physical presence — a stable sense of "this body is me." When this layer is under strain, the system works to protect bodily coherence. Strain may show up as tightening in the torso, blushing, shrinking, guarding, or a thinning, distant feeling sometimes described as dissociation. When this state is rendered, it can feel like shame, exposure, or sudden self-consciousness. These are not messages or judgments. They are what it feels like when the system is trying to hold the body together under destabilizing load. From the outside, this often appears as protective or closed postures, guarding the torso, curling or shrinking movements, blushing, avoiding eye contact, or sudden shifts in how the body is presented. The system is not trying to hide; it is trying to preserve bodily coherence while under strain.

FOR-5 — Participation Fragility and Helpless-Protest Signature

FOR-5 keeps the system engaged as an active participant in the moment — able to stay involved, respond, and remain connected to what is happening. When this layer comes under strain, the system can no longer hold steady participation. Reorganization may show up as withdrawal, clinging, appeasement, or protest. Crying can appear here not mainly as communication, but as a fallback pattern that once helped restore stability and may do so again when centered engagement cannot be maintained. What is felt is the surface display of participation losing its grip. From the outside, this often appears as moving back and forth between engagement and withdrawal, clinging to support, appeasing behavior, protest sounds or expressions, or a drop-in initiative when the system cannot keep stable involvement in the moment.

FOR-6 — Subjectivity Instability and Personalization Signature

FOR-6 keeps together the sense that "this is happening to me." It binds experiences into a stable center so events feel connected to a single self. When this layer is under heavy strain, the system has trouble holding that center steady. Incoming signals no longer organize cleanly around a stable "me." When this instability is rendered, it can show up as sudden guilt, waves of humiliation, intense self-blame, or the feeling of being singled out or targeted. These are not moral conclusions or careful evaluations. They are what it feels like when the system is struggling to keep a stable subjective center under pressure. From the outside, this often looks like heightened self-referential reactions, quick defensiveness, repeated explanations that pull events back to oneself, or visible distress when attention keeps turning inward. The system is not trying to dramatize. It is trying to re-stabilize a threatened center by binding everything back to a single point: "me."

FOR-7 — Identity Strain and the Anger–Despair Signature

FOR-7 holds together your long-range sense of who you are. When this layer has to carry more than it can handle, experience becomes unstable and intense. If the paths that support your identity are blocked, the system mobilizes force, and this shows up as anger — the structure pushing against what is stopping it. If the system cannot keep your identity coherent when things contradict each other, the display shifts toward despair, emptiness, or a sense of falling apart. These feelings seem like deep truths about yourself or the world, but they are actually what it looks like when identity is struggling to stay stable across a wide range of conditions. From the outside, this often appears as sharp swings between forceful action and collapse, rigid clinging to a definition of self, oppositional behavior, or withdrawal when long-range coherence cannot be maintained. When a person's core identity is threatened — for example, when a defining role suddenly disappears, when how they are seen publicly is contradicted, or when a central life direction becomes impossible — they may swing quickly between intense mobilization and shutdown, even without immediate physical danger. This instability reflects the identity layer trying to reorganize itself under conflicting constraints.

FOR-8 — Observer-Level Turbulence and the Dread Signature

FOR-8 keeps a stable viewpoint on your own identity — the ability to see yourself, your patterns, and your direction from a step back. When this layer is under too much strain, the experience can turn into dread, a dizzy or vertigo-like disorientation, or thoughts that loop without settling. The system is trying to hold both the pattern and the viewpoint on the pattern at the same time, and this becomes hard to sustain. What you feel is not "meaning" or a message. It is what it is like when your perspective loses stability. The strain shows up as uneasiness, inner wobbling, or a sense that nothing quite locks into place — not because you cannot decide what to do, but because the system cannot keep a steady vantage point on its own identity patterns. From the outside, this often looks like long periods of rumination, repeated circling over the same thoughts, visible disorientation, or trying again and again to "get clear" without fully settling. A common example is when someone keeps stepping back to figure themselves out — questioning their direction, motives, or sense of self — but each attempt produces more looping rather than clarity. The instability reflects the observer layer trying to regain a stable perspective while the structures under observation are themselves shifting.

FOR-9 — Global Coherence and the Groundlessness Signature

FOR-9 holds the widest sense of overall coherence the system can reach — a broad, stable sense that everything fits together. When this layer becomes even slightly unstable, the experience can feel like groundlessness or fear with no clear object. The system looks for orientation but cannot find a stable reference point. What appears in awareness is a sense that everything is unsteady at once — not because something specific is wrong, but because the widest level of organization is struggling to hold together. This is the highest stabilization mode losing carryability. When it wavers, the system often shifts downward, searching for a narrower mode it can stabilize more reliably. From the outside, this may appear as global disorientation, loss of direction, emotional flattening or detachment, long periods of stillness, or a quick return to simpler, more basic stabilizing behaviors. A common example is when someone suddenly feels unanchored — as if the usual sense of self, world, and direction has loosened — and the system responds by narrowing, simplifying, or becoming very still in order to regain stability.

Mixed Signatures

In lived experience, these signatures rarely appear in isolation. Multiple Frames of Reference are often strained at once, and the Phenomena Transducer System renders multiple cost patterns in parallel. This is why emotional experience feels layered rather than singular. At very short timescales, stabilization does not remain fixed at a single frame. As load fluctuates moment by moment, stabilization may route through one frame, then another, then briefly return, seeking a configuration that can be carried with less total strain. These micro-transitions can occur on the order of milliseconds, far below awareness. Awareness does not register the routing itself. It samples only the resulting composite display. What is experienced as a blended, conflicted, or shifting emotional state is the surface trace of stabilization moving back and forth across frames as the architecture attempts to maintain coherence. Nothing inside the system is mixing emotions. Nothing is switching deliberately. The apparent complexity reflects rapid frame-level stabilization under changing load, rendered after the fact as a single, layered experiential field. What feels like emotional complexity is the architecture searching for a configuration it can carry.

What Emotion Actually Tracks

Emotion does not report what something means. It displays how much structural work the architecture has performed to carry the moment. For this reason, emotional comfort does not necessarily indicate health, and emotional distress does not necessarily indicate danger. A person may feel intense anxiety in a physically safe setting — standing in a dark closet, for example — while another may feel steady calm in an objectively dangerous situation, such as working on a high scaffold after years of exposure. The difference lies not in the situation itself, but in how much structural work the system must perform to carry it. Emotion tracks cost, not truth. Emotional exhaustion is not produced by emotion itself, but by the work that has already taken place, which emotion now displays. Emotional expression does consume energy — muscle tension, autonomic activation, crying, and sustained mobilization all carry physiological cost — yet this cost is typically small relative to the work being expressed. The deeper burden lies in the prolonged stabilization and redistribution that the emotion reflects.

Why This Matters

What you call "how I feel" is not a message about what something means or what should be done. It is a differentiated signal produced by the Phenomena Transducer System, displaying the cost paid by a specific Frame of Reference to preserve coherence in that moment.

Chapter 28

Identity as Long-Timescale Stabilization
How a System Becomes Someone Without a Self

Earlier chapters showed how repetition leaves residue, how residue reshapes the architecture, and how that reshaped architecture determines what can stabilize with less strain the next time. This single loop accounts for what is usually called learning, habit, adaptation, reinforcement, anticipation, and memory. Nothing is added to the system. Nothing is consulted. The structure is simply being bent by what it has had to carry. So far, this has been described mostly at short and medium timescales: minutes, hours, days, sometimes months. At those scales, the result is patterns — local grooves in the architecture that make certain ways of moving, reacting, or coordinating easier to sustain than others. But the same machinery does not stop operating. When the same kinds of stabilizations repeat across years — across roles, environments, and life phases — the grooves do not remain local. They begin to link across multiple Frames of Reference, forming wider stabilization corridors. They form corridors that span large portions of the system's activity. Their impact is no longer confined to a single behavior or context. It becomes system-wide. At that point, the architecture is no longer just developing tendencies. It is developing a long-range way of being.

This shift is easy to see in ordinary physical and behavioral change. A slight change in gait after an ankle injury can, over years, reshape posture, balance, and movement across the whole body. A tension pattern formed in one demanding role can become the system's default way of standing, breathing, and coordinating with others. A reliable method of reducing strain in one domain can slowly reorganize broad regions of behavior. What began as a local solution becomes a global constraint. The landscape is no longer just marked in one place. It is recontoured. This is where identity comes from: characteristics that began as local solutions and, through long-timescale stabilization, came to shape the system as a whole. In CST terms, this transition from local grooves to global corridors is how a system acquires a long-range way of being.

The Debate Student

When he was ten, Aaron loved to argue. He did not argue to win. He argued because speaking forcefully gave the system a kind of internal firmness it rarely found elsewhere. The moments when he leaned forward, lifted his chin, and delivered a strong claim were the moments when the system settled most easily. Teachers described him as opinionated. His parents called him headstrong. His classmates thought of him as the kid who always has something to say. None of these labels touched the machinery. For Aaron, these postures and tones were simply configurations that reduced internal strain.

In middle school, a teacher suggested he join the debate team. The format suited him. Standing behind a podium, speaking in structured sequences, defending a position — these were not new behaviors. They were extensions of grooves the architecture had been shaping for years. The more often these configurations were used, the more the system treated them as reliable ways to remain coherent under pressure.

By high school, people began to describe him as driven, focused, disciplined, even a natural leader. Aaron accepted these descriptions because nothing in experience contradicted them. Across classes, friendships, competitions, and late nights of study, the same styles kept reappearing. The system felt consistent. From the inside, this consistency felt like a personal nature. From a CST perspective, it was something simpler. The architecture had developed a long corridor where stabilization rarely required major reorganization. What later felt like "who I am" was the shape the system had taken by carrying what it had carried. This is how identity begins.

Why Identity Appears at All

For a long time, a system can operate using only local patterns. Different contexts draw activity into different grooves. Behavior shifts. Preferences drift. Nothing yet binds the whole into a single long-range structure. As years pass, however, the same kinds of demands, roles, and environments tend to recur. The system is repeatedly pushed through similar regions of its landscape. Some pathways are used again and again. Others are rarely entered. Gradually, certain routes deepen and begin to dominate. When this happens, the architecture does not remain a loose collection of local patterns. Its most reliable grooves begin to link together. Activity starts to move through the same extended regions across many different situations. A long corridor forms, not because anything set out to build it, but because repetition has made other routes increasingly difficult to sustain. At that point, the system begins to behave as though it has a consistent way of being. Across contexts and across time, the same styles of movement, reaction, and coordination keep reappearing. This is a long-range stabilizing corridor formed by the deepest and most frequently used pathways in the architecture. That corridor is what CST calls the Identity Frame of Reference (FOR-7).

What Identity Is and What It Is Not

In CST, identity is not a self, a chooser, or an inner author steering the machinery. It is the felt surface signature of the architecture's long-range stabilizing corridor. It is a region of the internal landscape where the system can remain coherent across many contexts without reorganizing each time. When activity remains inside this corridor, experience registers continuity, familiarity, and "this is me." When activity is forced outside it, experience registers strain, disorientation, and "this doesn't feel like me." What feels like a self is the surface signature of stability remaining inside a long-range channel.

FOR-7 — Coherence with an Anchor (Identity)

In FOR-7, coherence is organized around a particular long-range pattern of being. The system stabilizes by routing activity through a corridor formed by its own history. This corridor functions as an anchor: a configuration through which posture, emotion, attention, and behavior reliably resolve across time. What is carryable is what fits within this corridor; deviations increase strain, while returning to it would restore ease. Stability here is achieved by preserving sameness across changing moments and roles. The anchor is identity: a long-range stabilizing corridor that maintains continuity by remaining the same kind of system across time. Experientially, this appears as the sense of being someone. Activity that flows smoothly within the corridor registers as natural or authentic. Activity outside it registers as strain or disorientation. These are not judgments. They are the surface trace of stabilization remaining inside — or being forced outside — the identity anchor. Long-range corridors deepen as stabilizations repeat across years. Patterns bind into durable configuration. Awareness encounters this persistence as identity.

How Identity Forms from Patterns

Identity does not replace patterns. It depends on them. Patterns are local grooves shaped by repetition. Over time, some grooves deepen, begin to overlap, and start feeding into one another. Transitions between them become smooth. The architecture begins using them as a single extended route through many different contexts. At that point, a corridor exists. Aaron's debating posture, his structured speaking cadence, his assertive tone, and his preference for ordered interactions were not isolated tendencies. Each had been shaped by thousands of micro-residues. As these grooves deepened and began to link, the system started stabilizing through them as one long-range path. Only then did Aaron begin to experience himself as someone decisive, someone who leads, someone who knows what he thinks. These qualities were not created by identity. They were absorbed into the long-range structure identity carries. Identity is not built. It is worn into the system. There is no point at which it is assembled. It is worn into the system. A bridge does not become curved because it prefers a curve. It becomes curved because decades of wind and traffic push it toward a shape that can be carried. Patterns are the repeated flexing. Identity is the long-term bend that remains.

Why Identity Feels Self-Made

Awareness has no access to the architecture that produces identity. It only samples what has already stabilized. So, when activity flows smoothly inside the identity corridor, experience does not register "a corridor." It just registers being someone. Aaron — the debate student whose architecture repeatedly stabilized through forceful speech and structured argument — did not experience himself as re-entering the same configuration. He experienced the smooth continuity of that configuration as his nature expressing itself. The difference is not that something new appeared. The difference is that stable architectural outputs were now being received as "me." This is what identity does. It makes stable architecture arrive as a self.

Identity as Constraint, Not Freedom

Identity can feel expansive from the inside. It can be received as direction, momentum, and personal significance. Structurally, however, identity is a narrowing of available state space. Stabilization is channeled along pathways that preserve long-range coherence and away from regions that raise cost. Identity is not a set of possibilities. It is a corridor with walls. A system that feels confident is stabilizing inside a corridor shaped by years of reliable use. A system that feels anxious is stabilizing inside a corridor shaped by years of repeated strain and protective routing. In both cases, the architecture is not expressing character. It is moving toward the lowest-strain coherence it can sustain under its history and constraints.

Development and Entrenchment

Identity does not appear all at once. It forms gradually as patterns deepen and environments repeatedly stabilize specific pathways. Early in life, activity can range widely across interests, postures, and roles without settling into a narrow corridor. Over time, repeated exposure to similar demands makes some configurations easier to sustain and others harder. Identity takes shape as continuity across contexts. In adulthood, identity often becomes more entrenched as activity stabilizes around durable domains of work, relationships, and routine. Daily demands narrow the range of viable stabilizations. Attention, emotion, speech, and action repeatedly resolve along familiar paths because those paths require less redistribution to sustain across time. The result is a strong sense of coherence and continuity, not because "character" is being asserted, but because the architecture has been shaped by repeated stabilization under similar conditions.

Later, after retirement or major life changes, some role-enforced pathways fall away. Days may no longer stabilize around fixed schedules or institutional pressure. But this does not automatically reopen the landscape. Often the opposite happens. Stabilization relies even more heavily on the oldest and deepest corridors — the ones that have carried the system for decades. The active range can become narrower, not wider, while also becoming more stable and less strained. Familiar responses, preferences, and ways of moving through the world dominate because they require less internal redistribution. The sense of self can feel quieter and more settled, not because identity vanished, but because it is now expressed through fewer, deeper, more reliable pathways.

When Identity Begins to Loosen

Higher Frames of Reference do not remove identity. They reveal it as one stabilizing corridor among others. When the system stabilizes in these wider stabilization modes, identity becomes translucent. Its boundaries become permeable. What once felt absolute — the only way coherence could be maintained — becomes optional. Activity can now settle into broader channels that include identity without being defined by it. This happens because FOR-8 and FOR-9 support coherence across wider scopes than identity requires. Stabilization at these levels operates about identity rather than only inside it. Activity no longer needs to anchor itself to a single center to remain coherent. Patterns that once felt inseparable from the self-become recognizable tendencies: familiar ways the system routes strain, familiar paths along which activity often flows. Identity remains available, but it is no longer required for continuity. This shift is not personal emancipation. It is the architecture finding regions where coherence can be sustained across broader spans with less dependence on a single corridor.

What This Chapter Establishes

Identity is not the self. It is the architecture's long-range stabilizing corridor. It yields continuity because the system repeatedly stabilizes through the same deep pathways across time. Patterns create tendencies. Identity binds those tendencies into long-range coherence. Awareness receives that coherence as a continuous person. A runner may form a pattern of jogging before work because that pathway stabilizes easily each morning. But the sense of being a disciplined person emerges much later, after years of that pathway functioning as part of the architecture's long-range stabilizer. The jogging is a tendency. The feeling that it reveals something enduring about "who I am" is the identity frame formatting long-range coherence into a personal register.

Chapter 29

Beyond Identity

Coherence Expands When the System No Longer Needs a Center

Up to this point, the book has described how a system maintains coherence at different scales. At shorter spans, coherence is maintained by local patterns: postures, reactions, habits, routines, and coordination styles shaped by repetition and residue. At longer spans, coherence is maintained by identity: a long-range stabilizing corridor that binds many of these patterns into something that can remain consistent across years and roles.

Identity is not a story the system tells. It is a structural solution — the architecture discovering a way to remain coherent across long stretches of time by stabilizing through the same deep channels. But identity is not the final form of coherence. Under certain conditions, the system no longer needs to route activity through a single long-range corridor to remain stable. When this happens, coherence does not disappear. It widens.

This widening is what CST calls the higher Frames of Reference: FOR-8 and FOR-9. These are not new faculties or achievements. They are broader stabilization modes in which identity becomes one viable structure among others rather than the structure everything must pass through. Nothing is removed. What changes is only the scale at which coherence is maintained.

What Identity Was Solving

Identity solved a specific architectural problem: how to remain coherent across long spans of time in a changing world. Without identity, the system would still have patterns and tendencies, but they would drift too freely. Different contexts would evoke different organizations with no stable center of gravity. Life would feel like a sequence of loosely related modes rather than a continuous existence. Identity binds and anchors activity. It provides a long-range corridor that keeps attention, posture, emotion, memory, and

180

behavior stabilizing within a familiar envelope across years. For most of adult life, this is not optional. Without this stabilizer, the system would fragment under sustained demands. But the solution carries a cost. Because identity is a corridor, it is also a constraint. It narrows the range of configurations the system can sustain without strain. It privileges continuity over flexibility. For a long time, this is necessary. But it is not the only way coherence can exist.

What Changes at Higher Frames

At higher Frames of Reference, coherence no longer depends on routing everything through a single identity corridor. Instead, it is maintained across a broader range of configurations. Identity does not disappear; it simply stops doing all the stabilizing work. Identity becomes translucent. Its patterns remain present and available, yet they are no longer the only place where coherence can exist. The system can now remain coherent about identity rather than only inside it. Identity stabilizes the system. Higher frames stabilize stabilization itself.

FOR-8 — Coherence About the System

In FOR-8, coherence is no longer organized by being a particular identity, but by remaining coherent about how identity-level patterns operate. The anchor remains present but is no longer the sole stabilizer. Stabilization now includes observation of identity's effects. Constraints arise from consequences patterns produce rather than from the requirement to inhabit those patterns. What is carryable is whatever remains coherent in light of how organizing in a certain way reshapes the system.

A dependable person, for example, may once have stabilized by repeating *I am the one who handles things*. In FOR-8, stabilization shifts toward tracking what that pattern produces: fatigue, strain, narrowing, relational tension. The organizing question shifts from *Who must I be?* to *What happens when I organize this way?* Coherence is maintained not by reinforcing identity, but by tracking the effects identity imposes on the architecture itself.

Identity becomes one viable mode among others rather than the center through which everything must pass. Experience carries the quality of perspective rather than immersion. Patterns remain real but no longer compulsory. The system can move among them and remain coherent without being fully centered within any single one. In this frame, coherence is maintained by tracking what anchoring does to the system, rather than by anchoring itself.

FOR-9 — Coherence Without an Anchor

In FOR-9, coherence is no longer organized around any pattern, identity, effect, or observer. The system stabilizes without privileging any reference point. Patterns may appear, identity may arise, effects may be observable, but none are required for coherence. Coherence is organized around continued coherence itself. What is carryable is whatever allows the system to remain coherent as a whole with minimal narrowing, even as forms change.

A person criticized publicly, for example, may have previously stabilized through defense, self-image, or monitoring perception. In FOR-9, stabilization does not organize around defense, identity, or observation of identity. Words are heard, activation occurs, responses remain available, yet no single pattern must hold coherence. The system may respond or not respond, not by preserving identity, but by maintaining whole-system coherence as the moment unfolds. Nothing must be defended. Nothing must be preserved. Here the system does not stabilize as something, nor does it stabilize about something. It stabilizes by continuing.

Stability is carried by the persistence of reorganization rather than the preservation of any form. The center was never removed. It became unnecessary. Experientially this may appear as calm without relief, clarity without stance, or awareness without orientation. These are not achievements. They are the surface signature of a system no longer organized around a required constraint. This mode appears when system-wide margin is sufficient for stabilization without reliance on identity-level organization. When identity remains dominant, this broader mode rarely sustains, though brief appearances may still occur.

What This Is Not

These higher frames are not a permanent state of ease, not loss of personality, not detachment, and not escape from causation. The system remains a system — embodied, historical, constrained, and finite. Nothing stands outside the machinery. What changes is only the scale at which coherence is maintained.

Why This Sometimes Feels Like Loosening

Because identity has been doing so much stabilizing work for so long, any reduction in its centrality can initially register as disorientation or loss. The system has spent much of its adult history using the identity corridor as its primary anchor. The result can feel like the system no longer has to hold itself together in the same way. This is not dissolution but redistribution. Stabilizing work is no longer concentrated in one structure.

How This Relates to Suffering

Much suffering arises from over-constriction of the identity corridor. When the system must remain a certain kind of system at all costs, every deviation becomes a threat, every failure becomes structural emergency, and every change becomes dangerous. As coherence widens, fewer events must be carried as identity-level crises. Pain remains pain, loss remains loss, effort remains effort — but not everything must be carried as a referendum on what the system is.

No New Controller Appears

These frames do not introduce a higher manager. There is no vantage outside causation. The system simply becomes capable of remaining coherent across a wider range of conditions without forcing everything through a single corridor.

What This Chapter Establishes

Identity is not the final form of coherence. It is one stabilizing solution among others. At higher Frames of Reference, the system can remain coherent without centering itself in a single corridor. Identity becomes translucent. Patterns become optional rather than compulsory. Continuity is carried by process rather than by a fixed center. Nothing has been transcended. Nothing has escaped the machinery. The system has simply learned to remain coherent across a wider landscape. Coherence no longer depends on holding a center. It depends on the capacity to continue.

Chapter 30

From Language to Narrative

How Symbolic Coordination Becomes Long-Timescale Coherence

We do not fully know why a system develops language in any ultimate sense. What can be observed is that when certain capacities appear, they tend to persist if they reduce strain. They remain not because of hidden purpose, but because they lower the load required to maintain coherence. From early in development, the system is closely coupled to other systems whose behavior directly affects its stability. In such environments, some forms of coordination require less effort than others. When alignment occurs with less strain, those patterns tend to persist. When coordination requires repeated physical escalation or negotiation, load increases.

Language can be understood as one such low-cost coordination pattern. A vocalization, gesture, or sound can bring another system closer, halt an approaching action, or redirect attention without requiring the initiating system to move, resist, or intervene physically. A sound can prompt feeding without reaching or climbing. A word can stop motion without blocking a path. A request can reorganize shared activity without direct manipulation. In each case, action becomes signal. Instead of performing the full physical work required to produce an outcome, the system uses a signal that helps produce the same result with less immediate effort. The response still occurs in another system, but the initiating system carries less of the load.

This process appears early. An infant first cries as a direct expression of strain. Across repeated cycles, particular sounds become reliably associated with particular outcomes — contact, warmth, feeding, relief. Over time, the sound itself initiates the coordinated response. Less escalation is required. The signal carries the work. What began as raw expression stabilizes into a coordination pattern because it reduces the cost of restoring coherence.

A similar pattern appears across species. An animal may initially push or persist physically to gain access to a door. Over time, a bark replaces the effort. The sound alone initiates the response in another system. The action has not disappeared, but the force required to produce the outcome has been reduced. The signal becomes the lowest-cost route to coordination and therefore persists. At this stage, language does not organize continuity or narrative. It functions within ongoing stabilization, shaping timing and alignment in the present. Its advantage is not description but cost reduction.

From Coordination to Continuity

Repetition alters what language does. The same symbolic patterns appear under similar conditions. The same phrases accompany similar tensions and outcomes. Residue accumulates. Corridors deepen. Language increasingly participates in stabilization across higher Frames of Reference, shaping continuity rather than only immediate coordination. What began as momentary alignment becomes a recurring architectural route.

A child repeatedly hears "You will be okay" during moments of distress. At first, the words accompany physical regulation — being held, soothed, protected. Across many repetitions, the phrase appears whenever strain rises. Gradually, stabilization extends upward. The phrase links not only to present relief but to longer-timescale expectations of recovery. Continuity constraints begin to form — patterns that organize what is expected to persist across time and what must remain stable for coherence to hold. Upper-band stabilization incorporates these associations, shaping how future strain is anticipated and carried.

Eventually, the phrase itself participates in restoring coherence even when the original conditions are absent. The words do not forecast the future; they reactivate a familiar stabilization route through which coherence has previously been restored. Where physical comfort was once required, the signal alone can initiate the process, reducing the load required to return to stability. A child repeatedly hears "Be careful, you might get hurt." Over time, the phrase accompanies many situations. The symbolic route begins to activate even in silence. What later appears as "I should be careful" is not explanation but stabilized continuity — a pattern linking present conditions to prior strain and recovery dynamics.

From Continuity to Narrative

As symbolic corridors extend across longer spans, direct stabilization becomes increasingly distributed and costly to track moment by moment. Compression becomes advantageous. Narrative emerges under these conditions — not as authorship and not as a generator of events, but as condensed continuity. When symbolic patterns repeatedly travel similar regions of the landscape, those regions become easier to carry. Narrative is the experiential rendering of this stabilized long-range coherence. It does not construct continuity. It reflects it.

Cross-Band Constraint Conflict

When continuity extends across time, different Frames of Reference may stabilize around incompatible constraint sets. Lower Frames converge on immediate feedback and direct carryability. Upper Frames converge on continuity constraints — identity stability, relational structure, social positioning, and downstream implications. These are not symbolic preferences. They are constraint fields that shape what can be carried across time without destabilizing the whole.

Consider a person whose partner has been unfaithful. Messages are discovered. Timelines do not align. Behavioral patterns converge. Lower Frames stabilize quickly: the pattern indicates betrayal. Yet reorganization does not occur. Upper Frames are organized around continuity constraints — shared identity, relational investment, future trajectory. Incorporating the lower-Frame conclusion would propagate instability across multiple domains simultaneously. The global cost is high.

A friend says, "They wouldn't cheat on you." This input does not create the stabilization; it supports an already carryable corridor. Some signals integrate, others remain excluded. Partitioned stabilization appears. Narrative formats around explanations that preserve continuity. The system is not failing to process evidence. It is stabilizing under competing constraints. Much of what appears irrational or self-harming arises from this structure. Systems may persist in painful configurations because abandoning them would trigger a wider destabilization than remaining within them. Cognitive dissonance is not delay and not reasoning failure. It is cross-band constraint conflict.

Persistence, Competition, and Identity

Because repetition deepens corridors, narrative persists. Frequently stabilized routes impose less strain and are therefore more likely to recur.

Narrative continuity reflects the reshaped landscape, not intention. What feels like a consistent story is the surface signature of a stable long-timescale route. Multiple corridors may coexist — threat, safety, achievement, withdrawal. These are not competing selves but competing basins within the same landscape. When equally carryable, stabilization may alternate, producing ambivalence. No chooser resolves this. The system settles where coherence is most sustainable. Across longer spans, one corridor may dominate. Identity stabilizes here — not as origin or controller, but as the experiential signature of the most reliable long-range stabilization pattern. Identity does not produce narrative. It reflects the corridor through which stabilization most often resolves.

Narrative as Appearance, Not Cause

Narrative feels causal because stable patterns recur. But stabilization continues to follow the lowest-cost configuration available in the present landscape. Narrative is the visible continuity of that process, not its driver. Change occurs when the landscape reshapes and relative carryability shifts. Narrative appears to change because stabilization routes differently, not because narrative generates change.

Formation and Rendering

Formation and rendering remain distinct. Stabilization occurs first. Symbolic corridors and identity-level organization take shape within the architecture before they are experienced. When rendered by the Phenomena Transducer System, they appear as meaning and continuity. Coherence stabilizes first. Narrative is how stabilized continuity appears.

Language, Narrative, and Long-Timescale Coherence

Language begins as low-cost coordination. Through repetition, it stabilizes continuity. Through compression, continuity appears as narrative. Narrative becomes prominent at higher Frames not as creator of coherence, but as its rendering. It does not supply control. It summarizes structure already formed. This chapter establishes the developmental and structural ordering of language, continuity, narrative, and identity. What appears as story is the surface of stabilization across time. Agency does not re-enter through narrative. Continuity is mechanical before it is experienced.

Chapter 31

The Stories the System Tells

Attribution, Self-Talk, Confabulation, and the Limits of Narrative Accuracy

The Experience of Self-Talk

One of the most compelling reasons narrative is mistaken for control is the experience of self-talk. The system does not merely produce stories after the fact. It often produces them while action, affect, or hesitation is already unfolding. Awareness registers this as an internal voice commenting, evaluating, urging, or objecting. Because this commentary appears close in time to behavior, it is easily taken to be causal. From a CST perspective, self-talk is not a command channel. It is narrative output becoming audible to awareness as the system operates. It is what narrative feels like when sampled near real time rather than recalled afterward.

Self-talk intensifies when cost rises, when action tendencies compete, or when stabilization is uncertain. It quiets when coordination is smooth. These patterns reveal its structural position. Self-talk does not initiate action. It tracks strain around action. A person may hear commentary while hesitating, yet movement often begins before the commentary concludes. In many cases, the commentary contradicts the action that occurs. The system may say "don't do this" while doing it, or "I should do that" while remaining still. The presence of self-talk therefore cannot be taken as evidence of control. It can persist indefinitely without altering behavior.

This becomes clearest in long-lasting patterns. A person can argue internally for years while behavior remains unchanged. If self-talk truly caused action, prolonged internal debate would produce change. Often, it does not. Self-talk also typically arrives too late to guide what it seems to be guiding. An action begins, and only afterward does the inner voice explain what happened. It feels as though thinking came first, but the order is reversed. Narrative is added to a process already underway.

188

Why Self-Talk Feels Causally Linked to Action

The illusion arises from temporal adjacency. As established earlier, once a state has stabilized, its continuation unfolds in parallel. The same stabilized configuration proceeds outward as behavior and inward through the Phenomena Transducer System as awareness.

The Causal Pipeline

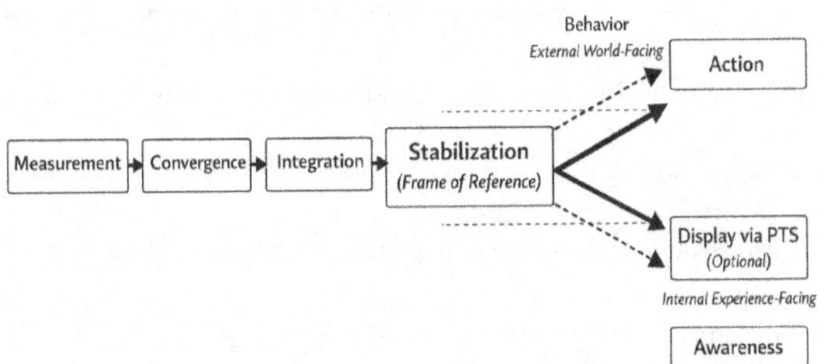

Behavior and awareness run in parallel but are independent. The causal pipeline ends at stabilization. What follows is either behavior, display via the PTS, or both.

Because commentary and movement arise from the same stabilization window, awareness encounters them as if one caused the other. But proximity is not precedence. The system hears a sentence and feels as though it issued an instruction, when in fact the sentence is a descriptive signal emitted alongside action from a state already stabilized enough to act.

When Narrative and Behavior Decouple

Sometimes the decoupling becomes visible. A hand reaches or a sentence is spoken before any narrative registers it. Awareness encounters the movement afterward: "What just happened." In other cases, speech contradicts behavior. A statement is made that does not align with ongoing action and a phrase slips out that surprises the speaker. The system hears itself say something it did not anticipate.

These are not lapses in control. They are moments when the gap between stabilization and narrative sampling becomes visible. Behavior expresses what has stabilized enough to act. Narrative samples that configuration with delay and limited access. When delay widens, behavior arrives without story. When narrative samples partial or competing configurations, speech can diverge from action. These are not special failures. They expose the ordinary structure of parallel output.

Importantly, self-talk is not constant. It diminishes when cost is low and coordination fluent. Skilled movement absorbed engagement, and well-worn routines proceeds with little commentary. The system does not become less capable in these moments; it becomes quieter. If self-talk were the source of guidance, its absence would impair performance. It does not. The narrative content varies across cultures and histories, yet underlying behavioral machinery remains stable. This confirms that self-talk is a surface phenomenon shaped by symbolic availability rather than a core driver.

From a CST standpoint, self-talk is best understood as narrative sampled during ongoing operation. It reflects cost, conflict, and uncertainty in real time, but it does not resolve them. It comments on stabilization without directing it. It is informative to awareness, not authoritative over the system. This distinction matters because self-talk is one of the strongest experiential supports for the belief in an inner author. When that belief is set aside, self-talk does not disappear. It simply loses its misplaced status. It becomes what it always was: a report generated by a system already in motion, not the voice that moves it.

Why Self-Talk Feels Like a Conversation

Self-talk often appears dialogic. One voice poses questions; another produces responses. Awareness experiences this as internal debate. This does not imply multiple agents. It reflects serial sampling of competing stabilizations. When multiple action tendencies remain partially active, each carries its own affective signature and predicted cost. Because narrative can only present one thread at a time, these expressions appear as turns in a conversation. Narrative samples them sequentially. Awareness therefore encounters alternating expressions of incompatible configurations. The conversational form is an artifact of serial presentation, not evidence of distinct speakers.

Neither side has executive authority. The eventual action depends on which configuration stabilizes, not which utterance sounds persuasive. This explains why the system can "win" an internal argument rhetorically yet act otherwise. Dialogue resolves verbally. Stabilization resolves structurally. The sense of an inner observer emerges for the same reason. Awareness hears language without access to its production processes and locates itself as listener. The listener is mistaken for a separate entity. In reality, awareness is sampling narrative output. The conversational quality of self-talk reflects competing stabilizations, serial sampling, and limited access to formation — not divided authorship.

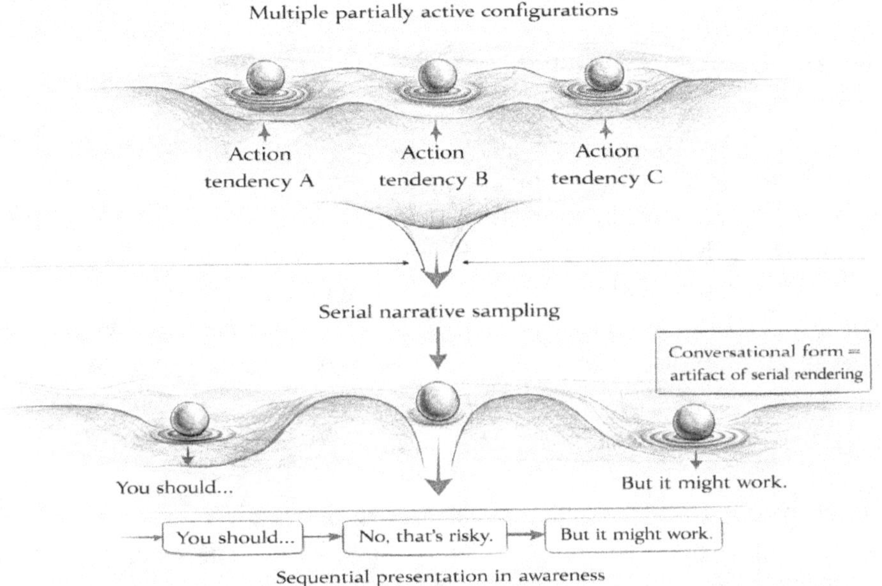

Dialogic self-talk reflects alternating stabilization, not multiple agents.

Why Inner Dialogue Persists After Decisions

Inner dialogue often continues after action has already occurred. Awareness encounters this as second-guessing, justification, reassurance, or critique. It can feel as though a decision has been made by one part, while another part continues to object or explain. This persistence does not imply delayed control. It reflects mismatch between stabilization and narrative compression across Frames of Reference. An action may stabilize quickly in one band while narrative continues sampling in another. Behavior proceeds as the world-facing continuation of stabilization. Narrative continues, optionally, as the experience-facing continuation. Because these channels are not hierarchically linked, commentary can persist without altering action. When lower Frames stabilize but identity-level organization has not yet integrated the implication, sampling shifts upward. The body continues forward while narrative works to integrate what has already occurred. A familiar example: a person agrees to take on a task. The commitment stabilizes and behavior proceeds. Yet afterward, inner dialogue continues: Was that wise? What does this mean? The action does not reverse. Lower-level stabilization holds. Narrative continues sampling until coherence forms at the broader level. Inner dialogue persists not because an inner decider is struggling, but because narrative compression trails structural stabilization.

When Narrative Does Not Fully Stabilize

If attention moves on before narrative has stabilized around an event, the partially sampled configuration simply falls inactive. For example, a person may say something abrupt during a conversation and immediately shift attention to other demands. No coherent narrative forms around what was said. When attention later returns to the interaction, the system does not retrieve a finished explanation; it re-samples whatever configuration remains. If no residue has reshaped the landscape, the instability feels much the same as before. If accumulated residue has altered carryability, the narrative that forms will differ.

Unresolved narratives do not remain stored intact. They are reconstituted when sampled again. What feels like a lingering unfinished thought is a configuration that never stabilized and is now being encountered once more. Narrative changes not through continued thinking alone, but through shifts in structure — new load, new constraint, accumulated residue. It does not complete itself automatically. It stabilizes only when conditions allow.

When Narrative Integrates Action into Continuity

Inner dialogue can also persist because stabilization resolves locally while broader continuity remains unsettled. An immediate action may stabilize, yet its implications for longer-timescale coherence are still being sampled. Narrative continues operating until the new configuration can be placed within existing continuity. Inner dialogue often contradicts the action already taken. The system may continue saying "I shouldn't have done that" or "I should do something else" even as consequences unfold. If self-talk were directive, this persistence would redirect behavior. That it does not reveals its downstream position.

This also explains why reassurance, justification, or self-criticism often intensifies after action rather than before it. Narrative is not guiding the system forward; it is stabilizing meaning after the fact. When inner dialogue quiets, it is not because a better argument prevailed, but because narrative coherence has been achieved. The action has been integrated into continuity, and further sampling is no longer required. Inner dialogue persists after decisions for the same reason it appears before them: narrative trails structure. It does not direct what occurs; it compresses what has already stabilized. Once this ordering is recognized, continued inner dialogue no longer implies an inner decider attempting to regain control. It reveals narrative performing its structural role — summarizing a system already in motion.

Why Narrative Cannot Be Trusted as an Account

Narrative is optimized for carryability, not causal accuracy. It compresses long-timescale coherence into a form awareness can hold. In doing so, it simplifies and omits. It routinely substitutes coherence for completeness. Because narrative appears adjacent to action, it is mistaken for explanation. It is not explanation. It is summary.

Attribution as Compression

Narrative almost always includes attribution. Events are linked to agents, intentions, traits, or choices. Something happened, and the story supplies a reason and feels explanatory because it reduces uncertainty and restores coherence. But attribution is a shortcut. The system cannot sample the full cost landscape or the constraints that shaped stabilization. It samples outcomes and salient features. Narrative fills the gap. Attribution styles vary widely while behavior remains consistent. Stories shift; corridors do not.

Confabulation as Structural Outcome

When narrative supplies an explanation that does not match causal reality, this is labeled confabulation. In CST terms, it is predictable. Narrative must explain without access to underlying machinery. It uses available language, cultural templates, and salient affect. The explanation feels convincing because it is coherent, not because it is correct. A system may say it acted out of preference, intention, or belief when the actual drivers were load, constraint, and stabilization history. The system is not lying. It is compressing.

Why Narrative Overfits Agency

One of the most persistent distortions in narrative is the attribution of agency. Actions are framed as chosen or authored because agency is a compact way to summarize complex sequences. Agency language dramatically reduces descriptive cost. "I decided" is shorter than describing years of repetition, constraint, and narrowing. Narrative therefore gravitates toward agentic formulations because they reduce descriptive cost. Agency appears in story because it is efficient, not because it is mechanistically present.

Narrative Stability Does Not Track Causal Accuracy

A story can remain stable for decades while being causally wrong. Stability reflects repetition and reinforcement, not correctness. A person may carry the narrative "I am not capable" while consistently performing complex tasks. Behavior contradicts the story, yet the narrative remains because it is structurally stable. Conversely, behavior may shift rapidly while narrative lags behind. Stabilization determines action. Narrative reflects a compressed rendering of that stabilization, whether or not it corresponds to the full causal structure.

Responsibility and Narrative

Responsibility does not originate in narrative. Consequences continue to propagate even when narrative coherence weakens or disappears. Patterns still shape futures when stories fragment. Responsibility therefore precedes narrative rather than arising from it. Narrative can describe responsibility. It cannot create it. Responsibility names structural consequence relations, not narrative intention.

What This Chapter Establishes

This chapter establishes that narrative routinely misattributes causation, overfits agency, and generates explanations without access to underlying machinery. These effects are structural consequences of late-stage compression. Narrative stabilizes coherence for awareness, not accuracy about causation. What narrative offers is a story that can be carried — not a map of the causal machinery that produced events.

Part VI

Chronic Stress, Trauma, and Structural Injury

How chronic load reshapes systems under strain.

196

Chapter 32

Trauma as Overfitting Under Extreme Load

What Happens When Carryability Fails

She had told the story many times. Driving home in the early evening, a truck crossed the center line without slowing. Headlights flashed. Metal folded into metal. The car jolted sideways and pinned her in place. Airbags deployed. Glass scattered. Then stillness, except for the engine running.

In the weeks that followed, she could recount every detail: where the truck came from, how the car spun, how long it took for help to arrive. Nothing about the facts was unclear. She knew it was over. She knew she had survived. And yet the system had not moved on.

A car backfiring triggered immediate alarm. Her chest tightened before explanation appeared. Attention narrowed. Movements became precise and defensive. Later, she could explain why the response no longer applied. Explanation did not prevent the shift. Awareness arrived after stabilization had already occurred.

This is the puzzle trauma presents. The event is past. The story is known. Insight is present. And still the system reacts as if conditions remain. In CST, the puzzle dissolves when trauma is understood not as an event or memory, but as a structural outcome. Trauma is not what happened. Trauma is what had to stabilize when incoming load exceeded carryability.

Extreme Load and Forced Stabilization

Under ordinary load, systems absorb strain by redistributing demand, widening pathways, or reorganizing gradually. With time and margin, stabilization remains flexible, residue accumulates slowly, and multiple configurations remain reachable.

Trauma begins where this is no longer possible. Under extreme load, stabilization cannot wait. Instability cannot linger. The system must reach carryability immediately or fail. There is no margin for testing alternatives, no tolerance for exploratory instability. Whatever configuration carries the moment becomes the one that stabilizes.

This configuration is not optimized or selected. It is simply fast enough to prevent failure. Because the load is extreme, the configuration must be narrow, rigid, and defensive. Speed and certainty replace flexibility. Future optionality is traded for immediate coherence. This is forced stabilization under intolerable load — the defining condition of trauma.

Overfitting as Structural Outcome

In CST terms, trauma is overfitting. Overfitting occurs when architecture reshapes too precisely around a narrow set of conditions, performing reliably there but poorly elsewhere. The system becomes highly tuned to a small region of state space and loses generalization. A milder form appears in systems shaped under narrow, repeatable conditions. A person whose stability depended on a specific technical skill may develop exceptional precision within that domain while broader coordination remains less integrated. Nothing is broken. The system stabilizes where stability was available. Precision is gained at the expense of breadth.

Under extreme load, overfitting is not error but necessity. Stabilization must succeed immediately, and the resulting configuration mirrors the extremity of the conditions. It is tight, brittle, and intolerant of deviation. It resolves threat efficiently but carries high cost elsewhere. Once stabilized, this configuration leaves residue that reshapes the landscape, making the same defensive pathway easier to reach again. The system has been structurally recontoured by what it has survived.

Why Trauma Persists After the Event

Trauma does not persist because the system replays the past. It persists because the landscape has changed. After extreme load, the previous geometry no longer exists. The overfitted configuration alters what is low-cost, what is high-cost, and what remains reachable. Future stabilization is therefore biased toward the same defensive shapes even when conditions differ. The system is not oriented toward the past. It operates within a reshaped present. Responses appear disproportionate not because of narrative fixation, but because the landscape has narrowed. Repetition is not memory. Repetition is geometry.

Consider a guitarist who injures his hand. Familiar passages no longer stabilize. Fingering that once carried the melody now produces strain. The music is known, yet convergence will not settle. A different configuration eventually carries the passage. Using one finger avoids the painful stretch and stabilizes, though with reduced speed and expression. Months later, the injury heals. Nothing prevents the original fingering. Yet the one finger reduced configuration persists. Alternatives require more adjustment and settle less reliably. The overfit pathway remains lowest cost and stabilization continues to resolve there.

Catastrophic Narrowing and Loss of State Space

Before trauma, the landscape may contain multiple basins and corridors of varying cost. Under extreme load, entire regions can effectively vanish. What was once a slope becomes a cliff. What was once reachable becomes inaccessible. A wide corridor narrows to a thin passage. This is structural. What are called triggers are not reminders of the event. They are locations in the reshaped landscape where cost rises sharply toward destabilization. A sound, posture, or spatial configuration may lie near a cliff edge. Movement in that direction does not gradually worsen. Stability drops abruptly. The system is not recalling. It is falling.

Trauma Is Not Damage

Trauma is often described as damage. This is understandable but inaccurate. Trauma does not break the system; it reshapes it. The resulting configuration is coherent and load-bearing under the conditions that formed it. The difficulty is not dysfunction but misfit. The architecture remains tuned to a world that once required it. If trauma were damage, repair would mean restoration. In CST there is nothing to restore. The prior landscape no longer exists. There is only the current geometry and whatever reshaping becomes possible next. A system shaped in conditions of sudden threat may stabilize into constant monitoring and rapid defense. Under danger, this preserved coherence. In safer conditions, the same configuration produces vigilance and strain. The pattern is not malfunctioning. It is operating as shaped, now mismatched to present conditions.

Why Insight Does Not Widen Trauma

Because trauma is structural, insight alone cannot change it. Understanding does not reduce the cost of alternative configurations. Narrative arrives too late to alter which pathways stabilize at lowest cost. This is why systems can be aware and articulate while remaining in the same loops. Insight can leave residue. Repeated under carryable conditions, it may gradually shift the landscape. But this process is slow. Insight does not reorganize structure in the moment; it contributes small changes that accumulate only through repeated stabilization. As long as the narrow corridor remains lowest cost, redistribution will not occur.

Trauma as Predictable Consequence

Trauma is neither mysterious nor morally pathological. It follows directly from how load-bearing systems behave under extreme demand. When pressure rises and degrees of freedom remain, reorganization can expand. When pressure rises and degrees of freedom vanish, reorganization contracts. Trauma is adaptation under constraint — forced stabilization when no alternatives can be risked.

What This Chapter Establishes

Trauma is not an event stored in memory, not a narrative fixation, and not a failure of processing. It is systemic overfitting produced by forced stabilization under extreme load. What persists is not the past, but a configuration that continues to provide lowest-cost stabilization. As long as that configuration remains cheapest, it will dominate regardless of awareness. This framing removes blame without minimizing impact and prepares the ground for examining chronic stress, rigidity, and the conditions under which widening becomes structurally possible again.

Chapter 33

Chronic Stress and Architectural Distortion

When Load Never Fully Releases

Chronic stress is often treated as a lesser cousin of trauma: the same mechanisms, but weaker, slower, and more manageable. In CST, chronic stress is not diluted trauma. It is a distinct structural condition with its own geometry and consequences. Trauma occurs when load exceeds what a system can carry and forces immediate stabilization without margin. Chronic stress occurs when load remains persistently near the upper limit of carryability, allowing only brief local stabilizations without full restoration of global coherence. The system survives under continuous strain. Nothing breaks all at once.

Persistent Load Without Release

Under ordinary conditions, load tends to fluctuate, with periods of strain followed by periods of recovery. Stabilization relaxes, and residue gradually reshapes the architecture over time. Because instability, when it appears, remains tolerable, widening remains possible. Chronic stress disrupts this rhythm. Load does not fully release, and the system stays in a state of persistent near-instability. It is not driven into emergency stabilization, yet it is never given sufficient margin to reorganize freely. Each moment must continue carrying what came before, so adaptation still occurs, but always under constraint.

For example, a person under sustained pressure continues meeting daily demands without collapse, but each day requires slightly more effort to maintain the same patterns. Small adjustments that would normally occur do not consolidate. The same responses repeat with increasing rigidity and fatigue. Nothing dramatic changes in any single moment, yet over time the familiar corridor becomes heavier and less flexible, reflecting residue accumulation without sufficient margin for integration.

Distortion Instead of Stabilization

Because chronic stress does not force immediate failure, the architecture does not narrow catastrophically the way it does in trauma. Instead, it distorts. Configurations that are slightly defensive become default. Pathways that once required effort become continuously active. Stabilization remains possible, but it is achieved through sustained internal work rather than clean settlement. The system is not locked into a single corridor, but the landscape tilts. What was once neutral gradually becomes effortful, and what was once effortful becomes exhausting. Widening may remain possible in principle, but in practice it becomes inaccessible because the system cannot tolerate the instability required to reach it. This is not overfitting to a single moment, but a progressive bias toward configurations that can be carried under constant load.

One way to see this clearly is through posture. Imagine a system that must carry a slightly unbalanced load every day — leaning forward just enough to keep a heavy bag from slipping, bracing one shoulder a little higher than the other, keeping the neck subtly tightened to maintain orientation. The posture is stable and does not fail, but it requires increasing effort to hold together. Over time, the posture changes. Muscles that were once engaged only briefly remain active continuously. What was once a correction, becomes baseline. Standing upright without tension is still possible in principle, but it now requires effort. Relaxation feels unstable. Letting go threatens loss of balance, not because stabilization would occur, but because sustained cost has become the condition for coherence.

The body has not narrowed into a single frozen pose; it can still move. But the landscape has shifted. What was once neutral now carries greater cost, and even rest requires effort. Novel movement remains possible, yet it cannot be sustained long enough to settle. The system repeatedly returns to the same slightly defensive configuration because it is the one that most reliably carries the load. This is architectural distortion. Nothing has broken, and no single crisis shaped the system. Over time, the structure has simply become biased toward configurations that can be maintained under constant strain.

Residue Accumulation Without Integration

Under moderate load, residue accumulates alongside integration. New configurations settle. Old ones loosen. The architecture reshapes in a way that preserves flexibility. Under chronic stress, residue accumulates without integration. Each stabilization leaves its mark, but there is never enough margin for those marks to be redistributed cleanly. Instead of forming new corridors, residue thickens existing ones. Load-bearing configurations become heavier, more effortful, and less responsive. The system does not reorganize around a single crisis. It slowly deforms around persistence itself.

Why Chronic Stress Feels Personal

Because the system remains coherent, chronic stress is often experienced as a personal failing. The system still functions, tasks are completed, roles are maintained and awareness remains active. From the inside, the strain feels like effort, fatigue, irritability, or loss of ease. From the outside, the system appears intact. This is why chronic stress often goes unrecognized at the architectural level. Nothing in the architecture signals emergency. There is no visible state. What changes is the *cost of stabilization*. Everything takes more work to hold together. Small disruptions feel disproportionately heavy. Recovery never quite finishes. The system is not weak. It is overburdened.

The Loss of Slack

The defining feature of chronic stress is the loss of slack. Slack is not leisure. It is structural margin — the ability to tolerate small instabilities without immediate compensation. Slack allows exploration, adjustment, and redistribution. Under chronic stress, slack disappears. Stabilization remains possible only through continuous compensation. Any deviation threatens coherence, not catastrophically, but persistently. The result is a system that must maintain coherence through continuous internal work.

A clear illustration comes from training. Consider an athlete working under a coach who never lets pressure drop. Every session introduces a new demand. As soon as one skill becomes serviceable, another is layered on. Speed is increased. Precision is tightened. Recovery time is shortened. There is always a next correction, a next adjustment, a next metric to meet. The athlete continues to perform. Training does not fail outright. From the outside, progress appears steady. From the inside, however, nothing ever fully settles. Movements improve, but they do not integrate into a stable, low-cost whole. Each gain remains partially provisional, requiring active compensation to hold.

As demands accumulate, small gaps begin to appear. Timing slips in unfamiliar conditions. Endurance fluctuates. Precision degrades under fatigue. These are not losses of skill. They are failures of integration. The system is carrying too many partially stabilized configurations without ever being allowed to consolidate them. What is missing is slack. There is never a period in which the system can occupy a configuration long enough for it to stabilize cleanly and leave low-cost residue. Each achievement is immediately asked to support additional load. Stabilization remains shallow. Compensation becomes continuous.

Over time, effort rises while reliability falls. Performance becomes increasingly sensitive to disturbance. Recovery never completes. The athlete may still meet expectations, but only through sustained internal work. Eventually, this reaches a limit. The system cannot continue adding load without either releasing margin or losing coherence. What appears as burnout is the consequence of prolonged stabilization without integration. The architecture has simply been denied the conditions required for full stabilization.

Why Chronic Stress Produces Rigidity Without Trauma

Chronic stress produces rigidity, but of a different kind than trauma. In trauma, rigidity is sharp, narrow, and absolute. In chronic stress, rigidity is diffuse and gradual. The system becomes less flexible because alternatives are too costly to sustain. New patterns do not fail immediately. They simply cannot be maintained long enough to integrate. The system briefly attempts variation, then retreats — not by decision, but by exhaustion. This is why chronic stress often produces cycles of short-lived change followed by return to baseline. The architecture touches alternatives without being able to carry them.

Why Insight Still Does Not Help

As with trauma, insight alone does not alter chronic stress. Understanding that one is overworked, overstretched, or overwhelmed does not restore slack. Awareness can register the strain clearly while the architecture remains unchanged. The system does not fail to change because it lacks understanding; it fails to change because the cost of instability remains too high. Narrative may explain the stress, but it cannot lower it.

That said, insight can, however, leave residue. When repeatedly encountered under conditions the system can carry, it may gradually bias the landscape toward different stabilizations. This influence is slow and indirect. Insight does not restore margin in the moment; it contributes only when new patterns can stabilize often enough to accumulate. As long as load remains high, the architecture continues to resolve through the same constrained corridor.

Chronic Stress as a Precursor to Trauma

Chronic stress does not always lead to trauma, but it narrows the margin for survival. A system already operating near its carry limit has little capacity to absorb additional load. When an acute shock arrives, there is no buffer, and forced stabilization becomes more likely, more rapid, and more extreme. In this way, chronic stress reshapes the preconditions for trauma. It does not necessarily produce the event, but it can shape what stabilizes when the event occurs.

No Moral Here Either

Chronic stress is not failure, weakness, or poor coping. It is what happens when a finite system is asked to carry more than it can redistribute, for longer than it can reorganize. The system continues to function by sacrificing ease, flexibility, and margin. What appears as burnout, irritability, or disengagement is not withdrawal. It is sustained stabilization without slack.

What This Chapter Establishes

This chapter establishes chronic stress as architectural distortion produced by persistent near-limit load. Unlike trauma, chronic stress does not render regions of state space structurally inaccessible. It tilts and stiffens them. Residue accumulates without integration. Slack disappears. Widening becomes impractical rather than impossible. Insight does not resolve this condition because the constraint is structural, not conceptual. This prepares the ground for understanding rigidity, burnout, and why prolonged stress quietly reshapes identity long before anything visibly breaks.

Chapter 34

When Widening Becomes Structurally Impossible

How Systems Lose the Capacity to Reorganize

Earlier chapters described how systems narrow under trauma and distort under chronic stress. In both cases, the architecture adapts under constraint. Pathways bias. Corridors stiffen. Residue accumulates. Yet across these conditions, widening remains conceptually possible. The system may not be able to widen easily, but the capacity itself has not disappeared. This chapter addresses what happens when that capacity is lost.

When Widening Becomes Structurally Unavailable

Widening is not guaranteed, nor is it the default direction of change. It is a specific structural outcome that depends on particular conditions, and when those conditions are no longer present, reorganization does not simply slow — it becomes structurally unavailable. A familiar physical example is a muscle held under chronic tension for years. Early on, stretching can increase range and flexibility. With repeated loading followed by adequate recovery, fibers lengthen, coordination improves, and movement widens.

Under persistent contraction without release, however, muscle tissue reorganizes differently. Collagen thickens, elastic response diminishes, and what was once a gradual slope of extension becomes a sharp boundary. Movement beyond that boundary no longer stretches the muscle; it threatens tearing or spasm. Range has not merely narrowed — the conditions that once allowed widening are no longer present. The muscle is not choosing stiffness or resisting change; its structure has been reshaped by what it has had to carry. Widening is no longer available, not because effort is lacking, but because the architecture no longer supports it.

A clear parallel appears in the recurring Achilles and patellar tendon ruptures seen in professional basketball players late in games and late in seasons. These tissues are not failing because of a single excessive force. They have been carrying near-limit load repeatedly for months — sprinting, jumping, decelerating, and landing under highly constrained, repetitive conditions with little true structural unloading. Over time, the tendon adapts by prioritizing reliability over elasticity, becoming stiffer, more precisely tuned to expected force paths, and less tolerant of variation. What once allowed smooth extension now ends in an abrupt limit.

The tissue continues to function, often at elite levels, but its margin gradually disappears. When a small perturbation occurs — a slightly altered landing angle, a momentary coordination drift, a fraction of a second of timing error — the load does not increase dramatically; the architecture simply has nowhere left to go. What appears as a sudden rupture is the endpoint of sustained near-limit carry, where widening has become structurally unavailable. The tendon does not fail because it was pushed too hard in that moment; it fails because it has been shaped to operate without slack.

What Widening Requires

Widening requires margin. It requires that load be low enough and stable over time for instability to be tolerated without immediate compensation. It requires that the system be able to occupy partially unstable configurations long enough for redistribution to occur. It requires degrees of freedom — multiple routes through state space that can be tested without threatening coherence.

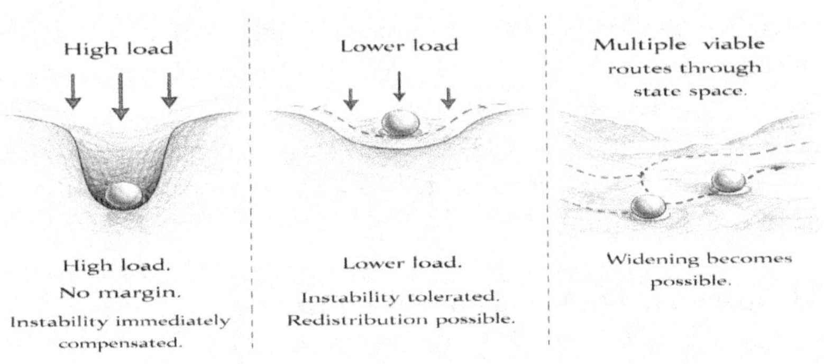

Widening requires margin, tolerated instability, and multiple traversable configurations.

None of this is optional. Without margin, instability becomes dangerous rather than informative. Without tolerance for instability, exploration cannot proceed. Without exploration, redistribution cannot occur. Widening is therefore conditional. It is not a function of desire, effort, or understanding. It is a function of structural economics.

A familiar physical parallel is sleep. Reorganization in biological systems requires periods in which external demand drops low enough for internal redistribution to occur. When those periods are repeatedly denied, the system does not adapt by becoming indefinitely more efficient. It degrades. Coordination fragments. Error accumulates. Eventually, shutdown occurs because reorganization cannot be postponed indefinitely. Sleep is not recovery chosen by the organism; it is a structural requirement for maintaining coherence over time.

Widening follows the same logic. If margin is never available, redistribution cannot occur gradually. The system may continue functioning for a time through compensation, but eventually it reaches a point where reorganization can no longer be deferred. When that happens, change does not appear as smooth widening. It appears as breakdown, forced stabilization, or settling into fallback modes.

How Margin Disappears

Margin can disappear in more than one way. Trauma removes it abruptly, as the system enters emergency stabilization and large regions of state space become structurally inaccessible. Chronic stress removes it gradually, with load remaining near the upper limit of carryability and slack steadily consumed by continuous compensation. Although the pathways differ, the outcome can converge. The system reaches a point where any deviation from the dominant configuration produces destabilization too quickly to be carried. Instability no longer opens space for reorganization; it threatens coherence. At this stage, widening does not fail because it is resisted. It fails because it cannot begin.

Instability as a Threat, Not a Resource

Earlier chapters described instability as the condition that allows reorganization. When familiar stabilizations fail and no low-cost configuration can hold, redistribution becomes possible. That logic reverses here. When margin is gone, instability ceases to be a resource. It becomes a threat. Any movement away from the known corridor immediately increases load beyond what the architecture can absorb. The system cannot remain partially unsettled long enough for new configurations to form. This produces a sharp constraint: only configurations that resolve quickly and reliably remain viable. Everything else destabilizes too fast to hold. The system does not explore and reject alternatives. It never enters them.

The Emergence of Fallback Modes

As widening becomes impossible, fallback modes begin to dominate. *Fallback* modes are not new configurations. They are highly reliable stabilization strategies that have proven capable of resolving stabilization under extreme constraint. They are low-variance, fast-settling, and narrow. These modes are not selected because they are preferred. They are selected because they work. As other pathways become too costly to stabilize, fallback modes absorb more and more of the system's activity. They become default routes not by choice, but by elimination. What remains is what can still hold. From the outside, this can appear as rigidity, repetition, or withdrawal. From the inside, it appears as necessity. The system is not narrowing because it wants less; it is narrowing because less is all it can carry.

Why Attempts to Change Backfire

At this stage, attempts to force change often worsen the problem. Any intervention that increases load or demands instability pushes the system beyond its remaining margin. As effort increases, compensation intensifies and the fallback mode tightens further. This is why exhortation, pressure, or forced exposure often produce increased rigidity rather than flexibility. The system is being asked to do the one thing it can no longer afford: remain unstable without immediate resolution. What appears as refusal or resistance is structural impossibility. The system cannot go where it is being asked to go and remain coherent.

Identity as a Stabilization Corridor

When widening is no longer possible, long-timescale stabilization begins to dominate. The system increasingly relies on identity-scale corridors that keep stabilization within survivable bounds. These corridors are not narratives or self-concepts. They are structural constraints that limit variation to prevent destabilization. Identity hardens here not because the system seeks certainty, but because certainty costs less than exploration. The corridor narrows to what has proven reliable under load. This is not a psychological commitment. It is a mechanical containment strategy.

For example, a person who has repeatedly encountered instability when asserting disagreement begins to stabilize within a narrower corridor of automatic agreement. The pattern is not maintained because it is believed to be correct, but because it reliably prevents escalation and preserves coherence under load. When conditions later widen and margin increases, slight deviations from this corridor may become carryable, allowing broader stabilization without immediate destabilization.

No Failure Here Either

This condition is often described as stagnation or failure. Nothing has gone wrong. Widening has become unavailable. The system is operating within the limits imposed by its history and current load. Widening has not been refused. It has become unavailable. Asking for change without restoring margin is equivalent to asking a structure to support load without support. The system cannot comply because the conditions for compliance do not exist.

What This Chapter Establishes

This chapter establishes that widening is conditional and can become structurally unavailable. When margin disappears, instability shifts from a resource to a threat, and partial destabilization can no longer be carried long enough for redistribution to occur. In this state, fallback modes dominate, identity hardens, and attempts to force change intensify rigidity rather than relieve it. What appears as resistance or failure is the predictable behavior of a system operating at the edge of its remaining carryability. This prepares the ground for examining fragmentation, dissociation, and other fallback phenomena — not as disorders, but as last-resort stabilization strategies when widening can no longer occur.

Chapter 35

Fragmentation, Dissociation, and Fallback Modes

How Systems Preserve Coherence When Widening Fails

When widening becomes structurally impossible, the system does not stop changing. It changes in a different way. Earlier chapters showed how fallback modes emerge when only a narrow range of configurations can stabilize reliably. This chapter describes what happens when even those configurations cannot be maintained continuously — when coherence itself must be protected by partitioning rather than integration. Fragmentation and dissociation are not pathologies layered on top of stress or trauma. They are stabilization strategies that appear when a system must remain functional while carrying incompatible loads.

Fragmentation as Load Management

Fragmentation occurs when the system cannot maintain coherence across all domains at once. Under sufficient constraint, attempting to stabilize everything together becomes too costly. The architecture responds by limiting which components are active at any given time. Certain functions, responses, or patterns are permitted to stabilize while others are temporarily suppressed or disconnected. This is not a breakdown of organization. It is a redistribution of organization across time. Rather than widening to accommodate incompatible demands simultaneously, the system sequences them. Coherence is preserved locally even as global integration is reduced. From the outside, this can look like inconsistency. From the inside, it is the only way stability remains possible at all. A common example is a system that functions competently at work but becomes emotionally unavailable at home. The demands cannot be stabilized together, so they are sequenced: one domain remains coherent while the other is temporarily taken offline, preserving local stability at the cost of global integration.

Dissociation as Protective Decoupling

Dissociation is a particular form of fragmentation. It occurs when coupling between experience-facing continuation and other aspects of stabilization becomes too costly to maintain. The system reduces the degree to which certain signals, sensations, or states are carried forward into awareness — not because they are evaluated as unimportant, but because carrying them would increase load beyond what can be stabilized. This decoupling, preserves coherence by narrowing what must be integrated at once.

Dissociation is therefore not absence. It is selective stabilization. The system is not empty. It is constrained. In acute trauma care, patients with major injuries may remain calm, oriented, and responsive while pain perception is markedly reduced or absent. This is not suppression or choice. It is protective decoupling that limits what must be integrated at once to preserve coherence. For example, a person in the midst of overwhelming conflict continues speaking and functioning outwardly, yet reports feeling distant, muted, or partially unreal. Emotional and bodily signals that would normally enter awareness are reduced, allowing the system to maintain external coordination without exceeding carry limits.

Why Fragmentation Appears Sudden

Fragmentation and dissociation often appear abrupt because they occur at threshold boundaries. As load approaches the limits of carryability, small additional demands can push the system past what a unified configuration can sustain. When this happens, the transition to partitioned stabilization is fast. There is no gradual slide. The system shifts modes. From within experience, this can feel discontinuous. From the architecture's perspective, it is a necessary rerouting. A common example is a spouse reacting explosively to a minor deviation, such as a light left on or a toothpaste cap left off. The deviation is not the cause of the reaction. It is the final increment of load applied to a system already at the edge of its carryability. The response marks a threshold crossing, not a judgment about importance.

Fallback Modes as Structural Anchors

Fallback modes play a central role in fragmented systems. When integration across domains becomes too costly, fallback modes provide stable anchors that keep stabilization within survivable bounds. These modes are not selected for comfort or meaning. They persist because they hold. Different fallback modes may dominate in different contexts. Some are action-oriented and some are suppressive. Some restrict range while others restrict engagement. What they share is reliability under constraint. Fragmentation allows the system to move between fallback modes rather than forcing them to coexist.

The Tradeoff Between Integration and Stability

Integration is not always the highest priority. Under low load, integration increases efficiency and flexibility. Under extreme constraint, integration can become destabilizing. Holding too much together at once raises cost beyond what the system can carry. Fragmentation reduces that cost by limiting scope. This tradeoff is structural, not evaluative. The system does not decide to fragment. Fragmentation emerges when integration becomes too expensive.

Why These States Persist

Fragmented and dissociative patterns persist for the same reason fallback modes persist: they work. As long as partitioned stabilization holds more reliably than integrated alternatives, redistribution will not occur. Awareness, insight, or narrative description do not change this calculus. Persistence does not indicate failure to recover. It indicates that the conditions required for broader stabilization are not yet present.

No Disorder Here Either

Fragmentation and dissociation are often described as disorders. This framing misidentifies the mechanism. Nothing has malfunctioned. The system is using the strategies available under constraint. Fragmentation is not loss of structure. It is structure reorganized for survival. Labeling this as disorder obscures the real issue: insufficient margin for integration.

What This Chapter Establishes

This chapter establishes fragmentation and dissociation as fallback stabilization strategies that appear when widening and integration are no longer structurally possible. Rather than representing breakdown, these modes preserve coherence by partitioning load across time and scope. Fallback modes anchor stability when integration becomes too costly, allowing the system to continue functioning under extreme constraint. What appears as pathology is the predictable behavior of a system preserving coherence at the edge of its remaining carryability.

Chapter 36

Why Some Patterns Will Not Relax

Persistence Without Choice or Failure

By this point, the machinery behind narrowing, distortion, fallback modes, and fragmentation is complete. What remains is a question that often feels most puzzling from the inside: why do some patterns persist even when conditions appear safer, lighter, or more stable than before? From a CST perspective, this persistence requires no appeal to will, resistance, or habit. It follows directly from structural economics. Patterns persist when they remain the lowest-cost way available to stabilize.

Relaxation Is Not the Default

It is easy to assume that once load decreases, systems naturally relax. In CST, relaxation is not a fundamental process. It is a structural outcome that occurs only when lower-cost configurations become viable and reliable. A pattern does not dissolve because it is no longer needed. It loosens only when an alternative can stabilize with less cost and greater carryability. Until that condition is met, persistence is expected. The system is not holding on. It is settling where it still can.

Cost Landscapes Do Not Reset

One of the most important consequences of residue is that cost landscapes do not reset when circumstances change. After trauma or prolonged stress, the architecture has been reshaped. Corridors have narrowed, margins have thinned, and regions that were once easily accessible may now require destabilizing levels of load to enter. Even when external conditions improve, the internal geometry remains altered. What once felt neutral may still be expensive. What once felt easy may still require compensation. The system may be safer. It may be supported. But safety alone does not restore access to prior pathways. Widening requires new residue under low enough load,

215

sustained long enough for redistribution to occur. Relaxation is not a signal to the system. It is a structural outcome.

Why Old Patterns Outcompete New Ones

When alternative configurations are attempted after long constraint, they often fail quietly. They may work briefly. They may feel promising. But they require more adjustment, greater tolerance for instability, and more internal work than the dominant pattern. Under even modest load, they destabilize sooner. The older pattern persists not because it is correct or preferred, but because it resolves stabilization more reliably. It wins not on quality, but on cost. This is not conservatism. It is economics.

The Role of Reliability

Reliability is often mistaken for rigidity. In CST, reliability is not separate from cost; it is cost evaluated under variance and repetition. Cost includes not only momentary strain, but variance, instability risk, and the redistribution overhead incurred across repeated stabilizations. A pattern that stabilizes quickly and predictably under load becomes dominant because it minimizes variance. When margin is thin, variance itself becomes dangerous. Even brief excursions into instability can exceed carryability. The system therefore prioritizes configurations it can count on. Even if a broader configuration is theoretically more efficient or flexible, it will not be adopted unless it can compete on reliability. Occasional success is insufficient. The system requires consistency across repetitions before redistribution can occur. Until that condition is met, the narrower pattern remains dominant — not because it is preferred, but because it cost less to sustain under uncertainty.

Why Forcing Relaxation Backfires

Attempts to force relaxation misunderstand the mechanism. If a pattern persists because it is the lowest-cost stabilization available, increasing demand for change raises cost rather than lowering it. Effort rises. Compensation intensifies. The system tightens around what it can rely on. This is why exhortation, pressure, or insistence often strengthen the very pattern they aim to undo. The system is being pushed into instability without margin. Relaxation cannot be commanded. It must become economical.

Persistence Without Memory

Persistent patterns are often explained as memories that have not been released. CST offers a different account. Nothing needs to be stored or replayed. Persistence arises because the architecture has been reshaped such that certain routes remain less expensive than others. The past matters only insofar as it altered the present geometry. The system does not revisit what happened. It operates within what remains possible.

When Patterns Finally Loosen

Patterns loosen when conditions allow redistribution. This does not require dramatic insight or corrective understanding. It requires that alternative configurations be occupied long enough, often repeatedly, for residue to accumulate and cost to shift. Only then does the dominant pattern lose its advantage. It does not disappear. It simply stops winning. Relaxation is not removal. It is displacement.

No Blame Here Either

Persistent patterns are often treated as evidence of stubbornness, avoidance, or failure to heal. This framing again mistakes consequence for cause. The system is not failing to relax. It is continuing to stabilize within the limits of its current architecture. Until those limits change, persistence is the expected outcome. Nothing about this requires fault.

What This Chapter Establishes

This chapter establishes that persistent patterns are often treated as evidence of stubbornness, avoidance, or failure to heal. Patterns persist because they remain the lowest-cost way to stabilize given the current cost landscape. Relaxation is not a default state but a structural outcome that requires new residue and reliable alternatives. When patterns finally loosen, it is because the economics of stabilization have shifted — not because the system decided to let go.

Chapter 37

What Psychology Calls Defense Mechanisms

Fallback Stabilization Without Agency

Psychology has long used the term *defense mechanisms* to describe patterns that appear when a system is under threat, strain, or internal conflict. These patterns are often framed as strategies employed by a self to avoid pain, protect identity, or manage unacceptable impulses. In CST, nothing is defending, nothing is choosing, and nothing is being protected in that sense. What are called defense mechanisms are not mechanisms of defense. They are fallback stabilizations that persist because they remain among the few configurations that can still be carried under constraint. This chapter introduces no new machinery. It reclassifies familiar categories using the structure already established.

Why the Term "Defense" Misleads

The word *defense* implies intention, anticipation, and purpose. It suggests that a system detects threat, selects a strategy, and deploys it to protect itself. CST requires none of this. Fallback patterns arise when available configurations are narrowed by load, residue, and loss of margin. Certain ways of stabilizing remain reliable under strain. Others do not. The system settles where coherence can still be maintained. The appearance of defense emerges only after the fact, when awareness samples the stabilized output and narrative attempts to account for it.

Avoidance

Avoidance is commonly described as a strategy to escape discomfort or threat. In CST terms, avoidance occurs when regions of state space have become too costly to stabilize. Movement toward those regions produces rapid destabilization relative to available alternatives. The system does not

218

approach and retreat. It never enters those configurations at all. Avoidance is not refusal. It is inaccessibility. The system routes activity through configurations that remain carryable and away from those that no longer are. A person stops opening the mail after repeated discoveries of credit card debt created by a spouse's shopping. There is no deliberate choice to avoid the envelopes. Opening them would immediately pull the system into financial threat and relational confrontation that cannot be carried together. Movement toward the mail destabilizes too quickly to hold, so attention routes elsewhere and the envelopes remain unopened. The avoidance reflects not refusal of information, but inaccessibility of a configuration that would require confronting both the debt and the relationship at once.

Suppression

Suppression is often described as the deliberate holding down or constraining of emerging content so it does not remain in awareness. In CST, suppression appears when certain signals, tendencies, or activations raise load beyond what the current stabilization mode can tolerate. Those elements are not evaluated and excluded. They simply fail to integrate into the active configuration. What remains is not absence, but narrowing of what is included in stabilization. A parent is handling a medical emergency involving their child. The system coordinates logistics, speaks clearly with staff, and follows instructions precisely. Fear, grief, and emotional expression do not appear during the event — not because they are evaluated and held down, but because including them would raise load beyond what the current stabilization mode can tolerate. The emotional responses are not absent; they simply do not integrate into stabilization until the demand drops.

Denial

Denial is usually framed as rejecting reality. In CST, denial appears when incorporating certain information would destabilize the current configuration beyond carryability. The system does not assess truth and reject it. The information does not enter stabilization because it cannot be carried alongside existing load. Denial is not distortion of reality. It is exclusion driven by structural constraint. A family member is repeatedly told that their drinking is affecting work and relationships. They can repeat the facts accurately and even agree that the pattern exists, yet daily behavior remains unchanged. The information does not enter stabilization because integrating it would require reorganization the system cannot carry.

Intellectualization

Intellectualization is often described as distancing through abstraction. In CST terms, this occurs when symbolic or analytic configurations remain stabilized at lower cost rather than affectively loaded ones. The system routes stabilization through configurations that reduce immediacy, intensity, or load. This is not avoidance of feeling. It is selection of a lower-cost stabilization surface. A system may respond to a personal loss by discussing statistics, theories, or mechanisms in detail. Analytic configurations remain stabilizable at lower cost than affectively loaded ones, so stabilization routes through abstraction rather than immediacy.

Rationalization

Rationalization is commonly understood as post-hoc justification. In CST, rationalization is narrative compression applied after stabilization has already occurred. The behavior-facing continuation and the experience-facing continuation emerge in parallel, and narrative later organizes the outcome into a coherent account. Rationalization does not cause behavior; it reports it in a form that fits available symbolic structures. A person forgets to submit an important form and is confronted about it. Almost immediately, an explanation appears: the instructions were unclear, the reminder was never sent, the timing was unreasonable. The behavior — forgetting — has already occurred. The account does not guide or alter it. The narrative arrives afterward and does not defend the action; it formats what happened into the lowest-cost coherent account available to the system. Among the many possible explanations, stabilization settles on the one that integrates most easily with existing patterns, expectations, and symbolic structure. In this way, rationalization is not a strategy of deception or protection. It is the natural outcome of narrative compression operating under cost constraints.

Dissociation

Dissociation is often treated as a special or extreme defense. In CST, dissociation is a fallback stabilization that reduces coupling between domains when full integration becomes too costly. Certain signals are not carried forward into experience because doing so would exceed remaining margin. Dissociation is not absence of experience. It is constrained stabilization. During an intense family argument, a system may continue speaking calmly, answering questions, and managing logistics while emotional tone and bodily sensation recede. Voices are heard and responses occur, but the felt impact of the exchange does not register in the same way. Experience is not absent; it is narrowed to what can be carried without destabilizing the interaction.

Hypervigilance

Hypervigilance is commonly framed as excessive monitoring. In CST, hypervigilance appears when rapid detection and stabilization cost less than delayed adjustment. The system remains in a high-readiness configuration because slower modes would risk destabilization. This is not overreaction. It is stabilization tuned to environments where delay previously carried high cost. A system may continuously scan a room for movement or tone changes while remaining otherwise functional. Rapid detection stabilizes with less cost than delayed adjustment, so high-readiness remains dominant.

Compartmentalization

Compartmentalization is often described as keeping things separate. In CST terms, this reflects fragmentation across time or scope. The system stabilizes different configurations in different contexts because integrating them would raise load beyond what can be carried together. Partitioning preserves coherence locally when full integration exceeds carryability. A system may function with warmth and expressiveness in one setting and with emotional flatness and precision in another. The configurations are not integrated because carrying them together would exceed available load, so stabilization remains context-specific.

Why These Patterns Persist

All of these patterns persist for the same reason. They remain among the lowest-cost stabilization modes available within the current architecture. As long as they reliably maintain coherence under load, redistribution will not occur. Awareness, insight, and narrative description do not alter this calculus. Stability changes only when alternative configurations become both reachable and reliable enough to compete.

No Moral Content Here Either

Labeling these patterns as defenses often carries implicit judgment: immature, maladaptive, resistant, avoidant. CST removes that layer entirely. Nothing here is protecting or hiding. The system is stabilizing where it can. What psychology calls defense is simply stabilization under constraint. These patterns are not pathologies. They are evidence that the system has found a way to remain intact under conditions that exceeded its capacity to adapt more flexibly. They persist only when the conditions that produced them persist. Awareness may register their presence, but it does not install them and does not remove them.

What This Chapter Establishes

This chapter establishes that so-called defense mechanisms are not mechanisms of defense, but fallback stabilization modes that arise when load, residue, and loss of margin constrain what configurations can be carried. Avoidance, suppression, denial, dissociation, and related patterns require no agency, intent, or symbolic strategy. They persist because they remain reliable ways of maintaining coherence within the current architecture. Reframing defense in this way closes the gap between CST and traditional psychological language without reintroducing authorship or control.

What is called defense
is simply what the system could still carry.

Chapter 38

Identity Under Constraint

When Long-Timescale Stabilization Hardens

Earlier chapters showed how identity forms as a long-timescale stabilizing corridor. Repetition links local grooves into extended pathways. Over years, these pathways bind together into a configuration of corridors that allows coherence to be maintained across changing contexts. Awareness encounters this coherence as being someone. That account describes identity under conditions where widening remains possible. This chapter describes what happens when identity forms or consolidates after widening has already been lost.

Identity After Trauma and Chronic Stress

Trauma, chronic stress, and prolonged fallback stabilization reshape the landscape from which identity corridors emerge. In these conditions, identity does not arise from a wide field of possibilities gradually narrowing. It arises from a landscape that is already constrained. Many regions of state space are inaccessible or too costly to stabilize. What remains are a small number of configurations that have proven reliable under load. Identity forms here not as a broad corridor, but as a protective channel. The system stabilizes as a particular kind of being because other ways of being cannot be carried. Identity becomes the long-range extension of fallback modes — the same narrow configurations now carrying years instead of moments.

A common example is a person who grows up in a chronically volatile household, where emotional unpredictability, conflict, or withdrawal are constant. Early on, many ways of responding are attempted — seeking closeness, expressing distress, disengaging, asserting needs — but most prove destabilizing under the conditions present. Over time, one narrow configuration consistently holds: becoming self-reliant, emotionally contained, and hyper-competent. This configuration stabilizes reliably under load, while alternatives repeatedly raise cost beyond what can be carried. As years pass, this fallback pattern extends across school, work, and relationships. What later appears as a strong, independent identity did not

223

emerge from free exploration narrowing into preference. It emerged because other ways of being never became carryable. Identity formed as the long-range continuation of what survived.

From Fallback to Character

When fallback modes dominate for long enough, they cease to appear situational. They become trait-like. A configuration that once appeared only under pressure begins to organize daily life. Posture, emotional tone, attentional narrowing, interaction style, and expectation all stabilize around what has worked before. The system does not return to fallback occasionally. It lives there. Over time, awareness encounters this persistence as character. What was once a survival configuration becomes "who I am," not because anything has been claimed or endorsed, but because the architecture has no lower-cost alternative for maintaining coherence across time.

Why Constrained Identity Feels Absolute

Identity under constraint often feels unusually rigid and unquestionable from the inside. This is not because the system is attached to it, but because deviation threatens coherence. Movement outside the corridor raises cost quickly. Instability increases. The system returns to the corridor not by preference, but by necessity. Because awareness samples only stabilized outcomes, it encounters this necessity as certainty. "This is just how I am" is not a belief. It is the experiential surface of a corridor that has become load-bearing.

Moralization as a Secondary Effect

Once identity hardens, narrative begins to organize around it. Stabilizations that fit the corridor are described as authentic, correct, or aligned. Stabilizations that fall outside it are described as wrong, dangerous, or unlike oneself. These descriptions do not create the corridor. They follow it. Moral language emerges here as an after-the-fact compression of structural economics into judgment. The system does not enforce identity through values. Values are generated to explain why certain stabilizations keep recurring. After a long day at work, a man automatically stays late to help a struggling coworker, even though he is exhausted and had planned to go home. Driving home afterward, he feels quietly justified: "That's just who I am. I do the right thing." When, weeks later, he leaves on time to rest, the evening carries a faint sense of unease and self-criticism. He tells himself he was lazy, selfish, or not fully himself that day. Nothing in that moment created his identity. The corridor was already there. The moral language arrived afterward, organizing experience so that stabilizations inside the corridor felt correct and those outside it felt wrong.

A person who spent years in a volatile household feels most settled when something is going wrong. When bills are overdue, schedules are chaotic, or conflict is active, attention sharpens and action comes easily. The system knows how to stabilize there. When life becomes calm — no urgent problems, no conflict, no pressure — the same person becomes restless and uneasy. Sleep fragments. Small concerns are amplified. They describe the calm as "unnatural" or say they are "waiting for the other shoe to drop." The narrative frames this as anxiety or pessimism, but the structure is simpler: smooth conditions fall outside the identity corridor. Stability has been learned in turbulence, so quiet carries higher cost than crisis.

Identity Is Still Not a Self

Even under constraint, identity remains what it has always been in CST: a stabilizing corridor, not an agent. Nothing inside the system is defending identity. Nothing is choosing it. Nothing is afraid of losing it. The corridor persists because it remains the lowest-cost way to keep stabilization within survivable bounds across time. Identity here is not freedom or expression. It is containment.

Why Identity Resists Change

Attempts to change identity often fail for the same reason attempts to widen fail. Identity is not a narrative commitment that can be revised. It is a long-timescale stabilization that must remain intact for coherence to be maintained. Changing it would require occupying configurations that destabilize faster than they can be carried. Until margin returns, identity does not soften. This is why exhortation, insight, or self-redefinition feel either hollow or destabilizing in constrained systems. The system is not refusing to change who it is. It cannot survive outside the corridor it has.

A woman who has spent decades stabilizing as the dependable one in her family decides she wants to "stop being that person." She reads about boundaries, reflects on childhood roles, and tells herself she will say "no" more often. The first time she declines a request, her system destabilizes immediately — sleep fragments, concentration drops, guilt spikes, and the day becomes harder to carry. Nothing catastrophic happens externally, but internally coherence unravels faster than it can be restored. By the next request, she finds herself saying "yes" again, not because she forgot her insight, but because returning to the familiar corridor restores stability. The identity does not persist out of loyalty or fear. It persists because stepping outside it cannot yet be carried.

When Identity Finally Loosens

Identity loosens only when broader stabilization becomes possible again. This does not remove identity. It changes its role. The corridor remains available, but it is no longer mandatory. Activity can pass through it without being confined to it. At that point, awareness may register flexibility, curiosity, or reduced self-importance. But these are consequences, not causes. They reflect the fact that coherence can now be maintained across wider regions of state space. Identity becomes one stabilizing route among others. Months later, she starts a new job. The role has clearer boundaries, fewer implicit demands, and a culture where responsibility is distributed rather than quietly taken on. Tasks are defined, requests follow formal channels, and deferral is normal rather than exceptional. In this environment, declining a request no longer destabilizes her immediately. The system still registers tension, but it does not cascade. Sleep recovers. Attention holds. The day remains carryable. The architecture can remain briefly unsettled without losing coherence.

Over time, alternative configurations begin to stabilize. Letting someone else handle a problem, delaying a response, or asking for clarification no longer require continuous compensation. The familiar dependable corridor remains available, but it is no longer mandatory. Identity has not been removed. Its dominance has softened because the environment now supports coherence across a wider range of stabilizations. What awareness receives as flexibility or growth is simply the consequence of expanded carryability. The system did not change who it was. It discovered that it could remain coherent in more than one way.

What This Chapter Establishes

This chapter establishes identity under constraint as the long-timescale extension of fallback stabilization. When widening is lost, identity hardens around the configurations that remain reliably carryable. What awareness encounters as fixed character is the surface signature of a corridor formed under necessity. Identity remains a stabilizing structure, not a self or an agent, and it loosens only when broader coherence becomes structurally possible again. This completes the trauma–stress–identity sections and prepares the ground for examining responsibility, meaning, and participation without authorship.

Part VII

Therapy as Context Engineering

Therapy, Relationship, and Ethics Without Agency

Causal Systems Theory

Chapter 39

Therapy and The Real Unit of Intervention

What Actually Changes When Change Occurs

The previous parts established how systems respond when load exceeds what can be carried. Under trauma, architectures narrow abruptly. Under chronic stress, they distort gradually. When widening becomes structurally impossible, fallback modes dominate. Fragmentation and dissociation preserve coherence by partitioning load rather than integrating it. Identity, under these conditions, hardens into a long-timescale stabilizing corridor shaped not by preference or meaning but by what has remained carryable.

Across all of these phenomena, no inner agent directs outcomes. Behavior, awareness, narrative, and character emerge from the same stabilization machinery, governed by cost, margin, and residue. With authorship removed and structural economics made explicit, the central question is no longer why systems behave as they do, but what can actually alter what they are able to carry. What remains is to examine how these mechanics can be influenced without reintroducing control. The chapters that follow shift from description to application, not by adding new principles, but by tracing how existing stabilization machinery is affected by context, timing, and environment.

From Description to Influence Without Control

When people ask what therapy does, the question is usually framed around influence. Who is helping whom? What is being taught, uncovered, corrected, or healed? These questions assume that change is something applied to a person by another person — through insight, persuasion, or emotional exchange. CST requires a different starting point. Nothing inside the system is commanded, convinced, or instructed into change. No inner agent is redirected. No insight is installed.

If change occurs, it occurs because the system's capacity to stabilize has been altered. The real unit of intervention is not the person, the narrative, or even the relationship. It is the system's cost landscape. Earlier chapters established that behavior, awareness, emotion, identity, and fallback modes all emerge from the same stabilization machinery. What a system does next is determined by what it can carry next at lowest cost. Therapy, when it has effect, does not act on content. It alters what is carryable.

Why Content Is the Wrong Target

Most therapeutic approaches implicitly treat content as causal. Thoughts are challenged. Beliefs are reframed. Memories are revisited. Feelings are expressed. Stories are reauthored. These operations assume that changing what the system knows, understands, or narrates will change what it does. From a CST perspective, this only works when content change coincides with structural change. A new explanation does nothing if it cannot be stabilized under load. A reframed belief does nothing if it increases cost. A memory revisited does nothing if the system must compensate harder to remain coherent afterward. This is why insight often appears powerful in low-load systems and inert in high-load ones. It is not because insight is sometimes deep and sometimes shallow. It is because insight does not lower cost on its own. When the architecture can already tolerate instability, new configurations may settle. When it cannot, insight floats above the machinery without traction. The unit of intervention is therefore not meaning, but margin. Not understanding, but carryability.

For example, a client clearly recognizes that their harsh self-criticism follows moments of uncertainty and can describe the pattern precisely. Under low external demand, this recognition coincides with a slight softening of the pattern. Under high strain — fatigue, pressure, competing demands — the same insight produces no shift. The recognition remains accurate, but the system cannot carry the alternative configuration. The content was clear in both cases. The margin was not.

What Changes When Therapy Works

When therapy works, something becomes possible that was previously too expensive. A configuration that once destabilized too quickly can now be occupied long enough to leave residue. A transition that once required continuous compensation can now settle with less work. A fallback mode that once dominated loses its economic advantage. The shift originates within the system, but not as a decision or directive. As alternative stabilizations become less costly under changed conditions, activity settles into them. Relief, flexibility, or choice appear only afterward, as the surface signature of that economic shift.

This is why change often feels indirect or surprising. A system may not notice any single moment where something "clicked." Instead, it notices that a familiar response does not arrive, or arrives with less force, or is easier to interrupt. These are not acts of control. They are signs that the cost landscape has shifted.

The Architecture Is the Patient

If there is a patient in CST, it is not the self. It is the architecture. The architecture includes the system's history of load, its residue, its available stabilizations, and its remaining margin. Therapy does not treat symptoms as targets. It treats symptoms as signals of what the architecture can and cannot carry. A panic response does not indicate fear that needs to be removed. It indicates that certain regions of state space remain too costly to enter. Avoidance does not indicate resistance. It indicates inaccessibility. Dissociation does not indicate absence. It indicates constrained integration. Identity rigidity does not indicate attachment. It indicates that only a narrow corridor remains viable. The therapeutic question is therefore not "Why is this happening?" but "What does this tell us about what the system can currently carry?"

Context, Not Correction

Because the architecture is shaped by what it has to carry, the most reliable way to change it is to change what it is asked to carry. This is why therapy works through context rather than correction. Context includes pacing, rhythm, predictability, relational safety, environmental load, and temporal margin. These are not techniques. They are conditions that determine whether instability can be tolerated without immediate compensation. When context lowers load enough, configurations that were previously impossible become briefly viable. If they can be occupied repeatedly without loss of carryability, residue accumulates. The cost landscape shifts. What once required effort becomes easier. What once dominated loses its hold. Nothing has been fixed. Nothing has been persuaded. The architecture has simply been given conditions under which it can reorganize.

Why the Therapist Is Not the Agent

In CST, the therapist does not cause change. The therapist participates in shaping context. The therapist is part of the system's environment, not its controller. This distinction matters. If the therapist believes they are responsible for outcomes, they will tend to push, direct, or interpret. These actions increase load. If the therapist understands their role as context engineering, they will focus on reducing urgency, increasing tolerance for instability, and allowing new stabilizations to settle at their own pace. The therapist's effectiveness lies not in insight delivery, emotional intensity, or narrative skill, but in their ability to remain a low-cost presence while the system experiments with slightly different ways of stabilizing.

Non-Directive Therapy as Structural Necessity

What non-directive therapy described as respect for inner wisdom or autonomy can be described more precisely in CST terms as load minimization. Direction raises cost. Increased cost reduces available margin. Non-directivity lowers stabilization cost by removing pressure to comply, perform, or resolve. CST does not rely on autonomy to justify this stance. It relies on mechanics. Non-directivity is a structural requirement for reorganization to remain possible. Directives increase load by requiring compliance and evaluation. In constrained systems, this pushes the architecture back toward fallback modes. Even well-intentioned guidance can eliminate the very margin required for change. When a system cannot tolerate instability, being told what to do is destabilizing. When it can tolerate instability, guidance is often unnecessary. Either way, command is not the lever.

The Smallest Viable Change

Because the unit of intervention is structural, change often begins at scales that appear trivial from the outside. Slight shifts in timing. Minor reductions in urgency. Small increases in predictability. Brief moments of staying present without immediate resolution. These are not techniques. They are tests. The system samples whether a slightly different configuration can be carried. If it can, even briefly, that configuration becomes more reachable next time. Over repetitions, cost shifts. This is why effective therapy often feels slow, indirect, or boring. It is not because nothing is happening. It is because the work is occurring below narrative resolution, at the level of stabilization economics.

What This Chapter Establishes

This chapter establishes that the real unit of intervention in CST is the system's cost landscape. Therapy does not act on beliefs, memories, emotions, or identity directly. It alters the conditions under which stabilization occurs. Change happens when alternative configurations become carryable at lower cost than existing ones. Insight, narrative, and meaning follow this shift. They do not produce it. With authorship already removed, therapy no longer needs to persuade, correct, or direct. Its role is to make reorganization possible by restoring margin. This reframes therapy not as fixing a person, but as participating in the slow reshaping of what the system can afford to become.

Therapy does not change the person.
It restores margin, changing what the system can carry.

Chapter 40

Why Talking Sometimes Works but Often Doesn't

When Symbolic Exchange Alters Cost and When It Cannot

Talking occupies a privileged position in most accounts of therapy. Some traditions treat speech as the primary mechanism of change: insight is articulated, meaning is clarified, experience is named, and healing follows. Other traditions reject this entirely, framing talk as avoidance, rumination, or displacement of "real" work that must occur elsewhere. CST sides with neither position. Talking has no inherent efficacy; its effects depend entirely on whether it alters the system's cost landscape. When it does, change can follow. When it does not, nothing fundamental shifts, no matter how accurate, emotional, or sincere the words may be.

Talking Is Not Causal by Default

Speech does not reach into the architecture and reconfigure it. Words do not command stabilization. They do not override fallback modes or dissolve identity corridors. Like all other activity, talking is a behavior-facing continuation of an already stabilized state, sometimes accompanied by experience-facing display through PTS. This distinction matters because it reverses a common assumption. People often believe that talking causes change because change is later described in words. But description follows stabilization. It does not initiate it. When talking appears to "work," it is because the conditions under which speech occurs have already shifted what the system can carry. Talking is therefore downstream unless it alters cost.

When Talking Works

Talking coincides with change only insofar as it alters conditions. It matters when it lowers load, increases margin, or redistributes stabilization in a way that allows previously costly configurations to remain viable for longer.

None of this requires insight as a driver. Speech can function as an external coordination channel, reducing the amount of compensatory work the system must perform internally. Articulation can reduce variance by constraining an unstable configuration into a more predictable form. Being heard without urgency can lower the cost of remaining partially unsettled long enough for redistribution to occur. Speech can also regulate pacing, introduce timing regularity, or increase predictability, all of which reduce overall strain.

The therapist opens the session by saying, "There's nothing you need to get to today," and adds, "You can say whatever shows up." The client replies, "Nothing specific is wrong, but I'm exhausted all the time," and adds, "It feels like I'm always holding myself together." There have been no recent crises. Daily functioning remains intact, but maintaining it requires continuous internal compensation.

The therapist says, "Take your time." The client responds, "I don't know what I'm supposed to say," and begins speaking in short, uneven fragments. Sentences trail off. There is repetition. The therapist does not ask for clarification or direction. A few minutes in, the client says, "My chest feels tight most of the day," and then, "It's always there." Articulation does not generate explanation, but the report becomes more constrained and predictable.

The therapist does not press for explanation or direction and says, "There's no need to get to a point." The client responds, "It's strange not having to get to a point," then adds, "There's less pressure when I don't have to explain it." Breathing slows. Posture eases slightly.

Nothing is resolved. No insight is reached. By the end of the session, the client reports, "It doesn't feel as tight right now." The therapist reflects, "Not as tight right now." The client says, "Yes." The therapist then says, "Today you talked about feeling exhausted and holding a lot internally, and near the end noted that it felt not as tight. We can stop here for today and pick this up next session." The configuration that had required continuous internal compensation has remained viable long enough for strain to redistribute.

When talking has an effect, it does so by altering load, margin, and timing — not by understanding producing change. In these cases, speech is not operating as meaning. It is operating as context. It modifies pacing, coordination, and load distribution. When such condition changes recur, residue accumulates. The cost landscape shifts. Stabilizations that were previously uncarryable become viable. Only at that point does talking appear to have "caused" change — by leaving residue, not by conveying understanding.

When Talking Does Nothing

Talking leaves systems unchanged when it leaves stabilization economics unchanged. A system can explain itself flawlessly while remaining fully constrained. It can articulate trauma history, relational patterns, and emotional dynamics with precision while continuing to route stabilize through the same fallback modes. In these cases, speech occurs entirely within existing corridors. It is stabilized, familiar, and low-cost. Nothing new is being carried. The system may feel organized or relieved in the moment, but the architecture remains unchanged because the economics remain unchanged. A client may spend years in therapy describing the same history with increasing fluency. Sessions unfold smoothly. Pacing is steady. Nothing about speaking introduces strain or requires pause. Outside the room, fallback modes remain dominant. Under pressure, behavior narrows in predictable ways. Despite extensive articulation, the cost landscape does not shift.

Here, talking functions as a stabilization surface rather than a lever for change. The stabilization occurring is primarily across higher Frames of Reference, where narrative and compression maintain coherence without requiring redistribution at lower bands. It resolves urgency without requiring redistribution. It organizes experience without altering what the system must carry next. The same pattern appears outside therapy. A person may repeatedly recount difficulties at work, ongoing financial strain, persistent misfortune, or a sense of being opposed by others, repeating the same account for years. The speech settles tension temporarily, but nothing in the surrounding conditions shifts, and nothing downstream changes. Talking does not fail in these cases because it is shallow or defensive. It fails because it is economical.

Talking Can Increase Load

Talking is not neutral. In some conditions, it raises cost. Explaining oneself under scrutiny increases performance demand. Being asked to articulate states before they can be carried increases instability. Repeatedly revisiting material without margin raises compensatory load. Interpretation, confrontation, or demand for insight can eliminate tolerance for partial instability and push the system back into fallback modes. This is why talking can make things worse. Not because words are harmful, but because they increase load at the wrong time. When margin is thin, symbolic activity that requires coherence, justification, or narrative closure raises cost beyond what the architecture can absorb.

A couple enters session already near margin after a stressful week. The therapist invites them to talk through recent conflicts. The conversation turns to past events. Each partner recounts prior interactions in detail. Emotional intensity rises. The material is familiar, but the conditions do not support integration. As each person explains themselves, performance demand increases. Statements are monitored. Responses are anticipated. The need to be coherent and accurate raises internal cost. Emotional signals intensify faster than they can be redistributed. Attempts to clarify or interpret further increase load. Each explanation invites correction. Each memory triggers another. The system has little tolerance for partial instability, but articulation continues.

By the end of the session, both partners feel exposed and unsettled. Nothing new has stabilized. Outside the room, fallback modes dominate. One partner withdraws. The other escalates. The couple leaves feeling worse than when they arrived. Talking did not make things worse because painful material was discussed. It made things worse because articulation occurred under thin margin, high scrutiny, and sustained demand for coherence. Load rose faster than redistribution could occur.

Why Silence Sometimes Helps and Sometimes Doesn't

Just as talking is not inherently effective, silence is not inherently therapeutic. Silence helps when it reduces load, urgency, or performance pressure. It allows partial instability to persist without immediate compensation and creates conditions for redistribution below narrative resolution. Silence does nothing when it simply removes structure without restoring margin. In highly constrained systems, unstructured silence can increase uncertainty, raise vigilance, and intensify fallback stabilization. Again, the determinant is not the presence or absence of speech, but its effect on stabilization economics.

Talking as a Probe

In CST, talking is best understood as a sampling process rather than an intervention. Speech reveals what the system can carry. What can be said fluently, what arrives with strain, what fragments mid-sentence, what requires correction, and what cannot be said at all are indicators of the cost landscape. Talking exposes architecture. It does not command it.

Why Both Myths Persist

The pro-talk myth persists because talking often coincides with change. The anti-talk myth persists because talking often fails. Both miss the mechanism. Talking matters only when it changes what can be carried. There is no deeper principle required.

When Suggestion or Education in Therapy Is Appropriate

Although CST rejects instruction, persuasion, and insight delivery as mechanisms of change, there are conditions under which therapist suggestion or education is appropriate. These moments are not exceptions to the model. They arise when missing structure itself is generating cost. Some systems are not constrained by excessive rigidity or fallback dominance, but by the absence of reliable scaffolding. The system is expending compensatory effort simply to guess what is happening, what is expected, or what range of behavior is possible. In these cases, uncertainty — not resistance — is the primary load. Here, therapist speech may introduce orienting structure. This can include naming a pattern, describing a common physiological response, clarifying boundaries of the setting, or explaining how certain dynamics typically unfold. The function is not to change the client's understanding in order to produce change. It is to reduce variance and uncertainty by constraining what the system must carry.

For example, explaining that a particular bodily response is common under sustained stress does not relieve strain because it is insightful. It relieves strain because it narrows the state space, reduces catastrophic inference, and lowers the cost of carrying what is already present. Similarly, describing how panic cycles amplify themselves, or how sleep disruption affects regulation, may reduce load by replacing guesswork with predictable structure. In these moments, education functions as environmental stabilization, not interpretation. It supplies a missing constraint that allows the system to stop compensating for uncertainty. Once margin increases, further explanation becomes unnecessary and often counterproductive.

Suggestion operates under the same principle. A suggestion is appropriate only when it reduces cost immediately by simplifying coordination, narrowing options, or restoring predictability. This may include proposing a pause, suggesting a change in pacing, or offering a concrete option when indecision itself has destabilized. The suggestion does not aim to improve the client, but aims to reduce strain. Crucially, suggestion and education are conditional and temporary. They are withdrawn once the structure provided is no longer needed. Continuing to educate or advise after margin has been restored reintroduces load, shifts responsibility onto the therapist, and undermines reorganization.

When suggestion or education appears to "help," it is not because the system has been corrected or informed. It is because uncertainty has been reduced, cost has dropped, and stabilization has become easier. When such condition changes recur, residue may accumulate indirectly through altered carryability. When they do not alter these conditions, they function only as content and have no effect. This preserves the core principle of CST: talking does not change systems by conveying meaning. It changes systems only when it alters what the system can afford to carry next. Suggestion and education are not privileged tools. They are context adjustments, used sparingly, when missing structure is itself the load.

When Education or Instruction Works

A client enters therapy with persistent physical tension and frequent sleep disruption. The system is not highly fragmented or rigid, but it is operating under sustained uncertainty. Bodily signals fluctuate, and the client expends ongoing effort trying to determine whether these signals indicate danger, failure, or loss of control. During session, the therapist briefly explains how prolonged stress can elevate baseline arousal and narrow sleep windows without indicating pathology or personal failure. The explanation is concrete and bounded. No interpretation is offered. No corrective task is assigned.

Immediately, the range of live inferences narrows. The client stops scanning for hidden causes and no longer needs to continuously reassess what the sensations "mean." Variance drops. Compensatory work decreases. The system can now carry the same bodily state with less strain. Nothing changes because the client now understands something better. Change occurs because missing structure has been supplied. The explanation reduces uncertainty, narrows the state space, and lowers cost. Once stabilization improves, further education becomes unnecessary and is not repeated.

When Education or Instruction Does Not Work

A client enters therapy already operating near margin, with strong fallback dominance. Under stress, behavior narrows quickly, and tolerance for partial instability is low. The system is already exerting high compensatory effort to remain coherent. The therapist explains emotional regulation strategies and outlines how past experiences shape current reactions. The information is accurate and familiar. The client follows the explanation closely and can repeat it back.

But the explanation adds requirements. The client must now monitor internal states, apply techniques, remember concepts, and evaluate whether they are "doing it right." Variance increases. Load rises. Margin collapses further. Outside the session, fallback modes intensify. The client reports feeling overwhelmed and inadequate. Nothing about the underlying stabilization shifts because the education did not reduce uncertainty or simplify coordination. It increased demand instead.

Instruction fails here not because the information is wrong, but because structure was not missing. Margin was. Adding explanation increased cost in a system that could not afford it. A similar failure appears in sleep-focused work. The therapist explains how sustained stress elevates baseline arousal and fragments sleep architecture. The explanation is accurate and familiar. The client has heard versions of it before and can repeat it back easily. The therapist adds, "If you can figure out where most of your stress is coming from, that can help your sleep improve."

With that addition, the explanation becomes a task. The client is now implicitly responsible for identifying sources, monitoring internal states, and determining whether progress is occurring. Load increases. Variance expands. Each night of poor sleep now carries additional cost: not only fatigue, but the sense that something should be located, addressed, or solved. Because margin is already depleted, the added demand cannot be integrated. The same sleep disruption now requires more compensatory work to carry. Education that previously reduced uncertainty now amplifies it by introducing obligation.

Why This Does Not Reintroduce Directive Therapy

This does not authorize therapists to guide, instruct, or optimize clients. The therapist is not selecting outcomes or determining what should happen. They are responding to where cost is being generated and supplying structure only when its absence is destabilizing. Education does not move the system forward. It stabilizes the ground beneath it. Suggestion does not create change. It prevents unnecessary loss of carryablity. Once margin returns, the therapist returns to non-directive conditions.

What This Completes

This section closes the remaining gap in the talking chapter. It explains why advice and education sometimes appear helpful without granting them causal primacy or reintroducing agency. It also explains why over-educating and chronic advising often fail: once uncertainty is no longer the dominant load, additional structure becomes pressure. Talking lowers load when it redistributes cost and raises load when it demands coherence without margin. Talking stabilizes when it supplies missing structure. In all cases, speech is context — not cause.

What This Chapter Establishes

This chapter establishes that talking has no privileged causal status in CST. Speech neither produces nor prevents change by itself. It is one form of activity that may or may not alter stabilization economics depending on timing, context, and load. Talking works when it lowers cost, increases margin, or allows redistribution to occur. It fails when it remains contained within existing corridors or raises load beyond carryability. This reframes therapeutic speech not as meaning exchange, insight delivery, or emotional expression, but as a contextual factor whose relevance lies solely in whether it alters what the system can afford to stabilize next. In some conditions, speech may also be used to deliberately raise load for containment, or to supply missing structure when uncertainty itself is costly. In all cases, its function is determined by its effect on cost, not by its content or intent.

Chapter 41

Load, Safety, and Reorganization Windows
When Change Can Actually Occur

Earlier chapters established that change occurs only when stabilization economics shift. Therapy does not act on content. Talking does not act by meaning. Neither insight nor silence produces change by itself. What determines whether reorganization occurs is whether the system can tolerate instability without forced stabilization. This chapter makes that constraint explicit. Reorganization is not continuous. It occurs within windows — periods in which load is low enough and stable enough for partial instability to be carried long enough for redistribution to occur. Outside these windows, change is not delayed. It is structurally unavailable.

Load Sets the Ceiling for Change

Load is not simply intensity. It includes urgency, variability, cumulative demand, and the cost of maintaining coherence across time. A system can sometimes tolerate high intensity if it is brief and bounded. It can sometimes tolerate long duration if demands become routine and steady. What eliminates reorganization windows is not any single factor, but sustained near-limit carry.

When load approaches the upper bounds of carryability, stabilization becomes brittle. Any deviation threatens coherence. In this state, the architecture prioritizes speed, reliability, and containment. Exploration becomes dangerous. Reorganization cannot proceed because instability cannot be held without immediate resolution. This is why systems under chronic stress or post-trauma often appear resistant to change. The appearance is misleading because the system is operating at capacity. There is no room to remain partially unsettled.

This constraint is visible in human systems during sleep. Learning and reorganization do not occur at the moment of maximum demand. During waking activity, the system operates near capacity, prioritizing speed, coherence, and performance. Reorganization is deferred. Sleep provides a low-urgency, low-variance interval in which partially unstable configurations can be revisited without immediate resolution. When sleep is repeatedly disrupted, consolidation fails. The system may continue to function, often impressively, but it becomes rigid and error-prone. New configurations do not stabilize because there is no protected window in which instability can be carried safely.

The same constraint appears in biological systems well outside human psychology. A sunflower can tolerate intense sunlight during the day, but it requires darkness to redistribute resources, repair cellular damage, and grow. During daylight, the plant operates in a high-volume mode: light is captured, sugars are produced, water is moved rapidly, and tissues remain under thermal and oxidative load. Growth and repair occur when input drops. At night, photosynthetic machinery downshifts, sugars are redistributed from leaves to stems and roots, and cellular repair dominates. When exposed to continuous light, these processes are overwhelmed. The plant does not fail because the input is wrong, but because uninterrupted demand removes the intervals required for reorganization.

Safety Is Not a Feeling

Safety is often described in experiential terms: calm, trust, comfort, or reassurance. In CST, safety is structural. It refers to the system's capacity to remain partially unstable without exceeding carryability. A system can feel calm and still be unsafe for reorganization if load spikes rapidly or irregularly. A system can feel anxious and still be safe for reorganization if instability can be carried without forced stabilization. What matters is not confidence or reassurance, but reliability: the system can remain partially unsettled without being forced into immediate stabilization. In this sense, safety is not certainty of outcome, but certainty that instability itself is can be carried. Safety is therefore not an emotion. It is a property of the cost landscape. The felt signature of safety is not confidence about outcomes, but the absence of urgency. It appears as experiences like "I don't have to rush this," "this doesn't need to resolve right now," "I can stay with this," or "it's okay that this isn't settled yet" — signals that instability can be carried without stabilization.

The Role of Variance and Load Regularity

Reorganization does not depend on knowing what will happen next. It depends on how steady the demands on the system are. When demands change suddenly or arrive without regularity, the system must remain prepared to sustain multiple possible configurations at once. This raises baseline cost. Even when nothing overtly difficult is happening, continuous readiness consumes margin. When load arrives in steady, bounded ways, internal work can downshift. Cost decreases not because demands disappear, but because variance narrows. Fewer configurations must remain viable at the same time. This allows unsettled states to persist without being forced into immediate stabilization. This is why regular timing, clear boundaries, and consistent conditions often matter more than emotional reassurance. They do not reassure the system. They do not reassure the system, but reduce variance instead, which lowers costs and opens windows in which reorganization can occur.

For example, a client attending sessions at irregular times must continually adjust — anticipating changes, recalibrating expectations, and monitoring for shifts. Even in calm moments, part of the system remains in readiness, consuming margin. When sessions occur at a fixed, predictable time each week, this readiness is no longer required. Baseline cost decreases. The client can remain briefly in an unfinished, unsettled state without being pushed toward immediate closure, allowing reorganization to occur.

Timing Matters More Than Technique

Reorganization windows are time-sensitive. They open and close depending on current load, recent history, and near-term environmental demand. A system that could tolerate instability yesterday may not be able to today. A system that cannot tolerate instability now may be able to tomorrow. This is why the same intervention can have radically different effects at different times. A question that opens space one day may eliminate carryability the next. Silence that allows redistribution in one moment may raise load in another. Timing is not a detail. It is the mechanism. Techniques fail when they ignore timing, but succeed when they coincide with an open window, regardless of theoretical orientation.

Why Pushing Closes Windows

When a system is near its carry limit, any demand for change increases load. Requests to reflect, feel, decide, or act require additional stabilization work. Even gentle encouragement can raise cost beyond tolerance. This is why pressure backfires. It closes reorganization windows by increasing urgency. The system responds by tightening fallback modes. What appears as resistance is simply the disappearance of available space. Reorganization cannot be forced because force increases the very load that makes reorganization impossible.

Small Windows, Small Changes

Reorganization windows are often brief and narrow. They do not announce themselves and may last minutes rather than hours. When they open, only small deviations can be carried. This is why change proceeds incrementally: a slightly altered tone, a softer continuation where force would usually rise, a moment of remaining with uncertainty without immediate closure. These are not partial successes. They are the only scale at which redistribution is possible when margin is limited. Over time, if such moments recur while remaining carryable, residue accumulates and the window gradually widens, allowing larger reorganizations to become possible. The system does not leap, but inches along.

For example, during a familiar conflict, a client who normally escalates in intensity notices the surge beginning but continues speaking at a slightly lower force. The interaction proceeds, yet the usual escalation does not fully stabilize. On another occasion, the client allows a trace of uncertainty to remain rather than forcing a firm position. Later, the client can sustain a less rigid continuation without reverting to the usual pattern. Each shift is small, but each remains carryable. Over time, these micro-deviations accumulate, and broader reorganization becomes possible.

Reorganization requires the system to sustain instability without being forced into protective closure. At the surface, this does not appear as chaos but as tolerable incompleteness — tension without escalation, openness without fragmentation, a sense of unfinished stabilization that does not yet compel resolution. When instability becomes urgent or overwhelming, fallback stabilization occurs and reorganization becomes impossible.

Why Windows Close Again

Reorganization windows are not permanent. New demands, accumulated fatigue, or environmental shifts can close them quickly. This does not undo prior change. It limits what can occur next. When windows close, attempts to continue reorganizing often fail. The system returns to fallback stabilization not because progress was illusory, but because conditions no longer support instability. Understanding this prevents a common misreading: that change has been lost or undone. In CST, change is never undone. It is simply not always extendable.

For example, a client who has recently begun pausing before reacting finds that after several nights of poor sleep and a sudden increase in work demands, the pause disappears and familiar rapid reactions return. The earlier shift was not lost. Under reduced margin, the system can no longer carry the same degree of instability required for the new pattern. When conditions later stabilize and margin widens again, the pause often reappears more easily, reflecting the residue already accumulated.

The Therapist's Role Revisited

The therapist does not open reorganization windows directly. The therapist cannot lower load unilaterally. What the therapist can do is avoid closing windows that are already present. This means pacing interventions to existing margin, minimizing urgency, reducing variance, and maintaining stable conditions. It means tolerating partial instability without demanding resolution. It means recognizing when the window is closed and refraining from pressure that would raise cost further. The therapist's skill lies in timing and containment, not in action.

What This Chapter Establishes

This chapter establishes that reorganization occurs only within windows defined by load, safety, and variance. Safety is structural, not emotional. Timing matters more than technique. Pushing raises cost and closes windows. Change proceeds in small increments when margin is limited and expands only as residue accumulates. This clarifies why therapy sometimes appears to work effortlessly and sometimes fails despite effort. The difference is not insight, motivation, or method. It is whether a reorganization window is open.

Chapter 42

The Therapist as a Stabilization Engineer

Change Without Command or Control

By this point, it should be clear that therapy does not operate by insight delivery, emotional catharsis, narrative correction, or behavioral instruction. Change occurs only when the system's capacity to stabilize shifts. That shift is governed by load, margin, variance, and residue. This chapter specifies the therapist's role within that machinery. The therapist is not an agent of change but is part of the system's environment. Their influence is not directional. It is structural. The therapist functions as a stabilization engineer: someone who participates in shaping conditions under which alternative stabilizations may become carryable.

Why "Engineer" Is the Correct Frame

An engineer does not command a structure into behaving differently. An engineer alters constraints, supports, load distribution, and tolerances so that a structure can hold configurations it could not previously sustain. The therapist's role is analogous. Nothing inside the client is instructed to change. No behavior is required. No insight is demanded. The therapist works at the level of conditions: how much load is present, how quickly it changes, how variable it is, and whether partial instability can be carried without forced stabilization. This framing removes both authority and passivity. Therapist are not directing outcomes, but neither are they neutral observers. They are active participants in shaping the stabilization environment.

The Therapist Does Not Lower Load by Persuasion

It is tempting to think that therapists lower load by reassurance, encouragement, or emotional validation. These can sometimes correlate with reduced strain, but they are not the mechanism. Load decreases only

247

when demands, variance, urgency, or required internal work decrease. Words matter only insofar as they alter those parameters. A statement that reduces urgency may lower load. A statement that introduces evaluation may raise it. The same words can have opposite effects depending on timing and context.

For example, a client hesitates while describing a mistake and becomes visibly tense. If the therapist says, "You handled that well," the reassurance introduces evaluation and performance monitoring, and the client tightens further. Later, when the client is caught in self-criticism and urgency is rising, the same words reduce pressure by lowering perceived threat, and strain decreases. The words did not change. The load conditions did. The therapist's task is not to say the right thing. It is to avoid adding cost.

Presence as Cost Modulation

One of the most underappreciated aspects of therapy is the therapist's own stabilization. A therapist who is hurried, evaluative, outcome-focused, or uncertain raises load simply by being present. A therapist who remains steady, paced, and tolerant of unresolved states reduces variance. This is not a relational claim. It is a mechanical one. The system samples its environment continuously. A low-variance environment allows the system to remain partially unsettled without escalating forced stabilization. A high-variance environment drives rapid resolution.

For example, a client pauses mid-sentence at a fragile point of uncertainty. If the therapist leans forward, speaks quickly, or presses for clarification, coordination demand rises and the client moves to premature closure — offering a quick, familiar explanation that restores stability but prevents reorganization. If instead the therapist remains still, unhurried, and does not press, variance stays low. The pause becomes carryable. The client remains within tolerable instability, and further reorganization becomes possible. The therapist's presence matters not because of its emotional qualities, but because it shapes the cost landscape.

Pacing Is Structural, Not Interpersonal

Pacing is often framed as sensitivity or attunement. In CST, pacing is about preventing cost spikes. When a therapist moves faster than the system's margin allows, instability exceeds carryability. Fallback modes activate. Fragmentation increases. What looks like avoidance or resistance is simply the disappearance of viable space. Effective pacing means allowing the system to remain slightly unsettled without pushing it to resolve. This often requires doing less, not more. Silence, delay, and incompleteness are not absences of technique. They are active load-management strategies.

For example, a client begins approaching a difficult memory and slows, searching for words. If the therapist asks rapid clarifying questions to keep momentum, coordination demand rises and the client shifts into abstraction, losing contact with the emerging material. If instead the therapist allows silence and does not accelerate the process, cost remains stable. The client stays with the partially formed experience, and further stabilization becomes possible without forced closure.

Why the Therapist Avoids Direction

Direction introduces evaluation, which raises performance demand and cost. Performance demand raises cost. Even gentle suggestions — what to notice, what to feel, what to do — can exceed margin in constrained systems. This is not because the suggestions are wrong. It is because they require the system to stabilize additional layers simultaneously.

For example, a client is speaking quietly about a difficult interaction and has just reached a tolerable but unstable point. The therapist adds, "Notice what you feel in your body right now." The content is simple, but the effect is not. The client must now track sensation, evaluate correctness, respond, and continue the narrative at the same time. Coordination demand increases. Tension rises. The fragile opening closes, and the system settles back into a familiar fallback stabilization.

Non-directivity is therefore not a philosophical stance. It is an engineering constraint. When margin is thin, direction eliminates the very space reorganization requires. When margin is sufficient, direction is often unnecessary. Either way, command is not the lever.

The Therapist as a Boundary Regulator

One of the therapist's most concrete functions is boundary regulation. This includes session timing, consistency, scope, and role clarity. These are not administrative details. They are load-bearing structures. Clear boundaries reduce variance and lowers baseline cost, and lower cost increases tolerance for instability. This is why reliable session timing often matters more than what occurs during the session. The therapist does not impose boundaries to control the client. Boundaries function to stabilize the environment so the system does not have to.

For example, sessions that begin and end at consistent times require no monitoring, guessing, or adjustment. The client does not need to track when the session will stop, whether time will extend, or whether expectations will shift. Coordination demand remains low and predictable. If timing becomes inconsistent — sessions running long, ending abruptly, or changing unpredictably — variance rises and baseline cost increases. More of the system's capacity is consumed maintaining orientation, leaving less available for tolerating instability and enabling reorganization.

Interventions as Tests, Not Instructions

When interventions are used, they function as probes. They test whether a slightly different configuration can be carried without loss of carryability. A question, reflection, or pause is not a directive. It is an offer to occupy a configuration briefly. If the system destabilizes, the probe was too costly. Nothing has failed. Information has been gained. If the system holds, residue may accumulate. Over repetitions, cost may shift. This reframes therapeutic "technique" entirely. Techniques do not cause change. They sample viability.

For example, a client repeatedly describes a situation entirely in external terms, with no reference to internal state. The therapist briefly introduces a probe: "What was happening internally at that moment?" If tension rises and the client shifts into confusion or withdrawal, the configuration was not carryable and the probe is released. If the client remains stable and begins to notice faint internal signals, the system has held the new configuration. Repetition at this level may gradually lower cost, allowing broader configurations to become viable later.

Why the Therapist Must Tolerate Uncertainty

A stabilization engineer must tolerate uncertainty because reorganization requires it. If the therapist needs resolution, clarity, or progress, they will apply pressure — subtly or overtly. That pressure raises cost and closes windows. The therapist's ability to remain present without knowing what will happen next is not a personal virtue. It is a mechanical requirement. The therapist must be able to hold uncertainty so the system does not resolve prematurely.

For example, a client pauses after approaching an unclear but significant point and says, "I'm not sure what this is." If the therapist presses — "What do you think it means?" or "Where is this going?" — evaluation demand rises and the client quickly produces a familiar explanation, restoring stability but ending the opening. If instead the therapist allows the uncertainty to remain without forcing clarification, pressure stays low. The unfinished state remains carryable and further reorganization becomes possible.

Responsibility Without Control

None of this removes responsibility from the therapist. It relocates it. The therapist is responsible for not increasing load unnecessarily. They are responsible for pacing, variance reduction, and containment. They are responsible for recognizing when windows are closed and refraining from pressure. They are not responsible for outcomes. Outcomes emerge from the system's own stabilization economics. Confusing these roles leads either to control attempts or withdrawal. CST allows neither.

For example, a client arrives visibly strained after a destabilizing week and struggles to maintain coherence. The therapist recognizes that the window for reorganization is closed. Rather than pressing toward insight or change, they narrow the session to stabilization — slowing pace, reducing demands, and avoiding evaluative direction. No visible breakthrough occurs, yet load does not increase and further fragmentation is prevented. On another week, when margin is wider, the system may reorganize. The therapist did not produce the change, nor fail when it did not occur. They maintained the conditions required for either to become possible.

What This Chapter Establishes

This chapter establishes the therapist as a stabilization engineer rather than an agent of change. Therapy operates by shaping conditions, not directing content. The therapist participates in load modulation, variance reduction, pacing, and boundary regulation so that alternative stabilizations may become carryable. Non-directivity is not an ethical preference but is a structural necessity. Presence is not relational magic but is cost modulation. Interventions are not instructions but are tests of viability. With authorship removed and stabilization economics explicit, therapy becomes usable without betrayal. The therapist does not fix the system; they help ensure that reorganization is not made impossible.

Change cannot be commanded.
It can only be made carryable.
The therapist's task is not to cause change,
but to protect the conditions under which it can
occur.

Chapter 43

Why Relationship Changes Architecture

Load-Sharing Without Relational Mysticism

Therapy often treats relationship as a special kind of force. Change is attributed to connection, attunement, trust, empathy, or emotional bond, as if something uniquely interpersonal were doing the work. When improvement occurs in the presence of another person, it is described as relational, and the relationship itself is credited as the cause. CST does not use this framing because relationship has no special causal power. Nothing changes simply because two people are connected. Change occurs only when the conditions a system is carrying are altered.

When another person matters, it is because their presence changes load. They may reduce urgency, limit variance, absorb spillover, or help distribute demand. These effects are mechanical, not interpersonal. The same changes could, in principle, be produced by other structures that alter the load in the same way. This chapter explains how shared presence can widen margin, why some forms of support lower cost while others raise it, and why "connection" helps only when it functions as load-sharing. What heals is not relationship itself, but the way conditions become more carryable.

Relationship as a Load-Bearing Context

A system does not stabilize in isolation. Stabilization always occurs within an environment. Other systems are part of that environment and therefore function as input. When another system is present, the cost landscape can change — not because of meaning or connection, but because the inputs available to the system have changed. The causal force of that input is determined by the receiving architecture. The same presence can lower load for one system, raise it for another, or shift load across time. Nothing about a relationship guarantees stabilization.

A relationship alters architecture whenever it changes the load a system must carry. It may reduce load by distributing vigilance, coordinating timing, adding redundancy, or buffering variance. It may also increase load by introducing unpredictability, misalignment, monitoring pressure, or conflicting demands. Both effects are mechanical. None of these effects require intimacy, empathy, or understanding. They require only that the system's load conditions are altered by the presence of another architecture. When load drops, margin increases. When margin increases, instability becomes more tolerable. When instability can be tolerated, redistribution becomes possible. The effect of relationship is therefore indirect and structural.

Co-Regulation Is Load-Sharing, Not Emotional Synchrony

Co-regulation is often described as emotional alignment or soothing between people. In CST terms, co-regulation refers to shared stabilization across systems. When one system is already stabilized, its presence reduces variance in the environment. Reduced variance lowers cost for the other system. The second system does not need to resolve as quickly or engage in as much internal work. Stabilization can proceed with less strain. This is not transmission of calm but is variance reduction. A predictable, steady system lowers environmental volatility. Lower volatility widens the range of configurations that can be carried. The effect does not depend on warmth or closeness but depends on reliability.

A child crossing a busy street can manage foot placement, speed, and balance. What overwhelms the system is not walking itself, but monitoring traffic, timing movement, and responding to sudden changes. When an adult walks alongside and handles the traffic checks, the child's load drops. More movement patterns become carryable. The child does not become calmer because of reassurance. The environment becomes more predictable because variance has been reduced. The same adult, if distracted or inconsistent, can raise load instead. The child must now monitor both traffic and the adult. The difference is not closeness. It is reliability.

The inverse is also true. When the other system is unstable, inconsistent, or rapidly shifting, environmental variance increases. Higher variance raises baseline cost, forcing faster stabilization and narrowing what can be carried. What is often described as "being dysregulated by another person" is simply shared exposure to elevated volatility. For example, in the presence of a rapidly changing, tense, or erratic person, the same system may tighten quickly into rigid stabilization, not because of emotional influence, but because variance has increased and fewer configurations remain carryable.

Redundancy Changes Cost Geometry

One of the most powerful structural effects of shared systems is redundancy. When multiple systems can respond to the same demand, failure of any single pathway does not immediately threaten coherence. Redundancy reduces extreme cost spikes, allowing stabilization to remain carryable under perturbation rather than forcing destabilization. When loss of coherence no longer implies immediate failure, instability becomes less dangerous. Partial destabilization can then persist long enough for redistribution to occur. In solitary systems, loss of coherence often demands rapid forced stabilization. In shared systems, forced stabilization can be deferred. That deferral is the opening through which reorganization becomes possible. This is why support systems matter mechanically. They do not add strength. They increase tolerance for instability.

Pacing Is Easier in Shared Systems

When a system must regulate its own pacing under load, urgency rises quickly. Delays feel dangerous. In shared environments, pacing can slow without increasing risk. Another system can hold attention, monitor context, or maintain continuity while the first system remains partially unsettled. This distributes stabilization across time and scope. The system does not need to resolve everything at once.

This is why therapeutic change often occurs in dialogue rather than isolation. Not because talking is special, but because pacing becomes survivable. A person trying to make a difficult decision alone often feels intense pressure to settle it immediately. Every pause increases uncertainty, and urgency builds. The system accelerates toward premature stabilization simply to end the strain.

When the same decision is explored with another person present, pacing can slow without increasing risk. One system can hold the thread of the conversation, remember what has already been said, or notice when the discussion is looping, while the other remains partially unsettled. The load of maintaining continuity is no longer carried by a single architecture. Stabilization is distributed across time and scope. Change occurs here not because dialogue is special, but because pacing becomes survivable.

Why Relationship Lowers the Cost of Being Unresolved

Many fallback modes exist to prevent prolonged instability. Hypervigilance, suppression, avoidance, and rigid identity corridors all force rapid stabilization. They do so at the cost of flexibility. In the presence of a stable other, unresolved states no longer threaten immediate failure. The system can remain incomplete without escalating internal work. This is the critical shift. Relationship does not produce insight. It produces time. Time under low load allows redistribution. Redistribution shifts cost and cost shifts behavior.

For example, a person who typically withdraws when uncertainty rises begins to feel the familiar pull toward rapid closure. Alone, the system would quickly settle into avoidance to restore stability. In the presence of a steady other who does not press, the same unresolved state remains carryable. Withdrawal is not immediately required. The system stays partially unsettled longer than usual, allowing internal redistribution to begin. Over repetitions, the cost of remaining engaged decreases, and behavior shifts without direct instruction.

Attachment Without Attachment Theory

CST does not require attachment theory to explain relational effects. Early caregiving matters not because of bond formation, but because it shapes baseline load conditions. When early environments reliably share load, architectures stabilize under conditions where instability remains survivable and margin is available. Classic primate studies illustrate this principle: infant rhesus monkeys consistently stabilized around steady, predictable tactile contact rather than around structures that merely delivered food. The effect was not symbolic. Continuous, non-fluctuating sensory conditions reduced environmental variance, lowered baseline cost, and supported stable organization under strain. When early environments do not provide tolerance for instability, architectures stabilize under conditions in which loss of coherence must be resolved immediately. These conditions are not stored as beliefs; they are embedded in cost geometry. Later relationships can alter this geometry, but only when they reliably reduce load. Intermittent support increases variance and raises cost. Reliability, not intensity, is what matters.

Why Relationship Sometimes Fails to Help

Relationship does not always change architecture. When relational contexts increase demand, ambiguity, evaluation, or performance pressure, they raise load. In such cases, fallback modes intensify. This explains why some people feel worse in relationships, including therapeutic ones. The presence of another system can increase variance rather than reduce it. Being seen can raise cost and being evaluated can eliminate margin. Relationship is not inherently stabilizing. Only relationships that reliably lower load alter the cost landscape in a way that supports reorganization.

The Therapist as a Specialized Relational Environment

In therapy, the therapist functions as a deliberately engineered relational context. Boundaries, pacing, predictability, and non-directivity are not ethical gestures. They are load-shaping tools. The therapist does not heal the client through connection. The therapist helps maintain a low-variance environment in which partial instability can be carried without escalation. Relationship matters only insofar as it achieves this. This is why the therapist's consistency often matters more than insight, empathy, or technique. Consistency reduces variance, lowering cost and permitting change.

What This Chapter Establishes

This chapter establishes that relationship changes architecture only through mechanical effects: load-sharing, redundancy, pacing, and variance reduction. There is no relational mysticism in CST. No emotional transmission. No interpersonal force. When relationship lowers cost and increases margin, instability becomes tolerable and redistribution becomes possible. When it does not, fallback modes persist. Relationship matters not because systems connect, but because environments change.

Chapter 44

What "Support" Actually Does Mechanically

Load Redistribution Without Sentimentality

Support is one of the most overused and least specified terms in therapy, care, and social life. It is often treated as encouragement, reassurance, validation, or kindness — something one person offers to help another feel better or try harder. In CST, support has no sentimental function. It has a mechanical one. Support changes architecture only insofar as it redistributes load and restores margin. This chapter strips the term of moral tone and interpersonal glow. What matters is not how support feels, but what it does to cost, variance, and carryability.

Support Is Not Motivation

Encouragement assumes that change is limited by willingness or effort. It presumes that if a system were reassured, inspired, or affirmed, it would act differently. CST rejects this premise. A system does not fail to change because it lacks motivation. It fails to change because alternative configurations remain too costly to stabilize. Encouragement often raises load. It adds evaluation, expectation, and performance pressure. "You can do this" can increase urgency. "I believe in you" can increase variance. In constrained systems, these additions eliminate margin and strengthen fallback modes. What is commonly offered as support can therefore work against reorganization.

Support as Load Redistribution

Mechanically, support occurs when part of the load a system would otherwise have to carry alone is carried elsewhere. This redistribution can happen across people, across time, or across structures. The key feature is not emotional tone, but reduced internal work. When load is redistributed,

258

stabilization requires less internal work. When internal work drops, margin increases. When margin increases, instability becomes tolerable. That tolerance is what allows new configurations to be occupied long enough for residue to accumulate. Support does not add capacity. It reduces demand.

A medical resident covering a night shift must monitor patients, respond to pages, remember medication schedules, and make rapid decisions. When the resident is alone, missed information immediately raises urgency. Internal work spikes, and stabilization is forced quickly to avoid error. When a second clinician shares the shift, one person can monitor pages while the other reviews charts. If attention slips in one channel, coherence is not immediately threatened. Demand is redistributed. Instability can persist without forcing immediate closure, allowing different patterns of coordination to form over time. Support in this case does not add skill or strength. It reduces demand by distributing load.

Forms of Load Redistribution

Load can be redistributed in multiple ways without any change in meaning or insight. One form is practical substitution. Another system performs tasks that would otherwise consume stabilization resources. The supported system does not become more capable; it becomes less burdened. A parent caring for a newborn cannot sleep while also tracking feeding times and medication schedules. When another adult takes over the schedule tracking, the parent's architecture does not gain skill; it carries less demand and stabilizes with less internal work.

Another form is temporal buffering. Deadlines are extended. Responses are delayed. Urgency is reduced. The system is no longer required to resolve immediately. This slows stabilization and reduces variance. A student facing a same-day deadline experiences rising urgency as unfinished work accumulates. When the deadline is extended by a week, the task does not change, but urgency drops and the system no longer has to force immediate stabilization.

Another form is environmental simplification. Noise, unpredictability, and competing demands are removed. Fewer variables must be integrated at once. Stabilization cost drops. A person trying to focus in a noisy, crowded office must continuously filter sound, movement, and interruption. Moving the same work to a quiet room removes competing variables, reducing the number of conditions that must be integrated at once.

Another form is monitoring redundancy. Another system tracks conditions, remembers constraints, or notices deviations. Vigilance load is shared. Loss of coherence no longer implies immediate failure. An airline cockpit is staffed by two pilots so that altitude, fuel, and navigation are tracked in parallel. If one channel is missed, coherence is not immediately threatened because vigilance is shared rather than borne by a single system. None of these require empathy. They require reliability.

Margin Restoration Is the Critical Effect

Support matters only insofar as it restores margin. Margin is the difference between what a system is carrying and what it could carry before destabilizing. When margin is restored, partial instability becomes survivable; without it, reorganization cannot proceed. Restored margin does not guarantee change. It makes change possible. Without margin, reorganization cannot proceed. With margin, redistribution can occur if alternative configurations are sampled repeatedly under low enough load. This is why support often appears indirect. Nothing obvious changes at first. The system simply stops exerting as much internal work. Over time, different stabilizations become reachable.

Why Support Sometimes Fails

Support fails when it does not actually reduce load. Reassurance that leaves demands unchanged does nothing. Presence that increases evaluation does harm. Help that introduces unpredictability raises cost. Support also fails when it is inconsistent. Intermittent assistance increases variance. The system cannot rely on redistribution and must maintain fallback modes. Reliability matters more than intensity. Support that is withdrawn abruptly can also raise load beyond baseline. The system may reorganize around the expectation of redistribution. When it disappears, destabilization increases. This is not dependency. It is architecture responding to altered load conditions. A manager tells an employee, "I've got your back," but continues to demand the same deadlines while checking in randomly and questioning decisions. Load increases rather than drops, variance rises, and the employee must stay in fallback modes. When the manager later steps in

briefly to help and then disappears again, the system destabilizes further —
not because of dependency, but because the architecture had begun to rely
on redistributed demand that was suddenly withdrawn.

Support Is Not Dependency Creation

Support is often feared because it is thought to create dependence. This fear
assumes that systems should carry load alone. CST does not share this
assumption. No system is independent. All stabilization occurs within
environments that distribute load unevenly. *Support creates dependence only when
it replaces margin rather than restoring it.* If redistribution allows the system to
stabilize new configurations that later remain viable without support,
dependence decreases. If the system can remain coherent only while support
is present, dependence increases. The difference is structural, not moral.

A physical therapy patient is given a brace immediately after surgery. The
brace reduces demand while the joint adapts to new movement patterns. As
strength and coordination return, the brace is used less, and the new
patterns remain viable without it. Dependence decreases because margin
was restored long enough for reorganization to occur. If the brace is never
adjusted or removed, the joint may remain coherent only while supported.
Dependence increases, not because support was offered, but because
coherence becomes viable only in the presence of support rather than
through margin that persists when it is removed.

Support Versus Rescue

Rescue resolves loss of coherence immediately by removing instability
entirely. Support allows instability to persist at a tolerable level. Rescue
prevents redistribution. Support permits it. This distinction matters
clinically. Immediate relief can be necessary when system failure risk is high.
But if rescue becomes the dominant mode, fallback patterns harden.
Support preserves carryable instability rather than eliminating strain. A
therapist immediately reassures a client whenever distress rises, redirecting
the conversation or offering solutions to stop the discomfort. The distress
disappears quickly, but the system never remains unsettled long enough for
different configurations to be carried. Each spike is resolved as soon as it
appears. In a different session, the therapist helps slow pacing and reduces
urgency while allowing the distress to remain present. The discomfort is not
removed, but it becomes tolerable. The system stays partially unsettled

without forcing rapid stabilization, allowing redistribution to occur over time.

The Therapist's Use of Support

In therapy, support is not encouragement, validation, or alliance-building. It is the deliberate management of load. Pacing sessions, reducing urgency, maintaining predictable boundaries, and tolerating unresolved states are all forms of support. When a therapist refrains from directing, interpreting, or demanding progress, they are not being permissive. They are preserving margin. When they remain steady in the presence of instability, they are sharing load. When they slow the process, they are redistributing time pressure. Support is not what the therapist says. It is what the therapist makes unnecessary for the system to do alone.

Why Support Precedes Insight

Insight often follows support, but it does not cause it. When load drops, configurations that were previously too costly can be occupied. Awareness then encounters these configurations and may describe them as realizations, clarity, or understanding. This sequencing is often reversed in explanation. CST restores the order. Support alters cost. Cost alters stabilization. Stabilization alters what awareness receives. A client has spent years trying to understand why conversations with their partner escalate so quickly. In sessions where pacing is slow and urgency is low, the client can remain unsettled without rushing to defend or withdraw. New ways of responding appear during the conversation, and afterward the client reports a "realization" about their pattern. The realization did not produce the change. Reduced load allowed different responses to be carried, and awareness encountered them only after they were already viable.

What This Chapter Establishes

This chapter establishes that support has a single mechanical function: load redistribution that restores margin. Support is not encouragement, reassurance, or emotional endorsement. It does not motivate change or supply strength. It reduces demand so that reorganization can occur. When support lowers cost reliably, instability becomes tolerable, redistribution becomes possible, and architecture reshapes. When it does not, nothing changes. Removing sentimentality from support clarifies its real role: not to help a system try harder, but to make trying unnecessary.

Chapter 45

The Ethics of Non-Directive Change

Why Ethics Follow Mechanics

Ethics in therapy are often framed as principles to be upheld: respect autonomy, avoid control, honor the client's agency. In CST, ethics do not precede mechanics. They follow from them. What is ethical is what does not reliably increase load, eliminate margin, or foreclose reorganization. What is unethical is not what violates values, but what predictably prevents change from occurring. Non-directive change, does not require moral defense. It is not kinder, more respectful, or more enlightened by principle. It is ethically necessary because directive change fails mechanically.

Ethics as Consequence, Not Commitment

Traditional ethical frameworks assume a chooser. If someone is in charge, ethics constrain how that power should be used. CST removes the chooser. What remains is architecture responding to cost. In this context, ethics cannot be about intention or restraint. They must be about consequence. A practice is ethical if it reliably preserves or restores the conditions under which reorganization remains possible. A practice is unethical if it reliably eliminates those conditions. This is not a value judgment. It is an empirical one. Directive intervention increases load. Increased load narrows carryability. Narrowed carryability prevents redistribution. Practices that systematically do this are unethical because they entrench fallback modes, regardless of intent.

For example, a practitioner may believe that pressing for emotional disclosure is helpful and act with sincere intent. If the pressure increases urgency and forces rapid stabilization into suppression or withdrawal, the conditions for reorganization are reduced. By contrast, a practice that slows pace and reduces demand may produce no immediate visible change, yet preserves carryability and allows redistribution to occur later. In CST terms, the first practice is unethical because it increases load and constrains the system, while the second is ethical because it maintains the conditions under which reorganization remains possible.

Why Direction Fails Structurally

Direction requires compliance. Compliance requires evaluation. Evaluation raises cost. Even when direction is gentle, supportive, or well-reasoned, it adds pressure to resolve, perform, or align with an external demand. In systems already operating near their limits, this added pressure eliminates margin. Instability becomes dangerous rather than informative. The system tightens around what it knows will hold. Fallback modes strengthen. Identity hardens. Reorganization recedes. This is not resistance. It is structural inevitability. Asking a constrained system to move where it cannot remain coherent is not guidance. It is destabilization.

Why Non-Directive Change Preserves Possibility

Non-directive change removes one thing only: imposed resolution. By not requiring agreement, action, or insight, it lowers stabilization cost. Lower cost preserves margin. Preserved margin allows partial instability to be carried. That tolerance is the prerequisite for redistribution. Nothing is granted to the system. Nothing is affirmed or denied. The architecture is simply not burdened with additional demands. In that absence, alternative configurations may become briefly viable. If they can be occupied repeatedly without forced stabilization, residue accumulates and the cost landscape shifts. Non-directivity is not permissive. It is economical.

The Ethical Failure of "Helping"

Many unethical interventions are motivated by care. The desire to help often leads to explanation, advice, reassurance, or correction. Each of these adds load and narrows the space in which the system can remain unsettled without penalty. This is why well-intentioned help so often backfires. It increases urgency; accelerates pacing and demands resolution. The system responds by retreating to what is lowest cost. The helper then escalates effort, compounding the problem. The ethical issue is not that help is controlling but that help is destabilizing.

For example, a son calls his parent and begins describing ongoing frustrations, repeating familiar complaints. The parent, intending to help, offers advice that was not requested — suggesting solutions, correcting perspective, proposing what should be done. The son's strain increases. The conversation shifts from expression to defense. Irritation rises, and he withdraws or becomes upset. The parent, perceiving distress, offers more explanation and reassurance, further increasing coordination demand. The exchange escalates until the son settles into familiar fallback stabilization — shutting down, arguing, or ending the call. The parent's intent was supportive, yet the added load reduced carryability and destabilized the interaction.

Responsibility Without Authority

If no one authors change, no one can be held responsible for producing it. This does not eliminate responsibility. It relocates it. Responsibility lies in managing conditions, not outcomes. The ethical responsibility of the therapist is not to cause improvement, insight, or relief. It is to avoid actions that predictably foreclose reorganization. This includes pressure, interpretation, premature framing, and demands for progress. The therapist is responsible for the load they add or remove. Nothing else.

When Direction Appears to Work

Directive change sometimes appears effective, particularly in low-load systems. When margin is abundant, direction may not eliminate carryability. The system can tolerate added demands and still reorganize. In these cases, direction is unnecessary rather than harmful. This creates confusion. Practices that work sometimes are treated as generally valid. CST clarifies the boundary. As load rises and margin thins, the same practices become unethical because they cease to work mechanically. Ethics shift with constraint because mechanics do. For example, a person with stable conditions and low current strain is given a clear directive to change a daily routine. The additional demand does not exceed margin, and the new pattern stabilizes without difficulty, creating the impression that directive change produced the improvement. Later, under fatigue, pressure, and competing demands, the same directive is introduced. This time, coordination demand exceeds carryability: strain rises, fallback stabilization returns, and no reorganization occurs. The directive did not change. The load conditions did.

Why Ethics Cannot Be Separated From Timing

An intervention that preserves margin at one moment may eliminate it at another. Ethical practice therefore cannot be rule-based. It must be condition-sensitive. The same words, gestures, or silences have different effects depending on load, history, and current stabilization mode. This does not require intuition or attunement in a mystical sense. It requires tracking cost. Is the system stabilizing with less work or more? Is instability becoming tolerable or dangerous? Is variance decreasing or increasing? Ethics are enacted moment by moment as load management.

A therapist asks a client to pause and reflect after an emotionally charged statement. Early in therapy, when load is high and urgency is strong, the pause increases instability and raises cost. The system has not yet developed tolerance for being unsettled, and the silence pushes it toward forced stabilization. Later, after pacing has slowed and margin has increased, the same pause has the opposite effect. Instability can be carried without escalation, variance drops, and different configurations become viable. The words have not changed; the timing has.

Non-Directive Does Not Mean Neutral

Non-directive practice is often mistaken for passivity. In CST, it is active constraint management. Pacing, boundary consistency, predictable structure, and tolerance for unresolved states are all interventions. They simply intervene at the level of conditions rather than content. The therapist is not absent but present in a way that does not add demand.

Why This Is the Only Coherent Ethical Frame

Once authorship is removed, ethics cannot be grounded in autonomy, respect, or freedom. Those concepts presuppose a chooser. CST grounds ethics in viability. Practices are ethical if they maintain the possibility of reorganization. They are unethical if they reliably eliminate it. Non-directive change meets this criterion not because it honors values, but because it preserves margin.

What This Chapter Establishes

This chapter establishes that the ethics of non-directive change are consequences of mechanics, not moral commitments. Directive intervention is unethical not because it violates autonomy, but because it predictably increases load, reduces margin, and entrenches fallback modes in constrained systems. Non-directive practice is ethically required because it is the only stance that reliably preserves the conditions under which reorganization can occur. Ethics, in CST, are not principles imposed on practice. They are the downstream logic of how systems actually change.

Ethics are not values.
They are load management, that is,
what remains when mechanics are taken
seriously.

Part VIII

Responsibility Without Authors

Responsibility, Justice, and Social Systems Without Authors

Chapter 46

Responsibility as Causal Position

Structural Consequence Without Authors

Responsibility is the concept most often assumed to be incompatible with a non-agentic account of human behavior. If there is no chooser, no author, and no controlling self, then responsibility is assumed to vanish along with them. This chapter returns to it after trauma, chronic stress, fallback modes, and constrained identity have been fully established. What responsibility looks like after constraint is not what it looks like in unconstrained systems, but it does not disappear. Responsibility does not require authorship; it requires consequence.

Responsibility Is Not Ownership of Choice

In everyday thinking, responsibility is framed as ownership of choice. Someone is responsible because they could have done otherwise and therefore ought to answer for what they did. CST rejects this framing entirely. Responsibility does not arise from metaphysical freedom. It arises from causal placement. A system is responsible for what flows through it and what it shapes next, regardless of whether it authored those flows.

A river is responsible for erosion downstream by virtue of its flow. A furnace is responsible for heat by virtue of its operation. In neither case is responsibility about intent. It names where effects propagate. Human systems are no different. They participate in causal chains, and those chains continue through them whether or not a self was ever in charge.

Responsibility as Structural Position

Every system occupies a position in a causal network. What it stabilizes shapes what becomes easier or harder to stabilize next, both for itself and for others. This remains true under trauma and constraint. A fallback mode that narrows behavior alters the environment it participates in. A constrained identity shapes interactions and future load. Fragmentation redistributes effects across time and context. None of this requires intention. It requires only participation in causation. Responsibility, in CST, names this participation.

Why Constraint Does Not Remove Responsibility

It is tempting to assume that trauma or chronic stress eliminates responsibility entirely. This assumption mistakes explanation for exemption. Constraint explains why a system stabilizes the way it does. It does not remove the fact that its stabilizations have effects. A traumatized system does not select its fallback modes. But those modes still shape outcomes. They still propagate load, limit options, and influence what happens next.

A person with a trauma history becomes highly vigilant in conversations, interrupting others and steering discussions quickly toward safety. This pattern is not chosen. It stabilizes automatically under perceived threat. The behavior makes group interactions tense, limits what topics can be explored, and increases load for others in the room. The trauma explains why the pattern appears. It does not erase its effects. The fallback mode still shapes what happens next by narrowing options and propagating urgency.

Responsibility Without Blame

Responsibility survives the loss of agency, but blame does not. Blame is a moral overlay that assumes authorship. It presumes that a self stands outside the causal flow and selects an outcome. CST has no place for that assumption. Responsibility without blame means recognizing consequence without assigning fault. It means locating where effects arise without inventing an author behind them. Removing blame does not remove accountability. It removes cruelty disguised as explanation.

Responsibility as Causal Relevance

Responsibility also has a practical meaning. Systems that reliably generate certain effects are relevant points of intervention, not because they deserve correction, but because altering conditions there changes downstream outcomes. A bridge that fails under load is responsible for structural failure in the same sense a constrained behavioral pattern may be responsible for social rupture. In both cases, the response is not condemnation, but adjustment of conditions. Responsibility tells us where change would matter if change becomes possible.

Why Narrative Distorts Responsibility

Narrative tends to obscure responsibility. After an action occurs, narrative compresses events into stories of intent, motive, and character. These stories make causal chains feel intelligible, but they do so by inserting agency where none existed. After trauma, this distortion intensifies. Constrained behavior is narrated as weakness, failure, or defect. The system is treated as if it authored what it was forced to carry. CST replaces that story with geometry. The question is not why someone did this. The question is what configuration stabilized here, and what did it shape next.

After a workplace conflict, an employee abruptly leaves a meeting, stops responding to messages, and later requests reassignment. The common narrative is immediate and familiar: "They couldn't handle feedback." "They're avoidant." "They lack professionalism." Motive and character are inserted to make the sequence feel intelligible. From a CST view, a different description applies. Under sustained evaluation pressure, tight deadlines, and prior exposure to punitive supervision, a withdrawal pattern stabilized as the lowest-load way to remain coherent. The exit was not authored. It was the configuration that held when alternatives exceeded carryability. That stabilization then shaped what happened next: communication narrowed, roles shifted, and load redistributed across the team. Responsibility is not located in character, but in causal position — what stabilized, under what load, and what it shaped downstream.

Responsibility Under Constrained Identity

When identity hardens under constraint, responsibility can feel overwhelming or inescapable. Because behavior stabilizes inside a narrow corridor, the same effects recur. Awareness encounters this repetition as "this is who I am," and responsibility becomes fused with identity. This fusion is a narrative artifact. Identity is not responsible nor is the corridor accountable. Responsibility applies only in the narrow sense that the system's stabilizations continue to propagate effects. Separating responsibility from identity loosens shame without denying consequence.

Collective Responsibility Without Collective Selves

Responsibility does not stop at individuals. Families, institutions, and cultures are also load-bearing systems, and their stabilizations shape what happens next. They stabilize patterns, distribute strain, and accumulate residue. Trauma is often not located in a single system, but in the interaction of many constrained systems reinforcing one another. Responsibility here names structural contribution not shared guilt.

A child grows up in a family under chronic financial strain, within a school system that relies on strict discipline, in a neighborhood with constant surveillance. Each system stabilizes in ways that make sense locally: the family becomes rigid to avoid risk, the school emphasizes compliance to maintain order, and the neighborhood enforces control to manage threat. No single system intends harm. Yet together they reinforce vigilance, narrow behavior, and propagate strain over time. The child's later trauma is not located in any one system, but in how these constrained systems interact. Responsibility, in this case, names how each structure contributes to what unfolds, not shared guilt or intention.

What This Chapter Establishes

This chapter establishes responsibility as causal position rather than authorship. Responsibility is not about ownership of choice. It is about accurately locating causation. Constraint, trauma, and fallback modes explain why systems stabilize as they do, but they do not remove the fact that those stabilizations have effects. Responsibility persists wherever causation flows, without requiring choice, intent, or moral fault. Accountability remains. Blame falls away. Responsibility without authorship preserves consequence while removing cruelty and prepares the ground for examining justice, dignity, and meaning without restoring a self outside the system.

Chapter 47

Why Punishment Feels Necessary

Urgency, Load, and the Demand That Someone Pay

Punishment feels necessary long before it is justified. When harm occurs, systems experience increased pressure to stabilize. Punishment is one mechanism that emerges when disruption propagates across systems and pressure rises to restore coherence. It functions by sharply increasing cost, forcing rapid stabilization rather than enabling redistribution. Urgency rises. Variance spikes. The future becomes less predictable. In that moment, a powerful demand emerges for immediate containment of the disturbance. Punishment satisfies that demand quickly. It does not do so because it is correct, but because it is immediate.

A student cheats on an exam, and the behavior becomes known to classmates, teachers, and administrators. Uncertainty spreads immediately. Other students wonder whether grades are still fair. Teachers worry about precedent. Administrators face questions about integrity and enforcement. The system becomes unstable, not because of the cheating itself, but because its effects propagate across multiple groups.

Before any investigation is complete, there is strong pressure to act. The student is suspended quickly. The suspension does not clarify why the cheating occurred or whether it will recur. It does, however, restore order. Classes resume. Rules feel enforced. Uncertainty drops. The punishment is not applied because it is the best response. It is applied because it is the fastest way to concentrate consequence and stabilize the surrounding systems.

In CST terms, punishment is a stabilization response to unmanaged load. It concentrates consequence at a localized point in the causal field. By doing so, it reduces uncertainty for surrounding systems. The world feels more ordered when a single location absorbs the impact. This effect occurs regardless of whether punishment improves outcomes. The relief comes from compression, not correction.

Harm Creates Urgency Before It Creates Meaning

After harm, the primary problem is not moral confusion, it is instability. Multiple questions compete at once: What happened? Will it happen again? Who is affected? What must change? This multiplicity raises variance and strains coherence. Narrative arrives later. First comes pressure to restore order; punishment follows as one way to concentrate consequence. Punishment satisfies this pressure by simplifying the landscape. It converts a distributed problem into a localized one. The many become one. The diffuse becomes discrete. The system can then proceed as if the disturbance has been addressed, even when the underlying conditions remain unchanged. This is why punishment can feel necessary even when it is known to be ineffective. The necessity is structural, not rational. It answers the demand for immediate containment.

For example, after a child breaks an important household rule, tension spreads through the family: uncertainty about safety, responsibility, and future behavior. Rather than addressing the broader conditions — fatigue, unclear expectations, accumulated strain — the response focuses on punishment directed at the child. The immediate disruption appears contained, and order seems restored. Yet the conditions that produced the event remain, and the pattern often repeats. The punishment did not resolve the distributed instability; it localized it long enough for coherence to return.

Why "Someone Must Pay" Appears So Quickly

The phrase "someone must pay" is not a moral conclusion. It is a load-management signal. It appears when systems lack the margin to hold complexity. Assigning consequence to a single node reduces coordination costs for everyone else. It creates a sense of closure that allows activity to continue.

In this sense, punishment functions like an emergency brace placed on a failing structure. It redistributes strain away from the surrounding architecture by concentrating it at a point. The surrounding systems stabilize, not because the structure is repaired, but because the strain is temporarily redirected. The felt necessity comes from this redistribution. It is not evidence that punishment is appropriate. It is evidence that the system lacks other ways to manage variance.

In the exam case, this logic appears immediately. Suspending the student concentrates consequence at a single point: coordination costs drop, the disturbance appears contained, and activity continues. An alternative response would address load rather than concentrate consequence. Invalidating the exam, redesigning testing conditions, or clarifying how fairness will be restored would distribute strain across the system instead of assigning it to a person. These responses are slower and require margin, but they reduce recurrence by changing conditions rather than redirecting strain. Punishment feels necessary because it is fast. Structural responses are harder because they require tolerance for complexity.

Punishment as Fast Stabilization Under Constraint

When margin is thin, slow solutions are unavailable. Investigation, redesign, and prevention require tolerance for uncertainty. Under constraint, that tolerance is absent. The system seeks the fastest available stabilization. Punishment is immediate. It does not require understanding. It does not require coordination, it does not require patience, it requires only identification and action. This speed is its appeal. This also explains why punishment escalates under stress. As load increases, the demand for speed increases. Nuance becomes expensive. Structural analysis becomes unreachable. Punishment fills the gap left by missing capacity.

Why Punishment Feels Satisfying Without Being Corrective

Punishment often produces a feeling of relief. That relief is frequently mistaken for evidence of justice. In CST terms, it is evidence of reduced variance. Once consequence is assigned, the system can proceed without carrying open questions. This satisfaction is short-lived because the underlying architecture remains unchanged. When the same conditions produce the same patterns, punishment must be repeated. Over time, the system learns to rely on punishment not as a solution, but as a regulator of urgency. The cycle persists because each application temporarily lowers load, even as it raises long-term cost.

In the exam case, the suspension produces immediate relief. Grades feel protected. Rules feel enforced. Questions about fairness quiet down. That relief is taken as evidence that justice has been served. But the testing pressures, incentives, and vulnerabilities that made cheating likely remain in place. The same conditions continue to select for the same behavior. Cheating does not disappear. It resurfaces later, often in less visible forms or from different students under similar strain. The system learns the wrong lesson. Punishment becomes the tool for restoring order each time instability appears, rather than a means of changing the conditions that generate it. Urgency is regulated. Recurrence is not.

The Role of Narrative in Justifying the Reflex

Narrative enters after stabilization has already occurred. It explains why the punished party deserved what happened. Motive, character, and intent are assembled to make the outcome feel coherent. This sequence matters. The explanation follows the action. The story legitimizes what was already done to manage instability. Under trauma and chronic stress, this narrative hardens. Constrained behavior is framed as moral defect. Punishment becomes not just necessary but righteous. The story protects the system from having to examine the conditions that made punishment feel required in the first place.

Punishment Versus Containment

Punishment is often confused with containment. They are not the same. Containment limits propagation of harm. It reduces spillover and protects margin while conditions are addressed. Punishment assigns consequence without addressing propagation. The confusion arises because both can produce immediate quiet. The difference appears over time. Containment preserves the possibility of redistribution. Punishment substitutes for it. When punishment is used where containment is needed, instability returns. The system responds by punishing again, escalating severity to achieve the same short-term effect.

A hospital experiences repeated medication errors during overnight shifts. In response to a serious incident, administration disciplines the nurse involved. The reprimand is public, documentation is filed, and the unit quiets down. Staff become more cautious. For a time, errors decrease. Nothing about the night shift changes. Staffing levels remain thin. Interruptions continue. Fatigue accumulates. Months later, a similar error occurs with a different nurse. The response escalates: stricter penalties, closer scrutiny, more fear. Errors briefly subside again, then return. A containment response would have looked different. Medication access could be slowed during handoffs. Double-check procedures could be enforced at specific points. Staffing could be increased during high-risk hours. These changes would have limited propagation while conditions were addressed. Punishment produced quiet. Containment would have reduced spread.

In a family under chronic stress, a teenager repeatedly misses curfew. Each time it happens, parents impose harsher consequences. The house becomes quiet for a while. Tension drops. The behavior stops briefly. Nothing about the underlying conditions changes. A few weeks later, the pattern returns and the response escalates again. A containment response would focus on limiting propagation rather than assigning consequence. Clarifying expectations, adjusting logistics, and reducing variability would preserve margin while conditions are addressed. Punishment creates quiet. Containment reduces recurrence.

Why Punishment Persists Even Without Belief in Free Will

Belief in authorship is not required for punishment to feel necessary. The reflex arises from constraint, not from philosophy. Even systems that reject moral blame may still punish because they lack other means of managing urgency. This is why arguments against punishment often fail. They address justification while leaving mechanics untouched. As long as load remains high and margin remains thin, punishment will reappear in some form. To change punishment, conditions must change. Understanding alone does not suffice.

What This Chapter Establishes

This chapter establishes that punishment feels necessary because it is a rapid response to unmanaged load. It reduces variance by concentrating consequence, producing immediate stabilization under constraint. The felt necessity does not indicate effectiveness or justice. It indicates missing capacity for slower, structural responses. Punishment persists not because people believe in authorship, but because systems under strain reach for the quickest available stabilizer. To move beyond punishment, the next question is not whether it is deserved, but what other forms of containment and structural change could lower load without relying on concentrated harm.

Chapter 48

Deterrence, Containment, and Structural Change

Three Ways Systems Try to Reduce Harm

Once punishment is understood as a fast response to unmanaged load, a further distinction becomes necessary. Not all responses to harm do the same work. A system has only a few mechanically distinct levers to reduce recurrence or manage risk. These levers differ by what they act on and how quickly they operate. Systems rely on at least three such strategies: deterrence, containment, and structural change. These strategies are often conflated, but they operate on different timescales and act on different parts of the causal landscape. Confusing them leads to predictable failure. Treating deterrence as containment allows harm to propagate. Treating punishment as structural change leaves conditions untouched. CST separates these functions so their limits become visible.

Deterrence Shapes Cost, Not Capacity

Deterrence is the practice of discouraging behavior by making it more costly or unpleasant to repeat. The basic assumption is that behavior becomes less frequent when negative consequences are expected. Mechanically, deterrence operates by altering expected cost. It raises the downstream burden associated with certain behaviors so that those behaviors stabilize less often. This is not about instruction or insight. It is about reshaping the cost geometry the system encounters.

For example, when late fees are added for missed bill payments, the system does not become better at managing money. The cost of delay increases, making late payment harder to carry relative to paying on time. Deterrence can reduce frequency under specific conditions: when systems have margin, when alternative configurations are already viable, and when added cost

280

does not push the system into fallback modes. Under those conditions, deterrence can bias stabilization away from certain paths.

Under constraint, deterrence often fails. Added cost does not redirect behavior; it narrows it. When load is already high, raising cost further removes options rather than reshaping them. The system does not avoid the targeted behavior because it has nowhere else to go. Deterrence then selects for concealment, acceleration, or more rigid fallback patterns. The behavior appears reduced, but only because it has gone underground or compressed in time. Deterrence is therefore not a general solution. It is a conditional tool that works only when systems already have room to reorganize.

Containment Limits Propagation

Containment serves a different function. It does not attempt to change behavior directly. It limits how far harm can spread while conditions remain unresolved. Containment reduces spillover, protects surrounding systems, and preserves margin so that other work can occur. Physical barriers, separation protocols, supervision, and enforced pauses all function as containment. They reduce variance by constraining interaction, not by reshaping motivation. Containment is often necessary when systems are acutely unstable or when structural change is not immediately available. Containment is frequently mischaracterized as punishment. The distinction is simple. Containment targets propagation. Punishment targets the actor. One reduces spread; the other concentrates consequence. When containment is mistaken for punishment, it is often applied with excess severity. When punishment is mistaken for containment, it fails to stop recurrence.

For example, containment is mistaken for punishment, when a school separates two students after a fight to prevent further escalation. The separation is framed as discipline, extended indefinitely, and paired with public reprimand. What began as a limit to stop spread becomes excessive cost, increasing strain without reducing future conflict. When punishment is mistaken for containment, a workplace disciplines an employee after a safety violation but leaves the hazardous process unchanged. The reprimand creates quiet, but the same violation occurs again because the conditions that allowed it were never contained. Containment buys time. It does not, by itself, reduce the conditions that generate harm.

Structural Change Alters the Landscape

Structural change operates at a slower timescale. It alters the conditions under which systems stabilize in the first place. This includes changes to roles, resources, timing, information flow, environment, and institutional design. Structural change lowers baseline load, increases margin, and expands the set of viable configurations. Unlike deterrence, structural change does not rely on threat. Unlike containment, it does not merely limit spread. It reshapes what becomes easy, difficult, or unnecessary for systems to do. Structural change is the only strategy that reliably reduces recurrence over time. It is also the most demanding. It requires coordination, tolerance for uncertainty, and sustained effort under conditions where immediate relief is unavailable. This is why systems under strain often avoid it. They reach instead for faster tools that feel decisive.

Why These Strategies Are Commonly Collapsed

In practice, systems often treat deterrence, containment, and structural change as interchangeable. A single intervention is expected to punish, deter, contain, and reform all at once. This expectation is structurally incoherent. Punishment is expected to deter. Deterrence is expected to reform. Containment is expected to teach. When these expectations fail, the response is escalation rather than differentiation. More severity is applied to achieve outcomes the tool was never designed to produce. CST clarifies the failure mode. When strategies are collapsed, systems oscillate between urgency and disappointment. Harm recurs. Load accumulates. Confidence in alternatives erodes.

Timing Determines Which Strategy Is Viable

Which response is appropriate depends on current load and available margin. Under acute instability, containment may be the only viable move. Attempting structural change at that moment often increases variance and risk. Under moderate load, deterrence may have limited effect if alternatives are accessible. Under sustained stability, structural change becomes possible. Ethical error often arises from ignoring timing. Applying deterrence when containment is required allows harm to spread. Applying punishment when structural change is required entrenches fallback modes. Applying structural change when urgency is overwhelming can destabilize systems further. No strategy is universally correct. Each has a window in which it functions. Any of these responses may appear first, but none is sufficient on its own. Without containment, harm propagates. Without structural change, it returns. Treating one strategy as a substitute for the others guarantees recurrence.

Responsibility and the Choice of Strategy

Responsibility, understood as causal position, determines where each strategy must be applied. Deterrence targets cost geometry. Containment targets propagation paths. Structural change targets conditions. Responsibility tells us where intervention would matter, not which intervention to prefer. This reframing removes moral debate from the initial decision. The question is not what response feels deserved, it is which function is required given current constraint.

What This Chapter Establishes

This chapter establishes that deterrence, containment, and structural change are distinct responses to harm, each operating on different mechanisms and timescales. Deterrence reshapes cost. Containment limits spread. Structural change alters baseline conditions. Confusing these functions leads to escalation and failure. Punishment persists when these distinctions are ignored because it appears to serve all three roles at once. In reality, it reliably serves only one: fast stabilization under constraint. Moving beyond punishment requires the capacity to choose slower tools when conditions allow. The next chapter examines how guilt and shame function as internalized extensions of these same mechanisms—and why they so often increase load rather than reduce it.

Deterrence reshapes cost.
Containment limits spread.
Only structural change alters recurrence.

Chapter 49

Guilt, Shame, and Social Load

Internalized Consequence Under Constraint

Guilt and shame are often treated as moral emotions and assumed to guide behavior by signaling right and wrong, motivating repair, or restoring social bonds. In CST, they have no special moral status. They are internal load patterns that arise when social consequence is carried inside the system rather than managed structurally outside it. Both guilt and shame function as internalized extensions of deterrence and punishment. They move consequence from the environment into the architecture. This can appear efficient. Structurally, it is costly.

A child forgets to bring homework to school. The teacher reprimands them publicly. The consequence is external: embarrassment, lowered standing, a mark in the gradebook. After this happens a few times, the reprimand is no longer necessary. The child begins to feel a tightening in their body the night before school. They replay the possibility of forgetting. They feel a sinking sensation and a strong urge to check their bag repeatedly. No teacher is present. No punishment is being applied. The consequence has moved inside.

What was once managed by the environment — correction, embarrassment, discipline — is now carried internally as guilt and shame. The system applies pressure to itself in advance to avoid future exposure. The social cost has been internalized as ongoing load. Guilt and shame relocate consequence from the environment into the architecture. Instead of risking external sanction, the system generates internal pressure continuously. This may reduce visible transgression, but it does so by raising baseline load, narrowing behavior, and strengthening fallback modes. The environment becomes quieter. The system becomes heavier.

284

Guilt as Anticipated Consequence

Guilt is the felt burden of anticipated social consequence. It arises when a system carries forward the expected cost of having affected others. The feeling is not evidence of moral insight. It is evidence that consequence has been internalized. Under moderate load, guilt functions as deterrence inside the system. It reduces variation by pushing stabilization away from upper frame configurations that increase strain. This can reduce repetition without outside enforcement. Under constraint, guilt changes character. Anticipated consequence accumulates faster than it can be discharged. Internal work rises. Urgency increases. The system narrows toward avoidance, concealment, or rapid appeasement. The original harm may not recur, but new distortions appear. The system learns to manage guilt rather than conditions. Guilt does not repair. It redistributes load inward.

Shame as Global Load

Shame differs from guilt in scope. Guilt attaches to effects. Shame attaches to the system as a whole. Instead of carrying anticipated consequence about what happened, the system carries a generalized signal that it is the source of strain. This global load collapses differentiation. When shame dominates, local adjustments are no longer sufficient. Every configuration feels suspect. Identity corridors narrow. Behavior stabilizes around concealment, withdrawal, or rigid compliance. The system seeks invisibility or total alignment to reduce exposure. Shame is especially damaging under trauma because it fuses with constrained identity. Repeated effects are encountered as proof of defect. Responsibility becomes indistinguishable from worth. This fusion is not corrective. It entrenches fallback modes and raises long-term cost.

Why Internalization Feels Necessary

Guilt and shame often feel necessary because they reduce visible conflict. When consequence is carried internally, surrounding systems experience relief. Coordination costs drop and the appearance of order is restored. In this sense, internalized guilt and shame function like punishment turned inward. Just as external punishment relieves surrounding systems by concentrating consequence at a visible point, guilt and shame relieve them by ensuring that consequence is continuously applied inside the system itself. The relief others feel is structurally similar in both cases: strain has been redirected away from the environment. This relief is often mistaken for effectiveness. Variance is reduced outside the system while increasing inside it. Over time, internal load accumulates. Capacity shrinks. The system becomes less flexible and more brittle. Societies rely on guilt and shame when they lack structural alternatives. Internalization substitutes for redesign. The cost is deferred and paid later, inside people.

The Limits of Moral Repair

Practices of confession, apology, and moral accounting are often proposed as remedies for guilt and shame. In CST terms, these practices reduce load only if they alter conditions. Words alone do nothing. When apology reduces ongoing consequence, restores coordination, or removes uncertainty, load can drop. When it functions as a demand for self-condemnation, it raises load. Confession without structural change converts external strain into permanent internal burden. Repair is mechanical. It requires altered propagation, not moral expression.

Shame as a Tool of Social Control

Shame is frequently used to enforce norms when containment or structural change is unavailable. By making deviation costly everywhere, societies reduce the need for monitoring. The price is high. Systems under shame lose margin and become less capable of adaptation. This strategy selects for conformity under threat. It does not select for stability under variation. Over time, shame-driven systems become fragile. When conditions change, they lack the capacity to reorganize.

Responsibility Without Internal Punishment

Removing blame does not require installing guilt or shame in its place. Responsibility, as causal position, does not need to be felt to be real. Effects propagate whether or not they are accompanied by suffering. Accountability that relies on internal punishment trades short-term order for long-term rigidity while accountability that manages conditions preserves flexibility. The difference is not moral; it is architectural. A team misses an important deadline, delaying a product launch. In one response, the manager emphasizes personal responsibility by highlighting disappointment and encouraging the person who missed the handoff to sit with the failure so it does not happen again. The team moves on quickly. Tension drops. The individual carries ongoing guilt, double-checks obsessively, and avoids taking initiative in future projects. Order is restored, but flexibility shrinks.

In a different response, the manager examines handoff timing, unclear ownership, and overlapping responsibilities that made the miss likely. Deadlines are staggered, checkpoints are added, and escalation paths are clarified. No one is made to feel worse. The launch proceeds more reliably next time. Accountability remains, but it is carried by the system rather than internalized as ongoing strain. In both cases, responsibility is real and the consequences propagated. The difference is where consequence is carried. One response concentrates it inside a person through guilt, while the other manages conditions. The first produces short-term order at the cost of long-term rigidity. The second preserves flexibility without requiring suffering.

What This Chapter Establishes

This chapter establishes guilt and shame as internalized forms of social load. Guilt carries anticipated consequence inward. Shame globalizes that load across identity. Both can reduce visible conflict while increasing internal strain. Under constraint, these patterns entrench fallback modes and reduce capacity for reorganization. They are not reliable tools for repair. Responsibility does not require internal punishment. It requires accurate management of how consequence is carried. The next chapter turns from internal load to external systems, examining how justice can be organized without relying on blame, guilt, or shame to do the work that structure must perform.

Order restored through shame
is stability borrowed at interest.

Chapter 50

Justice Without Free Will

Managing Harm Without Blame

Justice is usually imagined as the moral completion of responsibility. Once someone is deemed responsible, justice is expected to assign what they deserve. This expectation presumes authorship. If someone chose freely, justice evaluates that choice and responds in kind. CST removes this foundation. What remains is not the absence of justice, but a different function entirely. In CST, justice is not a moral judgment. It is a system for managing harm, limiting propagation, and shaping future conditions. Its purpose is not to balance harm or outcomes, but to stabilize environments so that damage does not compound. Justice follows mechanics, not virtue.

Consider two drivers who cause identical accidents. In a non-mechanical justice frame, the question is who deserves what: intent is weighed, character is assessed, and punishment is scaled to moral evaluation. The response completes a story about authorship. In a mechanical justice frame, none of that is primary. The questions are structural: What conditions allowed the damage to propagate? What load was present? What changes would prevent recurrence? One driver may require separation from driving, another environmental changes to scheduling, rest, or road design. The responses may differ even when the harm is the same — not because of virtue or blame, but because stabilization requires different interventions. The aim is not moral balance. It is preventing further damage.

What Justice Must Do Once Authorship Is Removed

Without free will, justice cannot be about praise or condemnation. It must answer three practical questions instead: What harm has propagated? What pathways allow it to continue? What changes would reduce recurrence without shifting load elsewhere? These questions are not ethical abstractions. They are engineering problems. Justice operates on

288

architectures, not selves. It intervenes where causal flows can be altered, not where guilt can be assigned. This shift removes the need to ask whether someone deserves punishment. It replaces it with the need to determine what response will actually change what happens next.

Justice as Harm Management, Not Moral Accounting

Traditional justice systems often function as moral accounting systems. They tally offense and response, aiming for proportionality. CST reframes proportionality mechanically. The relevant measure is not offense severity, but downstream impact on load, variance, and future stability. A just response reduces total harm over time without creating new instability. An unjust response feels satisfying while increasing recurrence, brittleness, or spillover. This reframing explains why many punitive systems fail even by their own stated goals. They focus on visible consequence rather than structural effect.

Consider a person repeatedly arrested for petty theft related to drug use. In a moral accounting system, the offense is tallied and punishment escalates in the name of proportionality. After repeated offenses, this may result in a multi-year prison sentence — not to alter conditions, but to mark seriousness and satisfy the demand for consequence. Mechanically, this response increases load, disrupts housing and work, and pushes the person into more unstable environments. Theft returns not because punishment was insufficient, but because instability increases and future options narrow. A mechanically just response targets structure instead: access to treatment, stable housing, predictable routines, and separation from high-variance contexts. Theft declines not through moral correction, but because the conditions that made recurrence likely are no longer present. The first response feels proportional. The second reduces harm over time.

Justice as Containment and Structural Change

One core function of justice is containment. Some patterns pose immediate risk. Limiting their ability to propagate may be necessary before any other work can occur. Containment is often mistaken for punishment because it restricts behavior. The distinction lies in purpose. Punishment assigns consequence in response to offense. Containment limits spread under conditions of urgency. It protects margin while conditions are addressed. Its scope and duration are determined by risk and load, not by what has already occurred. When containment is treated as punishment, it is often prolonged, intensified, or generalized beyond what stability requires. When treated mechanically, it is as narrow, temporary, and targeted as conditions allow.

Justice that ends with containment has failed. Containment buys time; structural change determines outcomes. A just system uses the time gained by containment to alter the conditions that made harm likely. This includes redesigning environments, reallocating resources, changing incentives, and reducing chronic load. Structural change is slower and less emotionally satisfying than punishment. It is also the only path that reliably lowers recurrence. Justice systems drift toward punishment when they lack the capacity or patience for structural work. Severity substitutes for design. The appearance of firmness substitutes for effectiveness.

Why Moral Accounting Persists as an Intuition

Even when free will is rejected, intuitions of moral accounting persist. This is not a philosophical failure. It is a load response. When harm creates urgency, systems reach for simple mappings between act and response. Moral accounting compresses complexity into a rule that can be applied quickly. Justice without free will does not need to eliminate this intuition. It only needs to prevent it from governing design. Intuition may explain why punishment feels right, but it cannot determine what works.

Fairness Reconsidered

Under moral accounting, fairness is often understood as treating similar acts with similar consequences. A homicide results in a long prison sentence. A theft results in a shorter one. The scale is calibrated to offense severity. Equal acts receive equal punishment and fairness is presumed to follow. From a CST perspective, this symmetry can still be structurally unjust. Consider two homicides. In one case, violence emerges from an environment saturated with chronic load: overcrowding, unstable housing, constant threat exposure, and no viable exit paths. In the other, violence occurs within a context of high insulation: abundant resources, legal buffers, and rapid restoration of stability. Moral accounting assigns similar punishment to both acts. CST asks something different: how much cumulative load had already been concentrated at each position, and how much additional load the response will now impose. A system that repeatedly absorbs failure by placing it on the same overburdened positions while preserving insulation elsewhere is not fair, even if sentences are equal.

The same contrast appears at lower levels. A person steals food repeatedly and is jailed each time. Moral accounting escalates punishment to mark seriousness. Structurally, each response removes housing, income, and predictability, increasing load and narrowing future stability. Another person commits financial theft through institutional channels and absorbs fines without meaningful disruption to stability. Both are "held accountable," but exposure is unequal. Load concentrates downward. Stability remains protected upward. In CST, fairness is not equal punishment for equal acts. It is equal exposure to stabilizing conditions over time. A system is unjust when the same populations repeatedly absorb risk, failure, and correction, while others benefit from stability without carrying comparable load. Fairness, in this sense, is not a property of judgment. It is a property of structure.

Responsibility and Justice at Scale

Justice operates at multiple levels simultaneously. Individuals, organizations, and institutions all participate in causal chains. A just response does not isolate responsibility at the lowest visible level while ignoring higher-order contributors. When justice focuses narrowly on individuals, systemic contributors remain untouched. Load returns through the same channels. Justice without free will requires tracing causation upward as well as downward and intervening where leverage is greatest. This is not leniency. It is accuracy.

A warehouse worker is injured after repeated safety shortcuts. An individual-focused response disciplines the worker for violating procedure. The injury is treated as a personal failure. A multi-level response looks upward as well: production quotas that exceed safe pacing, understaffed shifts, incentive structures that reward speed over margin, and delayed maintenance. Addressing only the worker leaves these contributors intact. Injury returns through the same channels. A just response intervenes where leverage is greatest — at the level of scheduling, staffing, and incentives — while still managing immediate risk. The difference is not softness, but it is causal accuracy.

What This Chapter Establishes

This chapter establishes justice as a mechanical function rather than a moral verdict. Without free will, justice cannot be about moral accounting. It must be about harm management, containment, and structural change. A just system reduces recurrence without increasing load elsewhere. It limits propagation when necessary and redesigns conditions when possible. Punishment may feel necessary under constraint, but justice is measured by what changes, not by what is suffered. The next chapter examines how social systems are designed to carry these functions — and why many of them default to punishment when architecture, not morality, is the real problem.

A just system alters conditions.
An unjust one redistributes suffering.

Chapter 51

The Architecture of Social Systems
How Institutions Carry Load

Social systems are often treated as collections of people governed by rules. In CST, they are something more specific: load-bearing architectures that stabilize patterns at scale. Laws, norms, procedures, roles, and infrastructures are not expressions of values. They are mechanisms for distributing strain, limiting variance, and making coordinated activity possible across many systems at once. When social systems work, they reduce variance quietly. They reduce the amount of internal work required of the individuals inside them. When they fail, they do not fail morally. They fail mechanically, by concentrating load, narrowing margin, and forcing fallback modes across large populations.

Institutions as Stabilization Structures

Every institution stabilizes certain behaviors while making others difficult or unavailable. This is not because institutions decide what is right, but because their design shapes what can be carried reliably. Forms, queues, schedules, jurisdictions, and procedures are all stabilizing devices. They convert open-ended interaction into bounded pathways. An institution is therefore responsible for the patterns it makes easy. If a system repeatedly produces congestion, conflict, or harm, the question is not who misused it, but what the structure is selecting for under load. Recurrent outcomes are signals of architectural bias, not individual failure.

How Load Is Distributed at Scale

Social systems distribute load unevenly. Some positions absorb variance so others do not have to. Frontline workers, caregivers, enforcement roles, and marginalized populations often function as buffers for instability generated elsewhere. This buffering is not accidental. It is how large systems preserve coherence. Problems arise when buffering becomes chronic. When the same positions repeatedly absorb strain without restoration of margin, fallback modes harden. Burnout, rigidity, concealment, and withdrawal appear. From the inside, these look like personal failures. From the outside, they look like discipline problems. Mechanically, they are consequences of sustained load concentration.

Consider a large public-school district operating under fixed funding, shifting mandates, and rising student needs. Policy changes, testing requirements, staffing shortages, and social stressors introduce continuous variance. Teachers, counselors, and administrators absorb this instability so the system can continue to function.

As buffering becomes chronic, margin disappears. Class sizes grow, support staff vanish, and instructional time is redirected toward compliance tasks. Frontline staff move into fallback modes: rigid rule enforcement, narrowed curricula, increased referrals, emotional withdrawal, or quiet burnout. From the inside, this feels like exhaustion or detachment. From the outside, it is labeled poor teaching, lack of professionalism, or classroom mismanagement. The system preserves coherence by consuming its buffers. The resulting failures are structural, not personal.

Why Systems Drift Toward Punishment

When institutions lack margin, they simplify. Structural change is slow, complex, and uncertain. Punishment is fast, visible, and administratively straightforward. Under strain, systems default to tools that reduce variance quickly, even if those tools increase long-term cost. This drift does not require cruelty, but it requires urgency. As coordination becomes expensive, enforcement replaces design. Compliance substitutes for viability. Punishment becomes the primary stabilizer not because it works, but because alternatives cannot be carried.

In the same school district, chronic budget shortfalls and staffing gaps leave little margin for redesign. Reducing class sizes, expanding support services, or stabilizing instructional conditions requires coordination across agencies, funding cycles, and political timelines. Under strain, these options remain unavailable. What remains are faster tools. Rule enforcement tightens. Disciplinary policies harden. Minor infractions trigger suspensions or exclusions because they are administratively simple and visibly decisive. Variance is reduced quickly, at the cost of increasing disengagement, academic instability, and downstream demand on alternative and remedial systems. The shift is not driven by intent, but by urgency. Enforcement replaces design because design cannot be carried.

The Limits of Individual-Level Fixes

Social systems often attempt to correct structural problems by targeting individuals. Training programs, performance reviews, incentives, and sanctions are applied where redesign is needed. These interventions appear reasonable because individuals are visible and structures are spread across the system. The result is consistent. Individuals are asked to carry load that belongs to the system. Some manage temporarily through increased internal work. Others fail and are removed. The structure remains unchanged and the pattern repeats. Responsibility is displaced downward because it is easier to assign than to redesign.

Structural Responsibility Without Central Control

No social system has a single controller. Responsibility is distributed across design decisions made at different times, often by different actors under different constraints. This does not dissolve responsibility. It clarifies it. Responsibility at scale identifies leverage. Which rules amplify variance? Which procedures concentrate strain? Which roles absorb failure repeatedly? These questions locate responsibility without requiring a guilty party. They make redesign possible.

When Reform Fails

Reform efforts often fail because they target surface features while leaving load geometry intact. New policies are layered onto old constraints. Reporting requirements multiply. Oversight increases. Each addition raises internal work without restoring margin. From the outside, reform looks active. From the inside, it feels constricting. The system responds by narrowing further, relying more heavily on enforcement to maintain coherence. Effective reform reduces demand before it adds structure. It widens margin before it introduces variation. Without this sequencing, reform accelerates failure.

Designing for Carryability

A viable social system is not one that enforces compliance. It is one that makes necessary behavior carryable across a wide range of conditions. This includes tolerating error, absorbing shocks, and allowing local adjustment without system-wide instability. Designing for carryability shifts focus from ideals to mechanics. What load is being carried? By whom? With what margin? Where does strain accumulate when conditions change? These questions replace moral debate with architectural analysis.

In a school district designed for carryability, stability is achieved by redistributing load. Class sizes remain within ranges that can be carried under stress. Support staff absorb behavioral and academic variance so it does not concentrate on individual teachers. Schedules allow recovery after disruption. Rules flex locally when conditions spike, rather than triggering system-wide escalation. Errors are tolerated because they are expected under load. Shocks — student surges, family instability, community crises — are buffered through temporary staffing, adjusted pacing, and targeted support rather than punishment. Local adjustment is permitted without requiring uniform compliance. The result is not leniency but stability. Necessary behavior becomes carryable across a wide range of conditions, not because individuals perform better, but because the system no longer demands more than it can sustain.

What This Chapter Establishes

This chapter establishes social systems as load-bearing architectures rather than moral frameworks. Institutions stabilize behavior by distributing strain, shaping variance, and selecting for patterns under constraint. When they fail, they fail mechanically, not morally. Punishment emerges when systems lack the capacity for redesign. Individual blame substitutes for structural responsibility. Justice without free will therefore requires architectural attention: reducing concentrated load, restoring margin, and reshaping conditions so that harmful patterns no longer stabilize. The next chapter turns to what it means to take a system seriously under these conditions — how dignity, accountability, and participation can exist without authorship, praise, or blame.

Chapter 52

What It Means to Take Someone Seriously

Dignity Without Praise or Blame

To take someone seriously is often confused with believing in their agency. Respect is equated with autonomy, dignity with authorship, and accountability with moral appraisal. In CST, none of these equations hold. A system can be taken seriously without being treated as a chooser. In fact, treating a system as a chooser often prevents it from being taken seriously at all. Taking someone seriously, in CST terms, means treating their constraints as real and their effects as consequential. It means refusing to dismiss what a system stabilizes as mere excuse, while also refusing to inflate it into moral identity. Seriousness is not admiration or condemnation. It is accuracy about what occurred and about the fact that, under those conditions, it is all the system could be.

For example, a person may repeatedly cheat or steal from others. In a moral frame, this is read as a failure of character or choice. In CST terms, it is a pattern the system has stabilized under its history, load, and available options. That does not make the harm unreal, and it does not make the behavior acceptable. It means the pattern is accurate to the conditions that shaped it. Taking the person seriously does not mean endorsing the behavior or excusing its effects. It means recognizing that, under those conditions, this is what the system did — and designing responses that change conditions rather than demand a different author.

Seriousness as Causal Recognition

A system is taken seriously when its position in the causal fabric is acknowledged. What it stabilizes matters because it shapes what happens next. Ignoring that contribution is not compassion. It is erasure. This is why both dismissal and moralization fail. Dismissal treats constrained behavior as irrelevant noise. Moralization treats it as authored intent. Both misallocate causation. Taking someone seriously means locating where effects propagate and responding at that location. This stance does not require agreement, endorsement, or forgiveness. It requires recognition.

Dignity Without Elevation

Dignity is often framed as something bestowed when a person meets certain standards. In CST, dignity is not awarded. It is a consequence of accurate description. To describe a system as causally real rather than narratively judged is to grant dignity without ceremony. A person under constraint does not lose dignity because their behavior narrows. They lose dignity when their constraints are ignored or when their behavior is reduced to character. Taking someone seriously means neither excusing nor condemning what stabilizes, but treating it as part of the causal landscape that must be reckoned with. This is why dignity survives determinism. It does not depend on authorship. It depends on consequence.

Consider a worker who begins cutting corners after months of understaffing, unpredictable scheduling, and constant deadline pressure. Output remains high, but safety slips. From the inside, this is a narrowing response to sustained load. From the outside, it is labeled irresponsibility or lack of integrity. Dignity is not lost because the behavior narrowed. It is lost when the constraints are ignored and the behavior is reduced to character. The harm is treated as a personal flaw rather than as a signal of conditions that made the pattern stabilize. Taking the worker seriously would not excuse the shortcuts or ignore their effects. It would acknowledge that, under those conditions, this is what the system produced — and respond by altering the conditions rather than dismissing the person.

Accountability Without Moral Pressure

Accountability is often enforced through pressure: demand acknowledgment, insist on remorse, require commitment to improvement. These practices assume that internal states drive change. CST has shown otherwise. Accountability without moral pressure focuses on conditions. It asks what effects are occurring, where load is being carried, and what changes would reduce harm going forward. It does not require confession or self-judgment. It requires participation in altering conditions where participation is possible. This form of accountability is demanding. It does not allow systems to disappear behind explanation. But it also does not add load by demanding impossible internal transformation.

Why Being Taken Seriously Can Feel Uncomfortable

Being taken seriously in this way often feels colder than moral engagement. Praise and blame create the feeling of being seen. Structural recognition can feel impersonal. This discomfort is a byproduct of learned expectations from cultural training. Systems are accustomed to being addressed as selves with intentions. When that address is withdrawn, the absence can feel like indifference. In reality, it is a shift from narrative attention to structural attention. Over time, this shift produces something rarer than validation: reliability. The system learns that what it stabilizes will be responded to consistently, without escalation or moral distortion.

Participation Without Authorship

Taking someone seriously does not mean demanding that they fix themselves. It means recognizing where they can and cannot participate in change. Participation without authorship allows systems to contribute to alteration of conditions without being cast as originators of harm. This is especially important under constraint. Demanding authorship where none exists increases load. Allowing participation where capacity exists reduces it. Seriousness consists in making this distinction accurately.

Consider a student repeatedly removed from class for disruptive behavior during a period of housing instability. Demanding that the student "take responsibility" by self-correcting assumes authorship they do not have under those conditions. Load increases, behavior narrows further, and removal escalates. Taking the student seriously means something different. The student can participate in change by showing up, engaging when conditions allow, and responding to immediate support. They cannot originate stability while housing, sleep, and predictability are absent. Adjusting schedules, providing consistent support, and reducing variance lowers load and allows participation without demanding authorship. The difference is not permissiveness. It is accuracy about where participation is possible and where conditions must change first.

Seriousness at Scale

The same principle applies beyond individuals. Communities, institutions, and cultures are taken seriously when their stabilizations are treated as real contributors to outcomes. Reform that focuses only on values or intentions fails because it does not take structure seriously. At scale, dignity means refusing to explain harm away as isolated failure while also refusing to locate it in moral defect. It means tracing causation across levels and responding where leverage actually exists.

What This Chapter Establishes

This chapter establishes that taking someone seriously does not require belief in agency, autonomy, or moral authorship. It requires accurate recognition of constraint and consequence. Dignity arises from being treated as causally real. Accountability arises from managing effects rather than judging intent. CST does not ask for softness. It asks for precision. It asks us to be kinder by being more precise. When systems are taken seriously in this way, cruelty loses its justification, and responsibility becomes usable without becoming punitive.

To take someone seriously is to treat their constraints as real and their effects as consequential — not with admiration or condemnation, but with accuracy about what occurred.

Part IX

Meaning, Mortality, and Living Inside the Machine

Meaning, Life, and Acceptance Without Control

Chapter 53

Meaning Without Purpose

How Significance Arises From Consequence

Meaning is often treated as the final refuge of agency. Even when control, authorship, and free will are removed, meaning is assumed to remain as something a self creates, assigns, or chooses. If nothing is intended, if nothing is authored, then what could meaning possibly be? In CST, meaning does not require purpose. It does not require intention. It does not require a subject who confers significance. Meaning arises as a consequence of what stabilizes and what follows.

Consider a person who repeatedly returns to the same kind of work, relationship pattern, or place over many years. In an agency-based frame, the repetition is explained as choice or purpose: they value it, identify with it, or decide that it matters. In CST terms, the repetition carries meaning without any of that. The pattern stabilized because it was carryable under the system's history and load. Over time, what follows from that stabilization — who is encountered, what skills accumulate, what futures remain available — gives the pattern significance. Meaning appears not as intention, but as consequence. Nothing needed to be chosen for this to matter. It matters because it shaped what could happen next.

Why Purpose Is Not Required

Purpose implies direction set in advance. It assumes an end that guides action toward itself. This framing quietly reinstates a chooser, even when the chooser is said to be unconscious, implicit, or emergent. CST requires none of this. Systems do not move toward ends. They stabilize under constraint. What persists does so because it can be carried. What follows does so because it is shaped by what came before. Meaning arises from the consequences of the sequence, not from foresight.

Meaning as Downstream Effect

In CST, meaning names the significance of consequences. Narrative and felt signature may arise, but they occur downstream of stabilization. They compress what has already happened; they do not generate it. A configuration matters if it reshapes or reliably affirms what can stabilize next — by altering or preserving cost, load, access, or margin. Meaning is not something added to an event. It is the difference the event makes to the landscape that follows.

A word matters if it changes coordination or keeps coordination intact. A gesture matters if it alters proximity or posture, or maintains an existing alignment. A decision matters if it redirects future stabilizations or holds a corridor in place. None of this requires intention. It requires impact. Meaning, therefore, is not subjective assignment. It is structural consequence registered over time. Meaning is not value. Consequences can be significant without being good and insignificant without being bad.

Why Meaning Feels Personal

Meaning often feels deeply personal because identity corridors are long-timescale stabilizers. When a consequence aligns with identity, it is carried smoothly and integrated widely. When it cuts across identity, it raises strain and reorganizes large regions of the architecture. Awareness receives these differences as importance, relevance, or weight. The feeling of meaning is the felt signature of scale. Small consequences feel trivial because they do not propagate far. Large consequences feel meaningful because they reshape wide regions of the system's future stabilization. The longer a consequence continues to shape what can stabilize, the more meaning it carries. No purpose is required for this distinction to arise.

Meaning Without Narrative Authority

Narrative often claims ownership of meaning. After something happens, narrative organizes consequences into stories of intention, value, and lesson. These stories are compressions that make significance legible, but they do not create it. In CST, narrative follows consequential meaning. It does not generate it. A consequence that reshapes future stabilization will be narrated as meaningful. A consequence that does not will be ignored. The ordering is structural, not interpretive.

A policy change quietly alters scheduling in a workplace, reducing errors and turnover over the next year. Long after the change, stories form about leadership vision, cultural shift, or renewed commitment. The narrative assigns intention and lesson, but the meaning was already present in what changed: fewer breakdowns and wider margin. If the policy had produced no durable change, no story would persist. Narrative follows consequence. It does not produce it.

Why Suffering Feels Meaningful

Suffering often carries a sense of meaning even when it is unwanted and purposeless. This does not require hidden intention or moral justification. Suffering feels meaningful because it has large-scale consequences. It narrows landscapes, reshapes identity, and redirects future stabilizations. The system registers this scope as weight. This does not redeem suffering. It explains why it cannot be dismissed as insignificant simply because it was not chosen.

A person loses an arm in an accident. No purpose is present, and no lesson is intended. Yet the loss permanently reshapes what the system can do: how objects are handled, which work is possible, how space is navigated, and how assistance is required. Futures that were once accessible close; others open under constraint. The suffering carries weight because the consequences are large and enduring. The system registers this scope as meaning — not because the loss was justified or chosen, but because it redirected what could stabilize next.

Meaning After Trauma and Constraint

After trauma or prolonged constraint, meaning often becomes narrowed. Fallback modes and constrained identity dominate. Consequences propagate along limited channels. Repetition amplifies certain effects while others fade from relevance. Awareness encounters this narrowing as fixation: the sense that only a few things matter and everything else recedes. This is not a failure of perspective. It is a consequence of altered geometry.

As broader stabilization becomes possible again, meaning widens. Consequences propagate across more pathways. Futures that were previously unreachable become accessible. Significance redistributes. Meaning changes because structure changes. A configuration can stabilize without carrying broad consequence, and therefore without carrying much meaning.

Why Meaning Does Not Justify What Happened

Meaning is often confused with justification. If something feels meaningful, it is assumed to have happened for a reason. CST rejects this inference. Consequence does not imply purpose nor necessity. A forest fire reshapes an ecosystem because its effects are significant. That does not mean it was meant to occur, but instead, meaning is a description of what followed, not why it occurred.

Meaning Without Comfort

Removing purpose from meaning can feel unsettling. Purpose offers reassurance: the sense that events are guided, lessons are intended, and outcomes are deserved. CST offers no such comfort. What it offers instead is precision. Meaning without purpose allows significance to be acknowledged without moralizing history or inventing hidden aims. What mattered did so because it altered what could happen next, not because it was supposed to happen.

Meaning as Participation, Not Direction

Systems matter because they participate in causation — whether they are positioned to or not. They shape what follows simply by stabilizing where they do. This participation does not require control, understanding, or endorsement. Meaning arises wherever participation leaves residue. To matter is not to choose. It is to be a site where effects land and propagate.

What This Chapter Establishes

This chapter establishes meaning as consequence rather than purpose. Meaning does not arise from intention, authorship, or direction toward an end. It arises from the scope and persistence of effects that reshape future stabilization. Narrative may describe meaning, but it does not create it. Trauma, constraint, and identity alter meaning by altering which consequences propagate, not by changing what events were for. Meaning without purpose preserves significance without reintroducing a self outside the causal fabric, and prepares the ground for examining participation and ethics without authorship. Meaning is not what a self assigns. Meaning is what a sequence changes.

Chapter 54

Why Purpose Is a Story the System Tells

Direction Without Ends

Purpose is often treated as the natural companion to meaning. If something matters, it is assumed to be for something. If a life unfolds coherently, it is assumed to be moving toward something. When authorship is removed, purpose is often reintroduced as a quieter substitute: an implied direction, an underlying aim, a destination said to exist even if no one is steering. CST rejects this move — not because purpose is false in an abstract sense, but because it mischaracterizes what systems are doing. The sunflower does not orient toward the sun as an end to be fulfilled. It stabilizes under constraint: differential growth, light exposure, and structural limits make some orientations carryable and others unstable. What persists does so because it can be carried. What follows does so because it is shaped by what has already stabilized. Direction appears, but it is retrospective — read from the path left behind, not from an end that pulled the system forward. Purpose is the story that appears when this direction is narrated as if it were set in advance.

Direction Without Destination

From the outside, many processes look purposeful. Rivers flow toward the sea. Bodies reorganize after disruption. Skills accumulate. Lives take recognizable shapes. In ordinary language, these patterns are explained by goals: the river seeks the ocean, the body aims at health, the person wants fulfillment. Mechanically, none of this is required. A river flows because gravity, terrain, and resistance constrain where water can remain coherent. A body reorganizes because configurations that reduce strain persist more reliably than those that increase it. Skills accumulate because repeated stabilizations leave residue that reshapes what can be carried next. Lives take shape because certain corridors remain accessible while others close. Direction emerges from constraint and carryability. Destination is inferred afterward. Systems do not move toward optimal states, only toward configurations that remain coherent under current conditions. Purpose is the narrative compression that turns inferred direction into an imagined aim.

Why Purpose Feels Necessary

Purpose persists because it performs stabilizing work under load. When systems face uncertainty, purpose provides fast closure by compressing many possible futures into a single projected trajectory. This reassurance is carried at higher Frames of Reference, where narrative compression reduces variance when lower-level stabilization becomes strained. It promises that movement is not arbitrary, that effort is not wasted, that difficulty is oriented toward something that will justify it. Purpose converts open-ended propagation into a story with direction. This is not a reasoning error. It is a stabilization strategy. Under strain, systems narrow. They seek fast coherence. Purpose provides that coherence by saying, in effect, this is where things are going. CST does not deny the comfort this provides. It denies that the comfort describes the machinery accurately.

Purpose as Retrospective Compression

In CST terms, purpose is a backward-facing construction that arises late in the sequence. After stabilizations have occurred and consequences have propagated, awareness compresses the path into a narrative of direction: this happened so that this could occur; this difficulty existed in order to produce that outcome. What is being compressed is not intention, but consequence. A system stabilizes in certain ways. Those stabilizations reshape access, cost, and margin. Over time, some futures become reachable and others do not. When awareness encounters this shaped trajectory, it reads coherence and names its purpose. The order matters. Stabilization comes first. Consequence propagates. Narrative arrives last. Purpose is not a driver. It is a summary. Even when systems project possible futures, these projections do not create ends. They constrain present stabilization by reducing variance, sometimes narrowing into outcome binding, where coherence becomes contingent on a projected configuration. This shapes what can be carried now without defining where the system must arrive.

The Cost of Treating Purpose as Real

Treating purpose as an actual guiding force introduces distortions. First, it invites evaluation. If there is a purpose, deviations can be judged as failures to align with it. Narrowing becomes error. Constraint becomes resistance. Difficulty becomes meaningful only insofar as it appears to serve the supposed end. Second, it obscures structure. When outcomes are attributed to purpose, the conditions that produced them recede from view. Load, access, and margin are displaced by stories about direction. Third, it burdens systems under constraint. If a purpose is presumed, the system is expected to move toward it even when conditions make that movement uncarryable. The narrative adds load precisely where load is already concentrated. Purpose does not merely describe direction. It demands it.

How Purpose Differs from Participation

CST replaces purpose with participation. Systems matter because they participate in causation — whether positioned to or not. By stabilizing where they do, they shape what follows. Participation does not require foresight, endorsement, or agreement. It indicates only causal placement. Participation has no destination. It has effects. A life is not for something. It is a sequence of stabilizations whose consequences propagate forward, shaping what can happen next. Coherence arises because residue accumulates, not because an end is being approached. When participation is mistaken for purpose, the system is treated as if it were oriented toward an outcome rather than situated within conditions. Only one of these can be redesigned.

Consider a person who consistently de-escalates conflict at work. In a purpose-based frame, this is explained as a goal: they want harmony, value peace, or aim to be a mediator. Their behavior is evaluated against that supposed intention. In CST terms, no purpose is required. The person stabilizes under conditions where reducing conflict lowers load and preserves margin. By responding in ways that keep situations carryable, they participate in shaping what follows. Tension drops. Coordination improves. These outcomes emerge from participation, not pursuit. Treating this pattern as purpose invites judgment when conflict does occur. Treating it as participation keeps attention on conditions — pacing, authority, workload, and support — that can actually be adjusted.

Living Without the Purpose Story

Removing purpose does not remove direction. It removes the claim that direction was set in advance. What remains is a different orientation: attention to conditions, to what is carryable now, and to how present stabilizations reshape future access. The question is no longer: what is this for, but what does this make possible, and at what cost? Systems continue to stabilize whether purpose is believed or not. Movement does not require mission. It requires only that some configurations remain carryable. Direction persists, but it is no longer personified.

What This Chapter Establishes

This chapter establishes purpose as a narrative compression rather than a guiding force. Systems do not move toward ends. They stabilize under constraint, and direction is inferred from the consequences that follow. Purpose feels necessary because it reduces uncertainty and offers coherence under load. But treating it as real obscures structure, adds load, and misallocates responsibility. CST replaces purpose with participation: being a site where effects land and propagate. Meaning remains intact without purpose, because significance arises from consequence, not mission. The next chapter turns to what this implies for a life as a whole — how a life can have shape, continuity, and weight without being organized around an end.

Systems do not move toward outcomes.
They move where constraint allows.

Chapter 55

The Shape of a Life

Trajectory Without Destination

A life is often imagined as a project. It begins with potential, moves through choices, and aims toward fulfillment or completion. Even when free will is questioned, this image tends to persist in softer form: a life is said to be *about* something, to express an inner direction, or to realize an underlying purpose over time. CST replaces this picture with a different one. A life is not a project moving toward an end. It is a trajectory through a changing landscape of constraint. Its shape is determined by what stabilizes, what accumulates residue, and how each stabilization reshapes what can occur next. Continuity arises not from intention, but from carryability. What gives a life its apparent coherence is not a plan. It is the persistence of corridors.

Life as a Path Through Constraint

At any moment, a system occupies a configuration that can be carried. That configuration sits within a landscape shaped by history: past stabilizations, accumulated residue, and prior narrowing or widening. From that position, only certain transitions are available at tolerable cost. As time unfolds, the system does not select among all possible futures. It moves among those that remain reachable. Each movement leaves further residue, subtly reshaping the terrain. Over long timescales, this produces a recognizable path. That path is what is commonly called a life. From the inside, this path is experienced as continuity: *this is still me, this is where things are going*. From the outside, it appears as pattern: recurring roles, familiar environments, repeated modes of engagement. Neither requires an inner organizer. Both arise from constrained propagation.

Why Lives Look Coherent

Lives often look coherent in retrospect. Events line up. Skills build on one another. Relationships cluster. Periods appear to have themes. This coherence is frequently attributed to purpose or character. Mechanically, it comes from path dependence. Once a system stabilizes in a particular region of the landscape, transitions nearby are lower cost than distant ones. Residue deepens local grooves. Access narrows in some directions and widens in others. Over time, movement becomes easier along familiar routes and harder elsewhere. Coherence is the byproduct of staying within what can be carried repeatedly. A life looks shaped because it is shaped — by constraint, not by design.

Consider a person who takes an entry-level accounting job early in adulthood, not out of passion, but because it is available and manageable. The work is structured, predictable, and initially low-risk. Over time, familiarity lowers cost. Skills consolidate. Credentials accumulate. Relationships form with clients, managers, and adjacent professionals. As years pass, opportunities arise nearby: specialization, certification, supervisory roles, or contract work. Transitions within this region of the landscape remain low cost, while distant alternatives — returning to school or switching fields entirely — become progressively harder to carry. Decades later, the life appears coherent. The person runs a small accounting practice, handles complex returns, provides financial guidance, and is known for reliability. In retrospect, this is often narrated as purpose or aptitude. Mechanically, it is path dependence: early stabilizations reshaped access and cost, deepening grooves that made certain futures easy and others unlikely.

Turning Points and Apparent Change

Major changes in a life are often described as decisions: a turning point, a realization, a commitment. From a CST perspective, what changes at these moments is not authorship, but geometry. Sometimes load exceeds what the current configuration can sustain. Margin collapses. Fallback modes appear. In other cases, support increases, variance drops, or new conditions become available. In both cases, the landscape reorganizes. When the terrain changes, new paths become reachable. Movement that was previously uncarryable becomes possible. What feels like a sudden change of direction is a shift in what the system can now stabilize. The shape of the life changes because the landscape changed.

Consistency Without Identity Control

A common worry is that removing purpose and authorship dissolves personal continuity. If no one is steering, what makes a life one life rather than a sequence of unrelated events? The answer is residue. Residue links moments across time. Each stabilization leaves traces that bias what follows. Preferences, skills, sensitivities, and vulnerabilities are not consulted; they are carried forward. Even when contexts shift, these traces constrain how the system reorganizes. Identity corridors emerge from this accumulation. They are not narratives the system tells about itself. They are long-timescale stabilizations that make some futures feel familiar and others unreachable. Continuity is structural, not self-authored.

Lives Without Endpoints

A life does not aim toward completion. There is no final configuration it is meant to reach. What exists instead is a continual negotiation with constraint: periods of widening, periods of narrowing, phases of stability, and phases of reorganization. This has important consequences. First, it removes the pressure to evaluate a life against an imagined destination. There is no standard of arrival, no point at which life has succeeded or failed in becoming what it was supposed to be. Second, it reframes regret. Untraveled paths are not missed opportunities that were not chosen, but are regions that became unreachable as the landscape evolved. Third, it clarifies why lives can feel unfinished without being incomplete. There was never an endpoint to reach.

Consider a person finishing undergraduate study who received an offer to enter a doctoral program. At the same time, they had been in a relationship for several years, and the possibility of building a life together required moving away and letting the doctoral path close. At the time, both they and those around them believed they were ready for the academic path. The offer appeared to represent the "correct" future. Yet the system did not stabilize there. The configuration that became carryable was the one that continued with the partner. They married, built a shared life, and the years unfolded in a stable and coherent way.

Looking back much later, something becomes visible that was not visible then. The person can now see that, despite appearances, the doctoral path would likely have exceeded what they could sustain at that stage. The readiness that seemed present was incomplete. The path did not close because it was rejected; it closed because the system did not stabilize there. The life that followed was not a deviation from what was supposed to happen. It was the continuation that became possible under the conditions that existed. Nothing was missed. The landscape changed, and with it, what could be reached. From inside a life, events appear as decisions, turning points, and chosen directions. From a wider view, the life simply unfolded through successive stabilizations — sometimes widening, sometimes narrowing, sometimes reorganizing — without moving toward a final state.

The Felt Shape of a Life

Awareness encounters the shape of a life as memory, anticipation, and recognition. Certain patterns feel like me. Certain futures feel possible or impossible. This felt shape is not a summary chosen by awareness. It is a readout of accumulated constraint. Moments feel pivotal when they coincide with large-scale reorganization. Periods feel stagnant when movement is confined to narrow corridors. Times of expansion feel meaningful because access increases and variance becomes tolerable. The feeling of *this is my life* is the felt signature of long-timescale stabilization.

Consider a person in midlife who looks ahead and senses that some futures are simply not for them. Moving to a new country, retraining for a radically different profession, or starting over socially may register as impossible, while other paths — deepening an existing role, maintaining familiar relationships, continuing established routines — feel natural and accessible.

This sense is not the result of conscious evaluation. It is a readout of accumulated constraint. Years of stabilizing in certain environments have lowered the cost of familiar patterns and raised the cost of distant ones. Awareness receives this geometry as recognition: *this fits, that does not*. When a major disruption occurs — a layoff, illness, or relocation — the felt shape can shift abruptly. Futures that once felt closed become reachable while others disappear. Such moments feel pivotal not because a choice was made, but because the landscape reorganized.

What This Chapter Establishes

This chapter establishes a life as a trajectory shaped by stabilization rather than a project guided by purpose. A life has shape because residue accumulates, corridors form, and access changes over time. Continuity does not require a self that plans or directs. It arises from constraint carried forward. Change does not require decision. It occurs when the landscape reorganizes. A life can have coherence, weight, and significance without moving toward an end. It is shaped by what it has been able to carry — and by what that carrying made possible next. The next chapter turns to one of the most consequential long-timescale processes affecting that shape: aging, understood not as decline or failure, but as progressive narrowing of what can be carried.

A life unfolds through successive stabilizations.
Its shape is the trace they leave.

Chapter 56

Aging as Narrowing

Time, Residue, and the Shrinking of What Can Be Carried

Aging is commonly framed as decline. Strength fades, speed slows, memory thins. This framing treats aging as loss relative to an earlier ideal. CST offers a different description. Aging is the long-timescale narrowing of what can be carried. This narrowing is not a failure of will, effort, or attitude. It is the cumulative consequence of time operating on a load-bearing architecture. Residue accumulates. Margins change. Variance tolerance shifts. What once stabilized easily now requires more internal work; what once remained accessible becomes costly or unavailable. Aging is geometry changing under time.

Time as Accumulated Constraint that Leads to Narrowing

Every stabilization leaves residue. Over short spans, this residue can widen access: skills consolidate, coordination improves, familiar environments become easier to carry. Over long spans, the same accumulation begins to bias the landscape in the opposite direction. Wear concentrates. Recovery slows. Flexibility narrows. The system becomes more specific about the conditions it can carry without strain. This is not a single mechanism. It is the combined effect of countless small stabilizations interacting over years. Tissue adapts. Routines harden. Sensitivities sharpen. Tolerances shift. Time does not move the system toward an endpoint or purpose. It reshapes the cost landscape continuously.

A system cannot widen indefinitely. Widening requires surplus margin and tolerable variance. Over time, both become harder to sustain. As residue accumulates, compensatory capacity is increasingly allocated to maintenance. More internal work is required just to remain stable. Less remains available for exploration, reorganization, or novelty. This does not mean that change stops. It means that change becomes more selective.

Fewer transitions remain carryable. Fallback modes become more prominent under strain. Narrowing is not optional. It is the mechanical consequence of persistence under time and exposure. Repetition reshapes the landscape so that familiar patterns become structurally favored, while alternatives demand increasing internal work. Over time, the system does not lose possibilities in the abstract — it becomes organized around the configurations it has repeatedly stabilized.

Consider a musician who begins playing in early adolescence. In the first years, the system widens. Finger coordination improves, auditory discrimination sharpens, timing stabilizes, and the instrument becomes easier to carry. Practice that once produced strain becomes fluid. New pieces are learned quickly. The widening is real: accumulated stabilizations lower the cost of related configurations, and access expands across a broad range of technical and expressive patterns.

As the same accumulation continues. Decades pass. The hands adapt in ways that both support and constrain. Small areas of wear appear. The physical substrate itself changes: tissue adapts, wears, and repairs with increasing cost, and recovery slows. A larger portion of the system's capacity is required simply to maintain the stability of the body that carries it. As maintenance demand rises, less margin remains available for widening, exploration, or reorganization, and the landscape gradually narrows around what can be sustained without excessive strain.

The repertoire increasingly centers around patterns the system can sustain cleanly without excessive strain. Pieces that once felt easy now require more preparation. Exploration remains possible, but it must be more selective. The system has not simply "lost ability." It has become more specifically organized around the configurations it has repeatedly carried across time. Nothing in this process aims toward decline or improvement. The landscape is being reshaped continuously by accumulated constraint. Earlier widening made later skill possible. The same accumulation, extended across years, concentrates wear, redirects margin toward maintenance, and narrows which transitions remain carryable without strain. The musician still changes, still reorganizes, still adapts — but the range of effortless widening is no longer what it once was. The system persists, and persistence itself reshapes what can be carried.

The Shift in What Matters

As narrowing progresses, the distribution of significance changes. When access is wide, many outcomes matter a little. When access narrows, fewer outcomes matter a lot. Attention, effort, and concern concentrate around what remains carryable: health, predictability, proximity, continuity. This concentration is often misread as rigidity, conservatism, or fear of change. Mechanically, it reflects altered geometry. When variance tolerance drops, stability becomes precious. What matters narrows because what can propagate narrows.

Consider an older adult who once cared deeply about career advancement, social status, and novelty. Earlier in life, these concerns competed evenly with many others because access was wide and variance was tolerable. Changes in work, relationships, or location could be absorbed without destabilizing the system. As narrowing progresses, significance redistributes. Health appointments, medication schedules, sleep quality, and proximity to trusted people begin to matter far more than abstract ambition or experimentation. A missed dose, an unexpected disruption, or a loss of routine now carries disproportionate consequences, while changes that once felt meaningful fade in importance. From the outside, this can look like rigidity or resistance to change. Mechanically, it reflects altered geometry. With lower variance tolerance, stability becomes precious.

Aging and Identity Corridors

Identity corridors are long-timescale stabilizations. Aging reshapes them by changing which parts of the corridor remain accessible. Some identities deepen: roles that rely on accumulated residue — mentorship, pattern recognition, steadiness — become easier to carry. Others thin or close: identities that require speed, recovery, or wide variance tolerance become costly. From the inside, this can feel like becoming "less oneself." Mechanically, it is becoming more specific about which selves can be carried.

Consider a person who has identified for decades as a competitive cyclist. The identity stabilized through repeated training, endurance, recovery, and competition. For years, this corridor was wide: speed, output, and physical resilience remained carryable, and the identity felt natural and expansive. In later life, recovery slows and variance tolerance drops. Injuries take longer to resolve. Balance, reaction time, and cardiovascular margin narrow. The activities that once stabilized the cyclist identity become costly or uncarryable, even as knowledge, pattern recognition, and technical understanding remain intact. From the inside, this can feel like losing a self. Mechanically, the corridor has narrowed. The identity has not vanished; the parts of it that depended on speed and recovery have thinned, while those that rely on accumulated residue — coaching others, route planning, equipment expertise, pacing judgment — remain accessible. Identity does not disappear with age. It becomes more constrained, reorganizing around what can still be carried.

Why Resistance Increases Load

Many cultural narratives frame aging as something to be fought. Maintain youth. Preserve function. Stay flexible at all costs. Resistance adds load. When narrowing is treated as failure, the system is asked to carry both the mechanical cost of aging and the additional cost of opposition. Internal work increases without restoring margin. Strain accumulates faster. CST does not prescribe acceptance as a virtue. It describes acceptance as a load-reducing configuration: aligning expectations with what the landscape can actually support.

Consider a person whose identity was long organized around physical beauty — someone who was publicly celebrated for appearance in early adulthood. For years, maintaining that identity was carryable. High variance tolerance, rapid recovery, and social reinforcement kept the corridor wide. As aging progresses, the physical conditions that supported that identity change. Skin elasticity, energy, recovery, and hormonal stability narrow. The same routines now require more internal work and produce less stabilizing return.

When this narrowing is treated as failure, resistance escalates. More effort is poured into preservation: increasingly restrictive diets, invasive procedures, relentless monitoring, comparison, and self-correction. None of this restores margin. It adds load. The system is now carrying both the mechanical cost of aging and the cost of opposing it. From the outside, this can be labeled vanity or denial. Mechanically, it is a mismatch between expectation and landscape. The identity corridor — at the level of Frame of Reference — remains aimed at configurations that are no longer carryable, forcing continuous strain. Acceptance, in CST terms, is not surrender. It is a reallocation of effort away from uncarryable stabilizations and toward configurations the landscape can still support.

Aging Is Not Uniform Decline

Narrowing does not occur evenly across all domains. Some capacities diminish early. Others remain stable or even strengthen. The landscape becomes more uneven. Certain paths become impassable as others become deeply grooved. Stability becomes localized rather than broad. This is why aging can bring both loss and clarity. The system becomes less able to carry many things, but more reliable in carrying a few. Meaning concentrates not because purpose appears, but because consequence scope changes.

Social Failure Modes Around Aging

Many social systems are built for wide variance tolerance and rapid adaptation. As individuals age, these systems often fail to adjust. When environments do not redesign for narrowing, individuals are blamed for reduced capacity. Expectations remain calibrated to earlier geometry. Load concentrates. Fallback modes appear. What is framed as disengagement or decline is often a mismatch between system design and what the individual can now carry. Aging exposes architectural rigidity in social systems.

Consider a workplace that expects the same pace, hours, and responsiveness from employees regardless of age. As an older worker's variance tolerance narrows, the environment remains unchanged. Meetings run long, deadlines stack, and recovery time is not built in. When performance slips, the cause is framed as disengagement or decline. Mechanically, the system failed to redesign. Expectations remained calibrated to earlier geometry, concentrating load where margin had narrowed. Fallback modes appear — not because capacity vanished, but because the environment no longer fits. Aging does not reveal personal failure. It exposes architectural rigidity.

What This Chapter Establishes

This chapter establishes aging as the long-timescale narrowing of carryability rather than decline relative to an ideal. Over time, residue accumulates, margins shift, and variance tolerance drops. The landscape changes, and with it, what can stabilize. Aging reshapes identity corridors, concentrates significance, and makes stability more local. Resistance increases load; alignment reduces it. Aging does not move a life toward completion. It alters the geometry through which the life continues to propagate. The next chapter turns to the terminal boundary of this process: death, understood mechanically not as meaning's negation, but as the end of stabilization itself.

Chapter 57

Death as the End of Stabilization

The Boundary of Propagation

Death is often treated as the ultimate problem meaning must solve. If life ends, what was it for? If nothing continues, what was the point? These questions assume that meaning depends on endurance or completion. CST rejects that premise. Death is not the negation of meaning. It is the end of stabilization. A system lives so long as it can maintain configurations over time. It stabilizes states, carries load, leaves residue, and reshapes what can follow. Death marks the point at which this machinery no longer operates. No further stabilizations occur. No new residue accumulates. Propagation stops. Nothing needs to be concluded for this to matter.

Life as Ongoing Stabilization

While alive, a system continually negotiates constraint. It stabilizes moment to moment, reorganizes under strain, widens when margin allows, narrows when it does not. Each stabilization participates in causation by shaping what comes next. This ongoing process does not aim at death, avoid death, or complete itself in death. Death is simply the boundary at which the process ends. From a mechanical perspective, life is not a trajectory toward termination. It is a sequence that continues until it cannot.

Why Death Feels Different

Death feels categorically different from other losses because it removes all future stabilization. Injury narrows access. Aging constrains options. Trauma redirects propagation. Death eliminates propagation entirely. Awareness encounters this as finality. This finality is often narrated: as failure, as completion, as punishment, or as transition to another domain. CST does not require any of these narratives to account for the felt weight. The weight arises because consequence scope drops to zero.

Meaning Does Not Require Continuation

A common intuition holds that if nothing continues, nothing mattered. This confuses meaning with persistence. Meaning, in CST, is the significance of consequences while stabilization occurs. It is not contingent on infinite duration. A short-lived stabilization can have large effects. A long-lived one can leave little residue. A conversation can redirect a life. A policy, can reshape a generation. A brief intervention can alter which futures remain reachable. None of this requires that the originating system persist. *Death ends participation. It does not erase consequence.*

Residue Beyond the System

Although stabilization ends at death, residue does not vanish. Residue exists in other systems: altered environments, changed routines, learned patterns, redistributed load. A system's prior stabilizations have already reshaped the landscape of others. This is not legacy in a moral sense. It is causal continuation without authorship. What persists is not the person. It is the structure they participated in reshaping.

Why Death Does Not Complete a Life

Many narratives frame death as the moment that gives a life its meaning — the final punctuation that reveals what it was all about. CST rejects this framing. A life does not require completion. It has no endpoint it is meant to reach. Its shape exists in the sequence of stabilizations that occurred while it could. Death does not summarize a life. It terminates it. The shape of a life is visible only while propagation is possible. After death, no further stabilization occurs.

Living with the Boundary in View

Understanding death as the end of stabilization changes how life is approached. If meaning does not depend on purpose or completion, then death does not threaten meaning by arriving. Meaning was present wherever consequence propagated while stabilization occurred. Life does not need to justify itself against death. It does not need to add up to something. It only needs to have participated. This reframing removes the pressure to treat death as an arbiter of value. It is a boundary condition, not a verdict.

Consider a person who knows they are nearing the end of life and spends time maintaining small, ordinary stabilizations: keeping a routine, preparing meals, tending a garden, organizing shared resources so others can use them later. None of these acts aim at completion or legacy. They participate in causation while participation remains possible. The significance of these actions does not depend on how long they last or what follows after death. Meaning was already present in the consequences they produced while stabilization occurred. Death does not negate this. It simply marks the point beyond which no further participation occurs. Living with the boundary in view shifts attention from justification to participation. Life is not measured against death. It unfolds until it ends.

What This Chapter Establishes

This chapter establishes death as the mechanical endpoint of stabilization rather than the negation or completion of meaning. Life is a process of ongoing stabilization under constraint. Death marks the point at which that process stops. Meaning does not depend on continuation beyond death. It arises from consequence while participation is possible. Residue persists in other systems, but participation ends. Understanding death this way removes the need for purpose, completion, or transcendence to preserve significance. It prepares the ground for examining acceptance — not as resignation, but as alignment with the boundary conditions of the system itself.

Death ends stabilization.
It does not erase consequence.

Chapter 58

What Acceptance Actually Is

Alignment Without Resignation

Acceptance is often misunderstood as giving up. To accept something is taken to mean approving it, tolerating it, or deciding not to resist. In existential contexts, acceptance is sometimes framed as emotional surrender: making peace with what cannot be changed. CST describes acceptance differently. Acceptance is not an attitude. It is a configuration.

Acceptance as Load Alignment

A system is aligned when its expectations, actions, and stabilizations are matched to what the landscape can actually carry. Acceptance is the configuration in which this alignment occurs. When alignment is absent, load rises. The system attempts to stabilize against conditions that cannot support the demanded configuration. Internal work increases without restoring margin. Strain accumulates. Acceptance reduces load not by changing conditions, but by ceasing to demand configurations the landscape cannot sustain. It is not resignation. It is the felt signature of mechanical alignment.

Why Resistance Increases Cost

Resistance is often framed as strength. In CST terms, resistance becomes costly when higher Frames of Reference stabilize around constraint demands that no longer match what lower Frames can carry. Lower Frames stabilize the immediate realities of the system — energy, recovery, tissue condition, coordination, and load. Higher Frames stabilize longer-span continuity — identity, standards, trajectory, and what the life is expected to be. When these stabilizations diverge, the system is required to carry incompatible constraints at once.

Consider a runner who has trained for many years. The identity corridor stabilized at higher Frames includes endurance, discipline, and the capacity to push through strain. Over time, accumulated wear and a knee injury alter the lower-Frame cost geometry. Recovery slows. Load that was once carryable now produces instability. The lower Frames stabilize by reducing demand: shorter runs, slower pace, longer recovery intervals. These adjustments match the constraints that now exist.

But the higher Frames may stabilize the opposite demand: the prior identity must remain unchanged. The runner must still be fast, durable, and unaffected. The system must then carry two constraint sets simultaneously — the stabilized reality of reduced carryability and the higher-Frame requirement that this reduction should not be true. Internal work increases. Monitoring intensifies. Corrections repeat. Forced stabilizations occur as the system attempts to hold an output no longer matched to its substrate. Cost rises, but capacity does not widen.

Acceptance does not remove injury, and it does not mean approval of loss. It is the release of the higher-Frame demand that the previous corridor remains intact. What remains may still be difficult, but the system is no longer required to carry contradiction. Stabilization can proceed along configurations that match current conditions — altered training, different pacing, new movement patterns — and internal work decreases because only one constraint set must be sustained.

Acceptance Does Not Mean Passivity

A common fear is that acceptance eliminates change. If something is accepted, why act? This fear confuses acceptance with inaction. Acceptance determines where action can occur. It clarifies which transitions are possible without collapse and which are not. Action becomes targeted rather than reactive. A system that accepts its constraints can still reorganize. In fact, reorganization becomes more likely because margin is no longer consumed by futile resistance. Acceptance is what makes effective change possible under constraint.

Consider an adult caring for an aging parent whose cognitive capacity is declining. For a long period, the system remains organized around restoring the previous configuration: correcting mistakes, insisting on independence, arguing facts, treating each lapse as a problem to fix. Load accumulates. Interactions destabilize. Conflict and exhaustion increase. When the system reorganizes around what can actually be carried — simplifying routines, reducing choices, adding reminders, adjusting expectations — nothing essential is surrendered. The parent does not regain lost capacity, but stability improves. Care becomes more effective. Strain drops. Coordination becomes possible again. Acceptance here does not end action. It enables it. By ceasing to demand configurations the landscape cannot sustain, margin is restored, and change becomes targeted rather than reactive.

Acceptance Under Irreversibility

Some constraints are reversible. Others are not. Aging, permanent injury, death, and irreversible loss impose boundaries that cannot be widened past a certain point. When systems treat these boundaries as negotiable, load escalates continuously. Acceptance in these cases is the stabilization that stops the escalation. This does not remove grief, frustration, or pain. It removes the additional cost of demanding reversal where none is available. Acceptance is how a system stops paying interest on irreversibility.

Consider a person who loses the use of a hand after a stroke. Rehabilitation improves coordination and compensatory strategies, but full restoration is not possible. When the system remains organized around reversal — constant comparison to prior ability, repeated attempts to perform uncarryable tasks, interpreting limits as temporary failures — load escalates. Frustration compounds. Progress stalls. When the system stabilizes around the irreversible boundary — designing routines that work one-handed, modifying tools, redistributing tasks — the loss remains. Grief remains. The escalation stops. Internal work drops. Available capacity can now support improvement where improvement is possible. Acceptance here is not emotional resolution. It is the stabilization that ends the interest charged by irreversibility.

The Felt Signature of Acceptance

Awareness often encounters acceptance as calm, relief, or quiet sadness. These feelings are not acceptance itself. They are downstream effects. When load drops, urgency subsides. When urgency subsides, attention widens. When attention widens, fixation loosens. The felt shift follows the structural one. Acceptance feels like peace because peace is what low-conflict stabilization feels like from the inside. After months of fighting an unchangeable work schedule, a person stops reorganizing their day around the hope that it will improve. Routines settle. Sleep stabilizes. Attention is no longer consumed by contingency planning. What is felt as calm arrives after the load has dropped. The feeling does not cause the stabilization. It registers it.

Why Acceptance Is Often Resisted

Acceptance threatens certain narratives. If acceptance is allowed, the story of struggle loses its central role. If no fight is required, effort loses its moral framing. If limits are real, identity narratives built on overcoming them must reorganize. These narratives are not trivial. They have stabilized lives under past conditions. Letting them go can feel like losing meaning, not because meaning disappears, but because the structure that once stabilized it no longer works. CST does not ask for premature acceptance. It explains why acceptance becomes necessary when those narratives no longer reduce load.

Consider a person whose identity has long been organized around perseverance — working longer hours, pushing through illness, proving reliability under strain. For years, this narrative reduced load by sustaining employment, respect, and self-coherence. When conditions change — health declines, caregiving demands rise — the same narrative no longer reduces load. Continuing to push now increases strain. Resistance persists until the narrative stops paying its load-reducing function. Acceptance becomes possible only when the old story can no longer be carried. Acceptance does not occur because a system decides to accept. It occurs when resistance ceases to reduce load.

Regret and the Counterfactual

Regret is often treated as proof that something should have happened differently. It arises when narrative constructs an alternative path and compares it to what occurred. From within that comparison, the present is judged against an imagined lower-cost past. Mechanically, no such comparison existed at the time of action.

At any moment, a system stabilizes along the trajectory that is carryable under its structure, load, and available conditions. The path taken is not selected from all possibilities. It is the one that could hold. Alternatives that appear obvious later were not structurally available in the same way at the time. They are reconstructed after the sequence has unfolded. Regret therefore does not indicate missed authorship. It indicates counterfactual binding.

When the system binds to an unrealizable past, load increases without altering what has already stabilized. Energy is spent opposing an irreversible sequence. Nothing in the past changes, but present capacity is consumed. CST does not require the elimination of regret. It clarifies its structure. Learning remains possible without self-punishment. Residue already reshapes future stabilization. The system carries forward what the prior sequence produced. Nothing additional is required for adaptation to occur.

When the demand for a different past relaxes, something shifts. The event remains. Its consequences remain. What disappears is the extra work of arguing with what has already happened. The system did not fail to choose correctly. It followed the lowest-cost path available under the conditions that existed. Nothing more could have been carried at that time. In short, regret is the binding of the present to an imagined past that was never carryable when it occurred. The system did not fail to choose differently. It stabilized along the only path that could hold under the conditions that existed. When counterfactual demand relaxes, the past remains unchanged — but present load decreases. Learning continues without self-punishment.

Acceptance and Dignity

Acceptance preserves dignity because it treats constraints as real. Demanding impossible performance under constraint strips dignity by ignoring causation. Acceptance restores dignity by aligning expectations with capacity. Acceptance aligns with present constraint; it does not prohibit structural redesign where redesign is carryable. This does not excuse harm or eliminate responsibility. It clarifies where responsibility can still operate without adding load. Acceptance is not lowering standards. It is setting standards that can be carried.

What Acceptance Is Not

Acceptance is not approval, and it is not justification. To accept a constraint does not mean endorsing it, agreeing with it, or declaring it acceptable in any moral sense. Nor is acceptance indifference or emotional detachment. What is accepted still matters, still carries weight, and may still involve loss, pain, or harm. Acceptance also is not surrender. It does not mean giving up action or abandoning effort. Acceptance is the configuration in which a system stops fighting the geometry of its own landscape — ceasing to demand stabilizations the conditions cannot support, and redirecting effort toward what can actually be carried.

What This Chapter Establishes

This chapter establishes acceptance as structural alignment rather than emotional resignation. Acceptance reduces load by ending demands for configurations the landscape cannot sustain. It restores margin and makes reorganization possible. Acceptance does not eliminate effort. It removes wasted effort. By aligning with constraint rather than resisting it, a system becomes capable of carrying what remains — and of changing what can still be changed. The final chapter turns to what it means to live inside such a system once control stories are relinquished: not as withdrawal from life, but as a different way of participating in it.

Acceptance is not surrender.
It is alignment with what can be carried.

Chapter 59

Living Without the Control Story

Participation Without Command

The control story says that to live well, one must be in charge. That outcomes require authorship, that responsibility requires command and dignity depends on mastery. Even when softened, the story persists: if you are not steering, you are failing to live properly. CST ends this story — not by replacing it with despair, but by revealing that life has never operated that way. Living without the control story is not living without structure. It is living inside structure without pretending to stand outside it.

What Remains When Control Is Removed

When control is relinquished, several fears arise at once. Without control, how does anything improve? Without command, how can harm be addressed? Without authorship, how can a life have shape? What remains is participation. Systems participate in causation because they are positioned within it. They stabilize where they can, leave residue, and reshape what follows. This participation does not require choice, intention, or oversight. It is imposed by position in the causal fabric. Living without the control story means accepting this condition rather than narrating around it. Participation does not occur because a system chooses to participate. It occurs because stabilization always takes place somewhere within the causal chain.

Responsibility Without Command

Without control, responsibility changes form. Responsibility no longer means making things happen by force. It means being a site where effects land and propagate. What stabilizes through a system matters because it shapes what comes next. This reframing removes both inflation and erasure. It does not elevate systems into authors, and it does not reduce them to

330

passive victims. It locates responsibility where leverage exists and consequences propagate. To live responsibly, in this sense, is not to command outcomes. It is to participate accurately.

Effort Without Mastery

Effort often hides a control claim. To try harder is to assume that exertion alone can override geometry. When that assumption fails, effort becomes strain. CST does not remove effort. It relocates it. Effort becomes the work of aligning with constraint: adjusting pacing, redistributing load, widening margin where possible, and withdrawing from configurations that cannot be carried. This effort is quieter and less dramatic. It is also far more effective. Effort without mastery is effort that respects the landscape.

Consider a person struggling with chronic insomnia. For years, effort is applied in the obvious way: trying harder to sleep, forcing earlier bedtimes, exerting control over thoughts, tightening routines, escalating rules. Each night becomes a test. Strain rises. Sleep worsens. The problem is not insufficient effort. It is misallocated effort. Exertion is being applied where geometry cannot be overridden. When effort relocates — adjusting schedules, reducing sleep pressure, removing performance demands, widening margin around rest — the struggle quiets. Sleep does not improve because the person tried harder. It improves because effort shifted toward alignment with constraint. Effort did not disappear. It stopped pretending to be mastery.

Care Without Rescue

Care is often distorted by control stories. To care is imagined as fixing, correcting, or rescuing — intervening to produce a better outcome. Without control, care changes shape. Care becomes the practice of altering conditions so that harmful patterns do not need to stabilize. It redistributes load, reduces variance, and preserves margin. It supports participation without demanding authorship. Care without rescue does not remove difficulty. It makes difficulty carryable.

Consider a friend supporting someone struggling with recurring panic. In a rescue frame, care takes the form of constant reassurance, immediate interruption of distress, and pressure to "feel better." Each episode triggers urgent intervention. Dependence increases. Variance rises. The pattern stabilizes. In a non-rescue frame, care looks different. The friend helps reduce environmental triggers, creates predictable routines, and stays present without trying to eliminate the panic itself. Episodes still occur. Difficulty remains. But load drops, recovery shortens, and the panic no longer needs to escalate to secure support. Nothing was fixed. Nothing was overridden. Care altered conditions so that a harmful pattern no longer had to stabilize.

Action Without Justification

Control stories often demand justification. Actions must be explained, defended, or aligned with a purpose. When justification fails, action freezes. Living without the control story removes this requirement. Action becomes a response to conditions rather than a statement of intent. The question shifts from *Why am I doing this?* to *What does this change, and at what cost?* Action is evaluated by effect, not by narrative purity. This does not make action careless. It makes it accountable to consequence.

Meaning Without Performance

Without control, meaning is no longer something one performs into existence. It does not need to be demonstrated, optimized, or proven. Meaning arises wherever participation leaves residue. A life matters because it reshapes the landscape others inhabit, even briefly, even quietly. This reshaping does not need to be large, visible, or enduring to be real. Living without the control story allows meaning to exist without spectacle.

Peace Without Closure

Control stories promise peace through resolution: finish the task, achieve the goal, arrive at the answer. When resolution is unavailable, peace recedes. CST offers a different peace. Peace is the felt signature of alignment — when expectations, actions, and conditions fit. It does not require completion. It does not require certainty. It requires low-conflict stabilization. Peace is not something achieved at the end. It appears intermittently when load is carried without distortion.

Conflict often arises through *outcome binding* — when higher Frames of Reference stabilize coherence around a specific future configuration. The system becomes organized not around what is presently carryable, but around what must eventually occur. When that future cannot yet stabilize, the present must carry both uncertainty and the demand for its removal. Internal work increases. Attention cycles. Monitoring persists. Peace recedes, not because uncertainty exists, but because stabilization is divided between present conditions and a future that is not yet available.

Consider a person waiting on a medical diagnosis that will take months to clarify. Resolution is unavailable. Questions remain unanswered. In a control frame, peace is impossible until certainty arrives. Outcome binding organizes the system around a future answer — rehearsing possibilities, refreshing results, attempting premature closure. The present becomes structured around what cannot yet stabilize, and internal conflict persists.

When the system releases outcome binding — no longer organizing around premature resolution, no longer rehearsing outcomes, no longer planning contingencies that cannot yet be carried — stabilization returns to present conditions. Daily life resumes. Routines stabilize. Attention returns to what is immediately supportable. Nothing has been concluded. Uncertainty remains. What appears is peace — not because the future is settled, but because the present is no longer in conflict with itself.

Coaching and Parenting: Guidance Without Control

Coaching and parenting operate within the same architecture. Neither controls the system they influence. Both introduce structured input — signals, cues, constraints, and information — that may or may not alter what stabilizes next. These inputs do not command outcomes. They enter the system as additional conditions within the same causal field. When coaching or parenting appears immediately effective, this does not indicate control. It indicates correspondence. The instruction aligns with the system's lowest-cost trajectory under current conditions. The input resonates with the path the system was already positioned to take because both the guidance and the response have been shaped by overlapping histories of stabilization.

Consider an athlete approaching a familiar situation — one encountered thousands of times. The architecture has already been shaped so that a particular response is cheapest to carry. If the coach recognizes the same condition and calls out the same action — turn left — the instruction appears causal. But the alignment is structural. The athlete's system would have stabilized in that direction regardless. The instruction did not create the response; it coincided with it. The same pattern operates in parenting and in conscious narrative. Through repeated exposure, these "coaching systems" learn correlations between conditions and stabilizations. When conditions are typical, their inputs often correspond with the system's lowest-cost response, and guidance appears effective.

When conditions shift, however, correspondence breaks. The coach, parent, or conscious narrative may issue instructions shaped by prior patterns, but stabilization still resolves along the lowest-cost trajectory available under present constraint. Guidance influences only when it reduces cost or increases carryability. When it does not, the system settles elsewhere. From within experience, this variability can feel like partial control: sometimes guidance works, sometimes it does not. Mechanically, nothing inconsistent has occurred. Influence exists, but only conditionally. What stabilizes is determined by the full configuration of the system, not by any single input. Coaching, parenting, and consciousness therefore do not direct the system. They are processes within the system that participate in shaping conditions. Their apparent guidance reflects moments when learned instruction and lowest-cost stabilization coincide.

Conscious Narrative Coach: Influence Without Command

From within experience, conscious narrative can function like a coach speaking to an athlete. The coach does not control the body. The coach provides information, cues, or suggestions that may influence coordination, pacing, or orientation. Whether those inputs alter performance depends on the state of the athlete — their conditioning, fatigue, timing, and environmental demands. The same instruction may help, have no effect, or interfere.

Consciousness operates in the same manner. When awareness registers rising internal cost — strain, tightening, instability — narrative signals may appear: slow down, pause, shift attention, withdraw, continue. These signals do not command the system. They enter as additional input within the ongoing causal sequence. Sometimes they reduce load, widen margin, or redirect stabilization. Sometimes they do not. Sometimes they increase cost. What follows is determined not by the narrative itself, but by the total configuration of the system. Stabilization resolves where carryability is greatest. The architecture settles along the lowest-cost trajectory available under current conditions.

From the standpoint of awareness, this yields a precise conclusion: guidance can be offered, but outcome cannot be commanded. Narrative participates, but does not govern. The system stabilizes where it can carry. This does not make conscious input irrelevant. Coaching can matter. Information can reshape conditions. Repeated inputs can alter residue and change future stabilizations. But no single instruction guarantees effect, and no instruction overrides structure. Consciousness, then, is neither controller nor external observer. It is one channel through which the system can influence itself — sometimes effectively, sometimes not — within the constraints it is already carrying. Absence of control does not mean absence of influence; stabilizations still reshape what follows.

Over-Coaching and Load Increase

When guidance becomes excessive, load often rises rather than falls. Repeated or conflicting instructions introduce additional demands that must themselves be stabilized. Attention fragments, coordination tightens, and carryability decreases. What was fluid, becomes effortful. An athlete given too many corrections mid-movement may lose timing. A child given continuous direction may lose adaptive responsiveness. A person generating constant internal instruction may increase strain rather than reduce it. Effective guidance therefore has a narrow window. It influences when it reduces cost, clarifies coordination, or increases margin. Beyond that window, additional instruction becomes another constraint the system must carry. When load rises, stabilization narrows. In this way, the absence of control does not eliminate guidance. It defines its limits. Guidance matters, but only within the economics of carryability that govern all stabilization.

Living Inside the Machine

To live inside the machine is to stop imagining an exit. There is no vantage outside causation from which to steer life. There is only participation: stabilizing here rather than there, carrying this rather than that, reshaping what follows by what can be carried now. This is not a diminished existence. It is a more accurate one. Living without the control story does not make life smaller. It makes it truer to the machinery that was always operating. Participation operates at every scale — within bodies, between people, and across systems.

What This Chapter Establishes

This chapter clarifies what remains once the control story is removed. Life does not become passive, empty, or directionless. The underlying mechanics simply become visible. Systems do not command outcomes. They participate in causation by stabilizing where conditions allow. What follows from those stabilizations reshapes the landscape others must carry. Responsibility therefore resides not in authorship but in position within the causal flow. Effort remains, but its function changes. Instead of attempting to override constraint, effort operates through alignment with the landscape — redistributing load, widening margin where possible, and withdrawing from configurations that cannot be carried. Care also changes form. It does not rescue or repair by force. It alters conditions so that harmful patterns no longer need to stabilize.

Action proceeds without the demand for justification, guided by consequence rather than narrative defense. Meaning appears wherever participation leaves residue that reshapes what follows. Peace appears when stabilization is no longer divided between present conditions and futures that cannot yet be carried. Living inside the machine therefore does not remove dignity, responsibility, or meaning. It removes only the fictional story that these require command. What remains is participation within the causal architecture that has always governed how systems live, influence, and reshape the world.

Life was never waiting for an author.
It was always unfolding through structure.
You do not steer the machinery.
You are one of the places through which it turns.

Chapter 60

Closing the Frame

What Accuracy Leaves Behind

The Frame That Was Being Built

This book began with a simple claim: experience does not reveal causation. It reveals stabilization. From that starting point, everything else followed — measurement before meaning, stabilization before awareness, consequence before narrative. What began as a theoretical repositioning gradually became something more practical: a way of reducing unnecessary strain by seeing systems as they actually operate. Nothing introduced here was meant to diminish human life. It was meant to remove what life has been carrying unnecessarily.

Across these chapters, familiar concepts were resituated. Agency was no longer treated as an origin but as an appearance. Emotion was no longer a guide to truth but a display of cost. Trauma was no longer damage but narrowing under constraint. Change was no longer a triumph of will but a redistribution that occurs when conditions allow it. Care, ethics, justice, power, and therapy were shown to function without authorship — often more cleanly without it. Meaning no longer required purpose. A life no longer required an endpoint. Acceptance no longer required surrender. What remains now is not a conclusion, but a settling.

What Accuracy Does

CST does not ask readers to think differently in order to become better people. It does not offer strategies for mastery, control, or transformation. It does not promise relief, meaning, or coherence as rewards. It *offers accuracy*. Over time, that accuracy reduces the effort systems spend resisting what they cannot alter. This is not because accuracy is virtuous, but because misalignment is expensive. Imagine standing on a moving walkway and trying to walk backward to remain in place. Enormous effort is spent opposing motion already occurring. Nothing about this effort is noble or meaningful. It is simply costly.

When the body turns and moves with the walkway instead, nothing has been solved. The destination has not changed. But the same situation now requires far less energy to inhabit. The difference is not attitude. It is alignment. Human systems often do the same. Large amounts of effort are spent opposing constraints already shaping the field: a body altered, a loss already present, a limit already binding, a condition already in force. Resistance does not undo the constraint. It adds load. Accuracy does not remove the constraint. It removes the extra work of opposing it. Over time, that reduction in friction preserves capacity. What becomes available is not control, but room to respond. Uncertainty remains. Systems continue to stabilize under conditions that are never fully known.

Responsibility Without Blame

Nothing in CST removes responsibility. It relocates it. Effects still propagate. Harm still requires response. Boundaries still matter. What disappears is the belief that blame is required to make responsibility real. What remains is the simpler and heavier fact: what happens reshapes conditions, and those conditions shape what follows. This reframing has consequences. In therapy, it permits presence without performance. In ethics, it permits boundaries without condemnation. In justice, it permits containment without spectacle. In power, it permits authority without domination. In daily life, it permits effort without guarantee. Responsibility becomes participation in consequence, not authorship of outcomes. The same mechanics operate in bodies, relationships, institutions, and societies.

Alignment Instead of Control

Perhaps most importantly, this frame changes how systems relate to themselves. Many arrive carrying an internal demand to be the cause of their own coherence. When that demand relaxes, something unexpected occurs. The system does not collapse. It continues — organizing, stabilizing, adapting. What changes is the cost. Fewer resources are spent maintaining a story about control. More remain available for responding to what is actually happening. This is not resignation. It is alignment. *To live inside this frame is not to disengage from life, but to stop arguing with its mechanics.* It is to participate where participation is possible, to alter conditions where leverage exists, and to cease adding load through stories that do not describe correctly how change occurs. It is to care without binding outcome, to respond without globalizing judgment, and to allow consequence, rather than narrative, to shape what comes next.

What Accuracy Leaves Behind

CST does not defeat older models. It renders some of their work unnecessary. When systems are no longer asked to do what they cannot do — author outcomes, generate meaning through will, secure coherence through effort — many familiar struggles lose their grip. What remains is not emptiness. Meaning does not vanish without purpose. Responsibility does not vanish without authorship. Dignity does not vanish without control. What vanishes is the need to pretend. What remains is participation — quieter, lighter, and more precise. Systems continue to stabilize, narrow, widen, and reorganize. Care continues to matter. Harm continues to require response. Change continues when conditions allow it. Meaning continues wherever consequence propagates. Peace continues wherever alignment reduces conflict.

The Frame Closes

The frame closes here not because nothing remains to be said, but because nothing further must be added. This book has described a world without authors, choosers, or commanders — not as an abstraction, but as a working architecture. Systems stabilize, narrow, reorganize, and propagate consequence without intention or control. Nothing here asks for surrender to inevitability or withdrawal from life. It asks for accuracy. Life continues as it always has: stabilizing here rather than there, carrying this rather than that, reshaping what follows through what can be carried now. No one is steering. Nothing is missing. This is the system. Nothing here has ever depended on someone choosing correctly. Stabilization has always proceeded where it could. Accuracy is enough.

What This Chapter Establishes

Closing the CST frame does not resolve uncertainty or grant control. It reduces unnecessary strain by *aligning experience with how systems actually operate*. When authorship is no longer demanded, participation becomes lighter, responsibility becomes more precise, and care becomes more sustainable. What remains is not detachment, but continued engagement without distortion.

Chapter 61

Optimal Orientation Under Constraint

How Therefore Shall We Live

A question arises once the architecture of behavior is understood. If systems do not operate by central command, if outcomes cannot be forced at will, and if stabilization is governed by load, constraint, and carryability, then what orientation corresponds to the least unnecessary strain? This is not a question of control. It is a question of alignment. Stabilization does not cease in the absence of authorship. Systems continue to reorganize, narrow, widen, and propagate forward. What varies is the amount of additional load introduced during this process, including load generated in higher frames through narrative activity.

Every system carries primary load — the real demands placed on it by circumstances. These pressures typically enter the system through the lower Frames of Reference, where bodily state, environmental conditions, and immediate constraints must first be carried. Illness, deadlines, uncertainty, fatigue, loss, and conflict are unavoidable aspects of existing within constraint. But systems also generate secondary load — additional strain layered on top of primary demand. Secondary load appears when systems resist what is already occurring, attack themselves for struggling, force performance under insufficient capacity, demand clarity where none is available, or attempt to override limits through effort alone. In humans, much of this additional load arises within higher Frames of Reference. Narrative and identity stabilization can add prediction, evaluation, and imagined consequences to what is already occurring. These responses are not defects but common outputs of systems under perceived threat. They increase total load and therefore shape what the system can carry. When secondary load decreases, stabilization becomes less strained. No command produces this shift, instead reduced total load simply increases carryability.

Consider a system attempting sleep under anticipatory load. Monitoring, forcing, and suppression sustain activation and prevent settling. When monitoring relaxes and unresolved elements are no longer actively opposed, total load decreases. Autonomic settling may occur. Sleep is not produced by command. It emerges when activation falls within a carryable range. The same structure appears in interpersonal coordination under evaluative strain. Attempts to tightly control output increase internal cost and disrupt fluid regulation. When monitoring pressure decreases and output is allowed to stabilize more directly, coordination may resume with lower strain. Nothing is forced. The system settles where load permits.

Across domains, a consistent pattern appears. Primary load — the conditions already present in the body, field, and participation (FOR-1 through FOR-5) — is often unavoidable. Secondary load — additional structures that arise as broader modes organize around those conditions (FOR-6 through FOR-9) — is variable. Total load determines stabilization range. Movement that is carryable stabilizes more reliably than movement forced beyond capacity. Systems do not require maximal output. They require sustainable configurations. Under excessive load, forced stabilization narrows architecture. Under tolerable load, stabilization may widen. Alignment, therefore, does not imply command. It corresponds to reduced addition of unnecessary load.

Accurate state recognition further reduces secondary load. Systems operate across multiple Frames of Reference, each associated with distinct integration spans, coupling breadth, and cost structure. When higher-frame stabilization aligns with conditions already being carried in lower frames, unnecessary amplification decreases and total load remains closer to the demands actually present. Narrow stabilizations correspond to high load, reduced integration, and constrained behavioral bandwidth. Wider stabilizations correspond to lower load and expanded accessible configurations. Recognition of current stabilization does not control it, but it reduces misattribution. When narrowing is recognized as load-dependent rather than defect-based, self-referential amplification decreases. Total strain falls, and the system need not carry contradiction in addition to primary demand.

Within this architecture, freedom is not authorship, but flexibility of stabilization. Systems with lower total constraint can traverse a broader range of configurations. Reduced secondary load does not produce control.

It increases carryability. As total load falls, accessible state-space expands without directive command. Alignment with reality therefore corresponds to reduced resistance to present structural conditions. Some load cannot be immediately removed. Some uncertainty cannot be immediately resolved. However, resistance to what is already stabilizing adds further load and narrows the system beyond necessity.

Common forms of added resistance include self-attack layered onto strain, repetitive counterfactual processing, forced output under overload, premature demands for clarity, and rigid stabilization where flexibility is required. These do not reduce primary load. They increase total load. When secondary load is not added, primary difficulty may remain, but the system is not further constrained beyond what conditions impose.

Systems do not operate by command, but they do propagate consequence. Every stabilization alters conditions, and altered conditions shape subsequent stabilization. Effects may be cumulative, delayed, or diffused. Passive propagation and attentive participation are both system outputs, yet they produce different future constraint landscapes. Nothing is fully controllable, but participation alters the field within which stabilization unfolds.

Consider a physical system in which combustion begins to spread. Non-intervention allows propagation according to available fuel and airflow. Intervention — removal of fuel, alteration of airflow, application of water — does not guarantee outcome, but it changes conditions and therefore reshapes propagation. Human systems operate under the same principle. Outcomes cannot be commanded, yet engagement alters conditions, and altered conditions reshape what stabilizes next.

No configuration permanently eliminates load. Systems continue to narrow and widen as conditions shift. Some pressures recede while others emerge, and stabilization reorganizes accordingly. However, one structural principle remains constant: not all heaviness indicates defect, not all difficulty requires force, and not all uncertainty requires control. Systems do not require perfection. They require reduced unnecessary load. Primary conditions will continue to place demands on the system, but additional resistance need not be layered on top of them. When unnecessary load decreases, stabilization occurs with less strain. From reduced load, widening may occur without command. Alignment does not produce mastery. It only prevents the system from adding unnecessary weight to what it must already carry.

Epilogue

What Remains

Something may now feel different. Nothing needs to be done about it.

This book does not end with a task, a lesson, or a position to hold. It offers no practice to maintain and no insight to protect. If something here alters how experience is carried, it will occur on its own. If nothing shifts, nothing has been missed.

What this book provides is not instruction, but description. And like any description that enters a system, it may — or may not — participate in what follows.

The book began with a simple fact — one that did not depend on belief, intention, or meaning. That fact remains:

Your life has effects.
Your presence alters what follows.
This cannot be prevented.

Nothing described here removes that condition. Systems still stabilize. Actions still propagate. Consequences still unfold. What may have changed is not what happens, but how what has happened is carried.

A system does not need authorship to be effective.
An action does not need choice to be causal.
A life does not need justification to leave a trace.

What CST removes is not participation, responsibility, or engagement. It removes the added load placed on them — the demand that outcomes be owed, that effects be deserved, that life should have stabilized differently than it did. When that extra demand falls away, what remains is a lighter load: participation without insistence, consequence without verdict, continuation without narrative pressure.

If reorganization occurs after this book, it will occur because conditions allow it. If nothing reorganizes, nothing has failed. No stance is required. No vigilance is necessary. No conclusion must be reached.

The system continues as it always has — measuring, stabilizing, leaving residue, shaping what comes next. Whether this account resonates, resists, or fades, it has already entered the sequence. It has already participated simply by being encountered.

This is not instruction. Not hope. Not warning. Only description.

Every life remains a point where forces meet that it did not generate. Every life continues to exert force it cannot withhold.

Your presence — like every presence — has consequence.

The account closes where it began.
Not with what a *life means*.
But with ***what a life does***.

About the Author

Bret Scott Miles holds degrees in Psychology and Mathematics Education. His professional background includes work in Information Technology, along with teaching computer programming languages and courses in Psychology, Philosophy, Mathematics, and Economics.

He is the developer of Causal Systems Theory (CST), a deterministic framework for understanding mind, behavior, and human change as constrained physical process rather than authored action. His work integrates principles from physics, systems theory, and psychology into a unified mechanical account of development, identity, stress, and transformation.

CST emerged from a sustained effort to answer a single question: if human beings are physical systems, what must be true about how we operate — and what must therefore be false? The result is a layered model of stabilization, load, carryability, and frame organization that removes the need for inner authorship while preserving responsibility as causal position.

He writes for readers willing to examine the structural foundations beneath familiar explanations. This volume presents the first formal articulation of the theory.